A Passionate Voice
In an Eternal Dialogue

Is man naturally selfish, aggressive, in need of strict controls to keep him in check, and of culture to raise him from his brutish state? Or is he naturally good —until the forces of government, society, school and family warp and cripple him?

The latter was the view of Jean Jacques Rousseau, as he broke away from the authoritarianism and rationalism of his day to champion inborn human rights and native intuition.

In his opposition to the forces of "law and order," and in his magnificently phrased arguments for a society designed to serve the many rather than the few, his is a voice that demands to be heard in a dialogue that continues to this day.

LOWELL BAIR is the noted translator of many classics of French literature, including *The Wanderer* and *Cyrano de Bergerac,* available in Signet Classic editions from New American Library.

MATTHEW JOSEPHSON, author of the now-classic *The Robber Barons* and the more recent *The Money Lords,* is also known for his highly acclaimed biographies, *Stendhal, Victor Hugo, Zola and His Times,* and *Jean-Jacques Rousseau.*

Other MENTOR Books You'll Want to Read

THE
ESSENTIAL
ROUSSEAU

The Social Contract

*Discourse on the
Origin of Inequality*

*Discourse on the
Arts and Sciences*

*The Creed
of a Savoyard Priest*

Translated by
LOWELL BAIR

A MENTOR BOOK
NEW AMERICAN LIBRARY

TIMES MIRROR
NEW YORK AND SCARBOROUGH, ONTARIO
THE NEW ENGLISH LIBRARY LIMITED, LONDON

Contents

INTRODUCTION

Rousseau: A Portrait

For more than two centuries since Rousseau's writings were first published, controversy over the man and his ideas has continued virtually unabated. In their diverse ways his admirers and his opponents both have affirmed his importance in world history: the supporting party has seen him as the Friend of Man, the prophet of the new democratic ages that were to come after him, and one of the fathers of the French Revolution; his antagonists have pronounced him a dangerous heretic who scorned organized religion, and as the inspirer of romanticism in literature and an unbridled libertarianism in politics. Indeed, they have somehow attributed to him the origin of many of the alleged evils of modern times, ranging from the restiveness of "hippie" youth to the rigors of totalitarian societies. However, those who have tried to judge Rousseau fairly have generally agreed that among the philosophical writers of his century he was the one who stated the problem of civilization with more clarity and force than any other of his contemporaries. Though his era was one of brilliant scientific progress and high civilization in Western Europe, he denounced the whole culture as spurious for having become separated in its purpose from the pursuit of human betterment. Too few men, only a tiny elite, then enjoyed the advantages of science and art. Let the light of civilization be extended into those wide areas of human wretchedness out of which he himself had arisen, he cried. "Everywhere I see men in chains," he wrote, and the laborious poor bereft of their "natural rights."

What of the man himself, the former Swiss waif and vagabond, entirely self-taught, whose genius long fascinated all literate Europe? During the years of fame passed among the aristocratic elite of feudal France, he would challengingly declare himself a commoner, Citizen Rousseau of Geneva, who, by choice, lived the simple life of the poor. But he was no ordinary fellow in that age of fierce individualists such as Voltaire and Diderot. He said: "I would rather be dead than be taken for an ordinary man." Some of his contemporaries held that he was not only singular, but sick-minded and "depraved." He himself, in his post-humous memoirs, *The Confessions,* wrote in deeply moving terms of his own sinful actions (resembling those of most men in his time) and of his sincere repentance. It is through his own account of his misdeeds, published by him (as if to discharge a burden of guilt), that the world learned of his wrongdoings, which might otherwise never have become known.

Jean-Jacques Rousseau was born in Geneva, Switzerland, on June 28, 1712; his father was Isaac Rousseau, watch-maker and descendant of French Huguenots, who a century and a half earlier had sought refuge from religious persecution in Calvin's city republic. On his mother's side, his ancestors, the Bernards, were Swiss of the well-to-do merchant class. Rousseau's forebears were not only devout Protestants but they had won the distinction of citizenship in the "holy city" (there were only 1,600 such out of 30,000 inhabitants). Both the Rousseaus and the Bernards seem to have been more given to the pleasures of books, of making music, and even of dancing, than was usual among the puritanical Genevese.

"My birth was the first of my misfortunes," wrote Jean-Jacques; his mother died of puerperal fever soon after the arrival of her second son. His father, an affectionate though light-minded man, brought up his younger son himself, with the aid of an Aunt Bernard, and taught the boy his letters at an early age. From the age of seven, Jean-Jacques was allowed to read whatever came his way; sometimes father and son stayed up to all hours of the night reading books indiscriminately, including classics such as Plutarch's *Lives* and Tacitus's histories. Jean-Jacques remembered the first ten years of his boyhood as happy and tranquil. There was music in his home, provided by his aunts, who often sang the pietist hymns and psalms that he loved.

The watchmaker in earlier years had sometimes been a wild young fellow. When Jean-Jacques was ten, his father began to neglect his business and took to hunting outside the town walls. He soon fell into deep trouble when an officer charged him with poaching and he slashed at his accuser with his sword. Condemned to a term in prison, the father fled to the neighboring canton of Vaud, leaving his two sons to the care of their Uncle and Aunt Bernard. The elder Rousseau remarried and never returned to Geneva.

Next, Jean-Jacques' elder brother, an apprentice to a watch-maker, by then seventeen, went "over the mountains" and was not heard from again. The younger son was then sent off for his schooling to the parsonage of an old pastor in a mountain village outside Geneva. There he received a some-what limited instruction, consisting mostly of Bible reading, arithmetic, and sermons.

Jean-Jacques was a slim, bright-eyed, good-looking boy who enjoyed the rough games of his fellow pupils but was more serious than they; he had a religious spirit, liked church services and sermons, and, even more, wandering about by himself in the open country or climbing the slope of Mount Salève that towered above the village. In the three years at that rude country school Jean-Jacques not only absorbed religious doctrine, but also acquired some vices. One of his teachers, the pastor's daughter, a spinster, used to punish him physically, and he observed keenly in his later recollections that this aroused in him precocious sexual impulses. On another occasion he was "whipped to pieces" for some alleged misdeed of which he was innocent; the unjust punishment, as he wrote in *Émile*, his famous work on education, hardened him in hatred of authority and made him "all the more rebellious, deceitful, and mischie-vous." The parentless boy pilfered apples and sweets there-after, telling himself he must use his wits to avoid being caught.

When he was thirteen, school ended for him; his guard-ians, seeing he appeared intelligent, thought of apprenticing him to a notary, but that did not work out. At length he was bound over for five years as an apprentice to an engraver, whose craft appealed to him. The master, however, was a harsh and violent man; the young Rousseau developed a fine hand with stylus and pen, but gained his skill at the cost of many beatings, of knowing much hunger in his master's house, and of feeling his spirit debased and his life dark-ened.

Like other ill-used, unhappy adolescents—and he was also virtually an orphan—Jean-Jacques tended to live a great deal in his fantasies as he wandered about, often alone, on his free Sundays. The many books he devoured, borrowed for three sous from an old woman vendor in Geneva's market, fed his compensating fantasies of high adventure, of fortune gained and beautiful maidens won. Yet, at sixteen, as he said of himself, he was ever "troubled, discontented and . . . without enjoyments."

Since his schooldays he had felt a passion for the outdoors. One evening toward sunset he was wandering in the fields beyond the city walls when suddenly he heard the bugles sound, and, running as hard as he could, he saw the great gates close before he could pass through. He must sleep in the open for the night and suffer a terrible beating for it in the morning. The thought came to him that it was like a sign from above—so be it! His father had abandoned him; he detested his uncle and the engraver, who beat him for reading books; the gates of his city had shut him out. Like so many other poor young Swiss he would run away. Thus began the incredible vagabond years of Jean-Jacques Rousseau.

On the morrow there was a beautiful day of early spring; he gloried in his liberty as he walked along the high road, all but penniless, wearing his little sword. After crossing the border of Savoy, territory of the Catholic King of Sardinia, he found a kindly village curé, who was on the watch for strayed Calvinists; the hungry boy was uncommonly well-fed, sheltered for the night, then sent on to a certain Mme. de Warens in the nearby town of Annecy. This good lady, herself a Swiss convert to the Catholic faith, seemed to make it her business to offer hospitality to Protestants and others who, like herself, might be persuaded to change their religion. She was a gracious widow, still in her thirties; the runaway, enjoying her charity, and good fare, was entranced by the pretty and buxom woman and readily yielded to her counsels. After being given a little money for the road, he was directed to journey to the Hospice of the Spirito Santo at Turin for further religious instruction. The dim, thick-walled monastery reawakened for a while his inbred aversion and fear of the Catholic Church. There were other proselytes here, and among them low creatures whose vile approaches shocked the youth; they too had come to change their religion for the sake of bread. Within a few days he was instructed, baptized, given a donation of twenty francs, and put out in the street.

Vainly he sought for work at his own trade; in his straits the son of free republican burgers of Geneva lowered himself to accept a place as lackey to an aged lady of Turin. A while later, amid the confusion of a funeral in the house, he stole a piece of ribbon, was caught, and then (as he confessed long years afterward) accused another servant of the theft; together with her he was dismissed. Again a kindly curé, the model of the "Savoyard Priest" in *Émile,* consoled him and placed him in service with another noble family. His intelligence and bits of erudition were noticed, and he would have been advanced to be secretary to a baron; but by then spring had come, the wanderlust possessed him, and he was off with a wild young companion on the roads over the Alps, in search of "treasures, feasts, and damsels eager to serve."

After a whole series of escapades and follies, the youth appeared again at the door of Mme. de Warens, whom he could not forget and whom he longed to serve. Though her house was always filled with priests and proselytes in transit, whom she was paid by the King of Sardinia to entertain, her scruples were not severe: she was outwardly pious but was also a discreet libertine. The seventeen-year-old Rousseau was allowed to stay for a while as one of her small staff. After failing to interest him in studying for the priesthood, at his own earnest demand she turned him over to a music master for instruction. Music he loved above all; soon he was giving lessons to others.

Departing on some secret mission to Paris, Mme. de Warens required Rousseau to accompany his music teacher on a journey to Lyons. But finding the man a sodden alcoholic, Jean-Jacques callously abandoned him at some tavern, where the teacher's precious music books were all stolen. The youth pushed on alone, enduring adventures along the road with increasing boldness and wit, like a Cagliostro, often encountering persons who trusted and sheltered him. Reason enough for him to attest in later years that, of his own knowledge, the plain people were "naturally good." Reaching Lausanne, he had the gall to give a music concert on his own. After that he agreed to serve as aide to an imposter posing as a Greek archimandrite gathering funds for his church. At Berne, where his accomplice was exposed, Rousseau narrowly escaped arrest and gained the protection of a French diplomat, who sent him on to people in Paris. There Rousseau found nothing to hold him, so back he went to Savoy and his beloved *maman,* Mme. de Warens, who forgave him for his sins. He was by now in his twenties, and she took him as one of her two current lovers, the other being her majordomo, an older man, making what the French call *un ménage à trois.* Rousseau served as her secretary.

Rousseau's youthful wanderings, so vividly described later by himself, were to be imitated by hosts of cultivated travelers, especially by the romantic poets who followed his steps. Before his time, almost no one journeyed for love of nature, but only on business bent. The young Rousseau was the kind of philosopher who often slept in the fields under the stars. He said: "Never did I think so much, nor exist so much, never was I so much myself as in the journeys I made alone and on foot. . . . Walking animated and enlivened my ideas."

No great writer was so little "literary" as he; his mind was formed not by received ideas at a school or university, but by exposure to life and by direct observation. Meanwhile, his intellectual growth, through formal education was retarded. This was a key principle of his innovative scheme of education as set forth in *Émile*. He learned much about real social forces in peasant huts or roadside inns, or even as a servant in the homes of the gentry. His fairly bewildering adventures in youth were in the deepest sense fruitful, for he remained a free spirit unreconciled to the values and usages of society in the declining phase of that *ancien régime* which he judged with the eye of an "outsider."

In 1738, at the age of twenty-five, while living at the villa of Mme. de Warens, who had removed to Chambéry, there began for him a truly happy interlude of repose and continuous study. While serving as Mme. de Warens' secretary he also gave lessons in music and tutored students. A small inheritance from his mother's estate, which he turned over to his mistress and benefactress, also contributed to his sense of security.

Love had come to him first in the form of a middle-aged woman. After a while he separated himself gently from her household and moved to a little cottage in the beautiful vale of Les Charmettes outside of Chambéry, where he lived alone. He had become so much her devoted "son," he explained, that he could no longer be her lover. There, surrounding himself with many books, setting up a little scientific laboratory for himself, quite in the eighteenth-century fashion, he gave himself wholeheartedly to his belated education. At the same time he composed songs and essayed his first piece of verse (poor enough), and some prose that was better. Living generally in solitude, in the rustic setting he loved, he enjoyed the three happiest summers of his life. His real companions now were "the divine Plato," Bacon, Copernicus, Newton, Galileo, Spinoza, and Locke, whose texts he read slowly but attentively.

By an extraordinary act of will, the former vagabond,

who had passed through the underworld of Europe, educated and also regenerated himself, becoming not only a man of learning but one strong on virtue. The heretical Christian reasserted itself in him; it was at this period that he adopted that "natural religion" which in later years he expounded so movingly in *The Creed of a Savoyard Priest*.

Those idyllic years came to an end in 1741, when he parted from his surrogate *maman* to serve as tutor to the children of the Provost Marshal de Mably of Lyons. Now he appeared as a man fully formed, high-minded and original in his ideas and speech. After about a year, having performed his duties admirably, he moved on to Paris again, armed with letters of strong recommendation to eminent persons in the capital. He had invented a new system of musical notation with which he hoped to establish himself in Paris; but it was offered in vain at the Conservatory. Yet his evident intellectual potential gained him new and influential friends, and especially such *grandes dames* as Mme. Dupin, a woman with both wealth and intelligence. At her salon he soon encountered the brilliant group of "the philosophes," among them Diderot, Condillac, d'Alembert, the Abbé de Mably, and the playwright Marivaux. Parisians, though they might seem "cold" and "sharp," have always been hospitable to any man who was not a bore. Rousseau was personable, had a very expressive physiognomy, and when stimulated spoke with a trenchant and often paradoxical reasoning power; in short he was an original who could rise to heights of eloquence. In 1742 one of his aristocratic patrons—for the educated class was virtually limited then to the well-born—won him an appointment as secretary to the French ambassador to Venice. There he did service as a diplomatic aide for more than a year and, it was said, performed ably; but his superior proved to be a fool; the independent-minded Rousseau quarreled with him, was dismissed, and returned to Paris. It was the last time he ever accepted a well-paid office under another person's orders. He cared nothing whatsoever for money, he used to say. Thereafter he chose to support himself in modest fashion by copying music in his spare time.

Now he began to write and also to compose music. Diderot, who at first was captivated by Rousseau, invited him to contribute articles on music and political philosophy to the French Encyclopedia, then in its momentous beginnings. He also had a first little opera produced in the private theater of a female Maecenas of Paris; her lover, the young

Duke of Richelieu, then commissioned Rousseau to retouch an opera ballet by Rameau and Voltaire for production at the court.

The Swiss watchmaker's son was fairly thriving in Paris, and acquired a mistress. His choice fell upon a young and illiterate servant-maid, Thérèse Levasseur, who remained with him for the rest of his life. At least, he used to say, he had found a simple, submissive type of woman who would never mock him, ever the timid lover who cared greatly for the other sex.

It was as if he had been gathering himself for some great effort during several years in the capital. In December, 1749, the Academy of Dijon announced as the subject of its annual essay contest the question: Has the advancement of civilization tended to corrupt or improve morals? At the time he learned of this, Rousseau was in a state of high excitement; his "brother" Diderot was in prison at Vincennes for his "godless" writings, and Rousseau now proposed to attack the establishment by choosing the paradoxical side of the debate initiated by the Dijon Academy. He would argue for (what became) his characteristic thesis—that a mounting corruption went hand in hand with the progress of the arts and sciences in a society wanting in justice and liberty. He went on to affirm that while primitive man (Rousseau's "noble savage") in the distant past had been "naturally good" and free, the present order of society made men increasingly vile and unhappy. Man must somehow strive to win back "the rights of nature" and the "primordial equality" he had once enjoyed. Rousseau's first full-fledged discourse was awarded the prize—was it a sign of a slow change of heart even among academicians? There was widespread debate over Rousseau's ideas in France as in all literate Europe, where thinking men grasped his essential message and kindled to his humane appeal for social justice.

His eloquence and freshness of approach brought him fame overnight. Not long afterward, he published his much stronger *Discourse on Inequality* (also included in this volume), which won him even wider fame. At the same period his simple, Italian-style opera, *Le Devin du village*, was produced before the King and Mme. de Pompadour and became popular. Paris was astonished to learn that the "wild man" from Geneva had refused to appear in court and thus forfeited the royal pension offered him. In a few strides, Jean-Jacques had won a celebrity rivaling Voltaire's, and he admitted to being "the most sought-after man in Paris."

Now he adopted a way of life that was in strict accord with his own teachings, that of a nonconformist in religion, of an abstemious Spartan in his daily regimen, and of a tireless advocate of egalitarian doctrine. Though he described himself as a commoner, who had the right to vote in town meetings as a Citizen of Geneva, he continued to frequent the elite, including diverse counts, dukes, and duchesses, while limiting the time he allotted them. He remained an odd hero in those same "artificial" salons of the French illuminati whom he criticized so severely. All the more did the reigning hostesses of the period, a Mme. d'Épinay or a Duchess de Luxembourg, pursue with their attentions and largesse this most difficult of literary lions, who dressed in outlandish costumes and wore a fur hat in summer.

Eventually, because he was so besieged by crowds in Paris, he made his way to the country outside the city, to the Forest of Montmorency, where he resided in a cottage on Mme. d'Épinay's estate—always with Thérèse and her mother—refusing place and money, and still copying music to gain his bread. In the late 1750's he was engaged in completing his long-prepared master works, which seemed to appear all together: the long romantic novel, *La Nouvelle Héloise,* which changed the whole course of European literature and moved men away from the arid neoclassicism that had gone before; this was followed within two years by *Émile,* his great tract on education, and *The Social Contract,* which prefigured the French Revolution and its Declaration of the Rights of Man.

The drama of Rousseau's late years when, a chronically ill man, he was persecuted by the governments of France and other nations and driven from one place of exile to another, made his appeal to the imaginations of men greater than that of any writer of his century. His most important books, *Émile* and *The Social Contract,* were burned by the common hangman in Paris, as well as in his native Switzerland, where religious fanatics forced him to take refuge for a year in England under the protection of David Hume. Suffering pain, distracted by his misfortunes, he became somewhat paranoid at the end, quarreling with old friends and even new ones. Yet he held his ground courageously enough, replying to his accusers in magnificent polemical discourses such as his "Letters from the Mountain." Thus in the eyes of the men of his century he assumed heroic

qualities as a man who lived in storm, undergoing martyr-
dom for having spoken great truths which the establishment
treated as Dangerous Thoughts. In 1767, in his old age, he
returned to France, where he lived until he died in 1778,
residing mostly in the country but sometimes staying in
Paris under a transparent incognito that the government
tacitly overlooked. Though his mind was somewhat clouded,
some of his finest writings date from those last days. His
works as moralist and political philosopher influenced and
fascinated minds as different as those of Hume, Kant,
Goethe, Byron, Schiller, and, in recent times, the American
behaviorist philosopher John Dewey. New opponents of
conservative bias have continued to write against him in the
present century, but he has also won new admirers, such as
the great French anthropologist, Claude Levi-Strauss.

The words you may freely read here in this volume of
new translations were once burned at the stake in Paris and
Geneva. But how can you burn ideas? How can you keep
the human spirit in exile? There were pages of Rousseau's
that were stronger than whole armies or the despots commanding them. He made history because, as Carlyle suggested, his writings were really *actions*. Though Carlyle
himself was an opponent of Rousseau's democratic teachings, he named him a "Hero as Man of Letters," adding:
"What could the world do, what could the governors of
the world do with such a man?"

—MATTHEW JOSEPHSON

The Social Contract
Or
Principles of
Political Right

By
J.-J. Rousseau,
Citizen of Geneva

—*foederis aequas Dicamus leges.*
AENEID, XI

CONTENTS

BOOK III

BOOK IV

FOREWORD

This little treatise was originally part of a larger work begun in the past without considering my ability to finish it, and long since abandoned. Of the various segments that could have been taken from what I had written, this one is the longest, and seems to me the least unworthy of being offered to the public. The rest no longer exists.

BOOK I

Taking men as they are and laws as they can be, I propose to inquire whether there can be any legitimate and reliable rule of administration in the civil order. In this inquiry I shall try always to combine what right permits with what interest prescribes, so that justice and utility will not be divided.

I shall go directly to my subject without first demonstrating its importance. I may be asked if I am a ruler or a lawmaker, since I am writing on politics. I answer that I am neither, and that that is why I am writing on politics. If I were a ruler or a lawmaker, I would not waste time saying what ought to be done; I would either do it or remain silent.

Having been born a citizen of a free state and a member of its sovereign,* I feel that however slightly my vote may affect public affairs, the right to vote on them is enough to make it my duty to inquire into them. When I reflect on governments, I am always happy to discover that my studies have given me new reasons to love the government of my own country.

CHAPTER I

The Subject of This First Book

Man is born free, and is everywhere in chains. This or that man may regard himself as the master of others, but he is more of a slave than they. How did this change

---

*For Rousseau, the sovereign is a collective being; see Book II, Chapter II. (Translator's note.)

come about? I do not know. What can make it legitimate? I believe I can answer that question.

If I were to consider only force and the effects it produces, I would say, "As long as a people is compelled to obey and does so, it does well; as soon as it is able to throw off its yoke and does so, it does even better, for it has recovered its freedom by the same right as that by which it was taken away, so either it is justified in recovering it or there was no justification for taking it away." But the social order is a sacred right that serves as the basis of all others. Yet this right does not come from nature; it is therefore founded on agreements. The problem is to determine what those agreements are. First, however, I must substantiate what I have just stated.

CHAPTER II

The First Societies

The oldest of all societies, and the only natural one, is that of the family; yet even in it, children remain bound to their father only so long as they need him in order to survive. As soon as that need ceases, the natural bond is dissolved. The children are released from the duty of obeying the father, he is released from the duty of taking care of them, and they all become independent. If they continue to be united, it is no longer naturally, but voluntarily, and the family itself is maintained only by agreement.

This common freedom results from the nature of man. His first law is to look after his own preservation, his first concerns are those that he owes to himself. As soon as he reaches the age of reason, he is the sole judge of the proper means of preserving himself, and he thereby becomes his own master.

It can thus be said that the family is the first model of political societies: The father corresponds to the ruler, the children to the people; and all, having been born free and equal, give up their freedom only for their own advantage. The only difference is that in the family, the father's love for his children rewards him for the care he gives them, while in the state, the pleasure of commanding takes the place of love, which the ruler does not feel for his people.

Grotius denies that all human power is established in favor of those who are governed. He cites slavery as an example. His usual procedure is to establish right on the basis of fact.[1] It is possible to use a more logical method of reasoning, but not one more favorable to tyrants.

It is an open question, according to Grotius, whether the human race belongs to a hundred men, or whether those hundred men belong to the human race. All through his book he seems to lean toward the first view, which is also Hobbes's. Thus the human race is divided into herds of cattle, each with a ruler who watches over it in order to devour it.

Since a herder is of a nature superior to that of his herd, the herders of men, their rulers, are of a nature superior to that of their peoples. Such was the reasoning of the Emperor Caligula, as reported by Philo. He concluded from this analogy that either kings were gods or peoples were animals.

Caligula's reasoning is equivalent to that of Hobbes and Grotius. Before any of them, Aristotle had also said that men were not naturally equal, but that some were born to be slaves and others to be masters.

Aristotle was right, but he mistook effect for cause. Nothing is more certain than that any man born in slavery is born to be a slave. Slaves lose everything in their chains, even the desire to be free of them; they love their servitude as Ulysses' companions loved their brutishness.[2] If, then, there are slaves by nature, it is because there were once slaves against nature. Force made the first slaves, and their cowardice perpetuated slavery.

I have said nothing of King Adam or the Emperor Noah, father of three great monarchs who divided the world among themselves, like Saturn's children, with whom some have identified them. I hope my moderation will be appreciated, for I am a direct descendant of one of those monarchs, perhaps of the eldest branch, and who knows but what a verification of titles might establish me as the lawful king of the human race? Be that as it may, it cannot be denied that Adam was the sovereign of the world as Robinson Crusoe was of his island, as long as he was its only inhabitant; and the advantage of that empire was that the monarch was secure on his throne, with no rebellions, wars, or conspirators to fear.

CHAPTER III

The Right of the Strongest

The strongest man is never strong enough to maintain his mastery at all times unless he transforms his strength into right and obedience into a duty. Hence the right of the strongest, a right that is taken ironically in appearance and established as a principle in reality. But will anyone ever explain what the term means? I do not see what morality can be derived from physical force. Yielding to force is an act of necessity, not of will; at the very most, it is an act of prudence. In what sense could it be a duty?

Let us suppose for a moment that this alleged right exists. I say that nothing results from it but a mass of nonsense. For if might makes right, the effect changes with the cause: Any might greater than the first will take over its right. As soon as one can disobey with impunity, one can disobey legitimately, and since the strongest is always in the right, one has only to act in such a way as to be the strongest. But what kind of right is it that ceases to exist when strength perishes? If a man is forced to obey, he no longer has any obligation to do so. It is clear that the word "right" adds nothing to force; in that connection, it means nothing at all.

"Obey the powers that be." If that means "Yield to force," it is a good precept, but superfluous, and I can guarantee that it will never be violated. All power comes ·from God. I acknowledge that; but all disease comes from him also. Does this mean that it is forbidden to call a doctor? If a bandit waylays me in the forest, I am forced to give him my money, but if it were possible for me to keep it, would I have a moral obligation to give it to him anyway? After all, the pistol he points at me is also a form of force.

Let us agree, then, that might does not make right, and that we are obligated to obey only legitimate powers. Thus my original question returns.

CHAPTER IV

Slavery

Since no man has natural authority over any other, and since force creates no right, we can only conclude that agreements are the basis of all legitimate authority among men.

If, asks Grotius, an individual can alienate his freedom and make himself the slave of a master, why cannot an entire people alienate its freedom and make itself subject to a king? There are many ambiguous words here that need explanation, but let us confine ourselves to "alienate." In this context, it can mean only "give" or "sell." Now a man who makes himself another's slave does not give himself; he sells himself, at least for his subsistence. But for what does a people sell itself? Far from giving his subjects their subsistence, a king draws his own only from them, and as Rabelais says, a king does not live on little. Do his subjects give themselves to him on condition that he will also take their property? If so, I do not see what they have left to preserve.

It will be said that a despot guarantees his subjects civil peace. Granted, but what do they gain if the wars in which his ambition involves them, his insatiable greed, and the harassments inflicted on them by his ministers distress them more than their dissensions would do? What do they gain if that civil peace is one of their miseries? Life in a dungeon is also peaceful; is that enough to make it desirable? The Greeks imprisoned in the Cyclops' cave lived peacefully, while waiting their turn to be devoured.

To say that a man gives himself for nothing is to say something absurd and incomprehensible. Such an act is illegitimate and invalid, from the mere fact that the man who does it is not in possession of his reason. To say the same thing of an entire people is to assume a people composed of madmen, and madness does not make right.

Even if a man can alienate his own freedom, he cannot alienate that of his children. They are born human and free; their freedom belongs to them, and no one else has a right to dispose of it. Before they have reached the age of reason, their father can, in their name, stipulate conditions for their preservation, but he cannot give them to someone else irrevocably and unconditionally, for such an act is contrary to the ends of nature and goes beyond the rights of fatherhood. In order, then, for an arbitrary government to be legitimate, each generation of the people would have to be free to accept or reject it; but then the government would no longer be arbitrary.

A man who renounces his freedom renounces his humanity, along with the rights of humanity, and even its duties. There is no possible compensation for someone who renounces everything. Such a renunciation is incompatible with the nature of man, and to remove all freedom from his will is to remove all morality from his acts. And finally, an agreement that stipulates absolute authority on one side and unlimited obedience on the other is vain and contradictory. Is it not clear that one has no obligation toward someone from whom one is entitled to demand everything, and does not that single condition, without reciprocity or compensation, nullify the agreement? What right could my slave have against me, since everything he has belongs to me? His rights are mine, and the idea of my rights against myself is meaningless.

Grotius and others see war as another origin of the supposed right of enslavement. Since the victor has the right to kill the vanquished, they say, the latter can save his life at the expense of his freedom, an agreement that is all the more legitimate because it is advantageous to both parties.

But it is clear that this supposed right to kill the vanquished does not result in any way from the state of war. Since men living in their original independence have no mutual relations stable enough to constitute either a state of peace or a state of war, they are not naturally enemies. It is a relation of things, not of men, that constitutes war, and since the state of war cannot arise from simple personal relations, but only from material relations, private war, or war between man and man, cannot exist, either in the state of nature, where there is no stable property, or in the social state, where everything is under the authority of law.

Individual combats, such as duels and other fights, are acts that do not constitute a state. As for the private wars authorized by the Establishments of Saint Louis and suspended by the Peace of God, they were abuses of feudal government, an absurd system if ever there was one, contrary to the principles of natural right and all good political administration.

War is therefore not a relation of man to man, but a relation of state to state, in which individuals are enemies only accidentally, not as men or even as citizens,[3] but as soldiers; not as members of their nation, but as its defenders. Finally, the enemies of a state can only be other states, not men, because there can be no real relation between things of different natures.

This principle is in conformity with the established rules of all times and the uniform practice of all civilized nations. Declarations of war are notifications not so much to rulers as to their subjects. A foreigner, whether a king, a private individual, or a people, who robs, kills, or imprisons a ruler's subjects without addressing a declaration of war to him is not an enemy, but a brigand. Even in the midst of a war, a just ruler takes possession of all public property in the enemy country, but respects the lives and property of individuals; he respects the rights on which his own are founded. Since the goal of war is the destruction of the enemy state, one has a right to kill its defenders as long as they bear arms, but as soon as they lay down their arms and surrender, they cease to be enemies or instruments of the enemy; they are now simply men again, and the right to kill them no longer exists. Sometimes it is possible to kill a state without killing a single one of its members, and war gives no right that is not necessary to the achievement of its goal. These principles are not those of Grotius; they are not founded on the authority of poets: They derive from the nature of things, and are founded on reason.

As for the right of conquest, it has no other foundation than the power of the strongest. If war does not give the victor the right to massacre conquered peoples, this nonexistent right cannot be used as the basis of a right to enslave them. One has a right to kill an enemy only when one cannot enslave him; the right to enslave him therefore does not come from the right to kill him, and it is an unjust bargain to make him pay for his life, over which the victor has no right, with his freedom. Is it not clear that there is a vicious circle in founding the right of life and death on the right of enslavement, and the right of enslavement on the right of life and death?

Even assuming that terrible right to kill everyone, I say that men enslaved in war, or conquered peoples, are under no obligation to their master; they must obey him only as long as they are forced to do so. In taking an equivalent of their life, the victor has not spared them: Rather than killing them unprofitably, he has killed them profitably. He is so far from having acquired any authority over them, in addition to force, that the state of war continues between them as before; their relation to each other is an effect of it, and use of the right of war does not imply a treaty of peace. It is true that an agreement has been made between the victor and the vanquished, but far from destroying the state of war, that agreement presupposes its continuation.

Thus no matter how we look at it, the right of enslavement is invalid, not only because it is illegitimate, but also because it is absurd and meaningless. The words "enslavement" and "right" are mutually contradictory; they exclude each other. It will always be nonsensical for a man to say to another man or to a people, "I make with you an agreement entirely at your expense and entirely to my advantage. I will keep it as long as I please, and you will keep it as long as I please."

CHAPTER V

We Must Always Go Back to a First Agreement

Even if I were to grant everything that I have so far refuted, supporters of despotism would be no better off. There will always be a great difference between subduing a multitude and governing a society. If separate individuals are successively subjugated to the domination of one man, whatever their number may be, I see only a master and his slaves, not a people and its ruler. The result can be called an aggregation, but not an association; there is no public good or body politic. Even if the man in question has enslaved half the world, he is still only a private individual, and his interest, separate from that of others, is still only a private interest. If he dies, his empire is left scattered and without cohesion, as an oak disintegrates and falls into a heap of ashes when it has been consumed by fire.

A people, says Grotius, can give itself to a king. According to Grotius, then, a people is a people before giving itself to a king. That gift is itself a civil act and presupposes a collective agreement. Therefore, before examining the act by which a people elects a king, it would be good to examine the agreement by which a people is a people. Since the latter necessarily precedes the former, it is the true foundation of society.

If there were no prior agreement, why—assuming that the election was not unanimous—should the minority be obligated to submit to the choice of the majority? Why should a hundred men who want a master have the right to vote on behalf of ten who do not? The rule of accepting the decision of the majority is itself established by agreement and presupposes unanimity on at least one occasion.

CHAPTER VI

The Social Pact

I suppose men to have reached the point where the obstacles to their survival in the state of nature have a resistance that cannot be overcome by the forces each individual has at his disposal for preserving himself in that state. The time has thus come when that original state can subsist no longer, and the human race will perish if it does not change its way of living.

Since men cannot engender new forces, but can only unite and direct existing ones, they now have only one means of preserving themselves: to form by aggregation a sum of forces capable of overcoming the resistance, then direct them toward a single goal and make them act together.

Such a sum of forces can be produced only by the collaboration of a group of men. But since each man's strength and freedom are his primary means of self-preservation, how can he pledge them without harming himself, without neglecting the care he owes to himself? The problem that arises here can be stated as follows:

"To devise a form of association which will defend and protect the person and possessions of each associate with all the collective strength, and in which each is united with all, yet obeys only himself and remains as free as before." Such is the fundamental problem that the social contract solves.

The terms of this contract are so determined by the nature of the agreement that the slightest alteration would make them null and void, so that even though they may never have been formally enunciated, they are everywhere the same, everywhere tacitly accepted and acknowledged, as long as the social pact is not violated, in which case each man regains his original rights and returns to his natural freedom, losing the contractual freedom for which he renounced it.

These terms, properly understood, can all be reduced to one, namely, the complete surrender of each associate, with all his rights, to the whole community. For in the first place, since each man gives himself entirely, the condition is equal for all; and since the condition is equal for all, it is to no one's interest to make it burdensome for others.

Furthermore, since the surrender is made without reserve, the union is as perfect as it can be and no associate has anything more to demand, for if individuals retained any rights, each would soon be his own judge on some point or other, there being no common superior to decide between him and the public; then eventually everyone would set himself up as his own judge on all points, the state of nature would subsist, and the association would necessarily become either tyrannical or ineffectual.

Finally, in giving himself to all, each man gives himself to no one, and since he acquires the same right over all the other associates as they acquire over him, he gains the equivalent of everything he loses, plus greater power to preserve what he has.

If, then, we exclude from the social pact everything that is not essential to it, we find that it reduces itself to this formulation: "Each of us puts his person and all his power in common under the supreme control of the general will, and we collectively receive each member as an indivisible part of the whole."

In place of the individual persons of the contracting parties, the act of association immediately creates a collective, artificial body, composed of as many members as the assembly has voters, and the same act gives this body its unity, its collective self, its life, and its will. Such a public person, formed by the union of all other persons, was formerly called a *city*,[4] and is now known as a *republic* or a *body politic*. Its members call it the *state* when it is passive, the *sovereign* when it is active and a *power* when they compare it with others of its kind. They themselves collectively take the name of the *people*, and are individually called *citizens* as sharing in the sovereign authority, and *subjects* as owing obedience to the laws of the state. But these terms are often used indiscriminately, one in place of another; it is enough to know how to distinguish them when they are used precisely.

CHAPTER VII

The Sovereign

This formulation shows that the act of association involves a reciprocal commitment between the public and the individuals who compose it, and that each individual, contracting with himself, so to speak, is under a double obligation: toward other individuals, as a member of the sovereign, and toward the sovereign, as a member of the state. But the principle of common law which says that a man cannot be held to a commitment he has made to himself does not apply here, for there is a great difference between assuming an obligation toward himself and assuming one toward a whole of which he is a part.

It should also be pointed out that while public decisions can obligate all subjects toward the sovereign, because of the two capacities in which each subject is considered, they cannot obligate the sovereign toward itself. It is therefore contrary to the nature of the body politic for the sovereign to impose a law on itself that it cannot infringe. Since it can be considered only in a single capacity, it is in the position of an individual contracting with himself. Hence we see that there neither is nor can be any kind of fundamental law binding on the people as a body—not even the social contract. This does not mean that the body politic cannot assume obligations toward others, insofar as they do not violate that contract, for in relation to outsiders it is an indivisible being, an individual.

But since the body politic or the sovereign draws its being only from the sanctity of the contract, it can never obligate itself, even to an outsider, to do anything contrary to that original agreement, such as alienating some portion of itself, or placing itself under the authority of another sovereign. To violate the agreement by which it exists would be to annihilate itself, and that which is nothing can do nothing.

Once a multitude is thus united in a body, no one can offend one of its members without attacking the body, much less offend the body without affecting its members. Duty and interest therefore equally oblige the two contracting parties to help each other, and the same men must seek to combine, in their double capacity, all the advantages that pertain to it.

The sovereign, being formed only by the individuals who compose it, neither has nor can have any interest contrary to theirs; consequently there is no need for the sovereign power to give guarantees to the subjects, because it is impossible for the body to want to harm all its members, and as we shall see later, it cannot harm any one of them in particular. Merely by virtue of existing, the sovereign is always what it should be.

This, however, is not true of the subjects in relation to the sovereign, which, despite the common interest, could not count on them to fulfill their obligations unless it devised means of making sure of their fidelity.

Each individual can, as a man, have a private will different from or even contrary to the general will which he has as a citizen. His private interest may speak to him quite differently from the common interest; his absolute and naturally independent existence may make him regard what he owes to the common cause as a gratuitous contribution, loss of which would be less harmful to others than payment of it is burdensome to him, and considering that the artificial person that constitutes the state is an imaginary being because it is not a man, he may want to enjoy the rights of a citizen without fulfilling the duties of a subject, an injustice that would bring about the ruin of the body politic if it were to spread.

In order, therefore, that the social pact shall not be an empty formality, it tacitly includes one stipulation without which all the others would be ineffectual: that anyone who refuses to obey the general will shall be compelled to do so by the whole body. This means nothing else than that he shall be forced to be free, for such is the condition which gives each citizen to his country and thus secures him against all personal dependence. This condition is essential to the functioning of the political machine, and it alone legitimizes civil obligations, which would otherwise be absurd, tyrannical, and subject to the most outrageous abuses.

Chapter VIII

The Civil State

The passage from the state of nature to the civil state produces a remarkable change in man by substituting justice for instinct in his conduct and giving his acts the morality they previously lacked. Only then, when physical impulses have yielded to the voice of duty, and appetite to right, does man, who so far had considered only himself, find that he is forced to act according to different principles and to consult his reason before listening to his inclinations. In this state he is deprived of some advantages given to him by nature, but he gains others so great—his faculties are exercised and developed, his ideas are broadened, his feelings are ennobled, his whole soul is uplifted—that if the abuses of this new state did not often degrade him below his previous level, he would constantly have reason to bless the happy moment when he was drawn out of the state of nature forever and changed from a stupid, short-sighted animal into an intelligent being and a man.

Let us reduce the balance to terms that can be easily compared. What man loses by the social contract is his natural freedom and an unlimited right to anything he wants and can get. What he gains is civil freedom and ownership of everything he possesses. To avoid error in evaluating this exchange, we must make two clear distinctions: first, between natural freedom, which is limited only by the individual's power, and civil freedom, which is limited by the general will; and second, between possession, which results only from force or the right of first occupancy, and ownership, which can be based only on juridical title.

Another gain can be added to those that come with the civil state: moral freedom, which alone makes man truly his own master, for impulsion by appetite alone is slavery, and obedience to self-imposed law is freedom. But I have already said too much on this point, and the philosophical meaning of the word "freedom" is not part of my subject here.

CHAPTER IX

Real Property

When the community is formed, each member gives himself to it as he is at that time, with all his resources, including the goods he possesses. This act does not make possessions change their nature in changing hands; they do not become property in the hands of the sovereign. But just as the might of the state is incomparably greater than the individual's public possession is, *de facto,* stronger and more irrevocable, though not more legitimate, at least so far as foreigners are concerned. For the state, in relation to its members, has control of all their goods by virtue of the social contract, which, within the state, is the basis of all rights; but it has control of them in relation to other powers only by virtue of the right of first occupancy, which it derives from individuals.

The right of first occupancy, though more real than the right of the strongest, does not become a true right until the right of property has been established. Every man has a natural right to everything that is necessary to him, but the juridical title that makes him the owner of one piece of property excludes him from all others. Having received his share, he must limit himself to it and can name no further claim to what is held in common. That is why the right of first occupancy, so weak in the state of nature, is deemed worthy of respect by every man in the civil state. In this right we respect less what belongs to others than what does not belong to us.

In general, to authorize the right of first occupancy to a certain piece of land, the following conditions are necessary. First, the land must not yet be inhabited by anyone; second, one must occupy only so much of it as one needs for one's subsistence; third, one must take possession of it not by a vain ceremony, but by work and cultivation, the only sign of ownership that must be respected by others in the absence of a juridical title.

In granting the right of first occupancy to need and work, are we not carrying it as far as it can go? Is it possible to leave that right without limits? In order for a man to lay claim to a piece of land held in common, shall it be enough for him to set foot on it? If he has the strength to expel others from it for a short time, shall that be enough to divest them forever of the right to return to it? If a man or a people seizes a vast territory and deprives the rest of the human race of it, is this not a punishable usurpation, since it robs other men of the habitation and food that nature had given them in common? When Nuñez Balboa stood on the shore and took possession of the Pacific Ocean and all of South America in the name of the Castilian crown, was that sufficient to dispossess all the inhabitants and exclude all of the world's other rulers? If so, such ceremonies were repeated unnecessarily, for the Catholic King could have sat in his study and taken possession of the whole world all at once, later deducting from his empire what was already in the possession of other monarchs.

It is easy to understand how adjoining parcels of land held by individuals are united and become public territory, and how the right of sovereignty, extending from subjects to the land they occupy, becomes real and personal. This places the possessors in greater dependency and makes their resources themselves a guarantee of their fidelity. Ancient monarchs apparently did not realize the advantage of this: They called themselves King of the Persians, Scythians, or Macedonians, and seemed to regard themselves as rulers of men rather than masters of a given country. Today's monarchs are clever enough to call themselves King of France, Spain, England, etc. By thus holding the land, they are sure of being able to hold its inhabitants.

Oddly enough, when an individual surrenders his goods to the community, the latter does not deprive him of them, but on the contrary, assures him of their legitimate possession. It changes usurpation into a genuine right, and tenure into ownership. He is then regarded as a depositary of public wealth; his rights are respected by all members of the state and upheld against foreigners by all its strength, so that by a transfer that is advantageous to the public and still more so to himself, he has, so to speak, acquired everything that he has given up. This paradox is easily explained by the distinction between the sovereign's and the owner's rights to the same piece of property, as we shall see later.

It may also happen that men begin to unite before they possess anything, then afterward occupy a territory large enough for all of them and either use it in common or divide it among themselves, the shares being either equal or of different sizes established by the sovereign. No matter how this acquisition is made, each individual's right over his own piece of land is always subordinate to the community's right over all the land, for otherwise there would be no strength in the social bond and no real power in the exercise of sovereignty.

I shall end this chapter and this book by pointing out something that should be the basis of the whole social system: Rather than destroying natural equality, the fundamental pact substitutes a moral and legitimate equality for whatever physical inequality nature has produced among men, so that while they may be unequal in strength or intelligence, they all become equal by agreement and rights.[5]

BOOK II

CHAPTER I

Sovereignty Is Inalienable

The first and most important consequence of the principles established above is that only the general will can direct the forces of the state in such a way as to achieve the goal for which it was instituted, namely, the common good; for while the creation of societies was made necessary by the clash of individual interests, it was made possible by the fact that those same interests also coincide. It is what they have in common that forms the social bond, and if there were no point at which all interests coincided, no society could exist. It is solely on the basis of this common interest that society should be governed.

I therefore say that sovereignty, being only the exercise of the general will, can never be alienated and that the sovereign, which is only a collective being, can be represented only by itself; power can be transferred, but will cannot.

While it is not impossible for an individual will to concur with the general will on a particular point, it is at least impossible for such a concurrence to be lasting and constant, for an individual will, by its nature, tends toward partiality, and the general will tends toward equality. It is still more impossible to have any guarantee of this concurrence; even if it were always to exist, it would be by accident and not by design. The sovereign can say, "I now will what this man wills, or at least what he says he wills," but it cannot say, "Tomorrow I shall still will what he wills," because it is absurd for the will to bind itself with regard to the future, and because no will can consent to anything contrary to the good of the being that wills. If, therefore, a people promises to obey unconditionally, it thereby dissolves itself and ceases to be a people; as soon as there is a master, there is no longer a sovereign, and the body politic is then destroyed.

This is not to say that the commands of rulers cannot

pass for general ills; they can, as long as the sovereign is free to oppose them and does not do so. In that case, universal silence must be assumed to indicate the people's consent. This will later be explained at greater length.

CHAPTER II

Sovereignty Is Indivisible

For the same reason that it is inalienable, sovereignty is indivisible. For either a will is general[6] or it is not; it is either the will of the whole people or of only a part of it. In the first case, when the will is declared, it is an act of sovereignty and constitutes law. In the second, it is only an individual will, or an act of administration, or at the very most, a decree.

But our political theorists, unable to divide sovereignty in its source, divide it in its object. They divide it into force and will; into legislative power and executive power; into the rights of taxation, justice, and war; into internal administration and the power to negotiate with foreigners. Sometimes they mingle all these parts and sometimes they separate them. They make the sovereign a fantastic being put together from various bits and pieces; it is as if they composed man of several bodies, each one with eyes, arms, or feet, and nothing more. Japanese conjurers are said to dismember a child before spectators, throw all the pieces into the air one after the other, then make the child fall to the ground, alive and whole. This is essentially the same as the legerdemain of our political theorists: After having dismembered the social body by a sleight-of-hand trick worthy of a fair, they reassemble the pieces in a manner known only to themselves.

This error comes from not having formed precise ideas concerning sovereign authority, and from mistaking mere manifestations of it for parts of it. Thus, for example, declaring war and making peace have been regarded as acts of sovereignty, which they are not. Each of these acts is not a law, but only an application of the law, a particular act which determines how the law applies in a given case, as will be seen clearly when the idea attached to the word "law" has been delineated.

If the other divisions were examined in the same way, it would be found that anyone who thinks he sees sovereignty divided is always mistaken, that all the rights taken for parts of it are subordinate to it and always presuppose supreme wills which they merely put into execution.

This lack of precision has introduced vast amounts of obscurity into the conclusions of political philosophers when they try to judge the respective rights of kings and peoples on the basis of the principles they have previously established. Everyone can see, in Chapters III and IV of the first book of Grotius, how that learned man and his translator Barbeyrac become entangled and embroiled in their own sophistries, for fear of saying too much or too little to suit their purposes, and of offending the interests they set out to conciliate. Grotius, a refugee in France, dissatisfied with his own country and wishing to win the favor of Louis XIII, to whom his book is dedicated, spares no effort to strip peoples of all their rights and bestow them on kings as artfully as possible. That would also have been very much to the liking of Barbeyrac, who dedicated his translation to the King of England, George I. But unfortunately the expulsion of James II, which he calls an abdication, forced him to maintain an attitude of reserve, to equivocate and be evasive, in order to avoid making William out to be a usurper. If those two writers had adopted the right principles, all their difficulties would have been removed and they would always have been consistent; but they would have sadly told the truth and won favor only with the people. Telling the truth is not a way to make one's fortune; the people appoints no ambassadors or professors, and grants no pensions.

CHAPTER III

Whether the General Will Can Err

It follows from what has been said above that the general will is always well-meaning and always tends toward the public good; but it does not follow that all decisions made by the people are equally sound. We always will our own good, but we do not always see what it is. The people is never corrupted, but it is often misled, and only then does it seem to will what is bad.

There is often a great difference between the will of all and the general will. The latter looks only to the common interest, while the former looks to private interest and is only a sum of individual wills. But take away from those same wills the pluses and minuses that cancel each other out,[7] and the general will remains as the sum of the differences.

If the people always decided on the basis of adequate information, and with no discussion among the citizens beforehand, the general will would always result from the larger number of small differences and the decision would always be right. But when there are factions, lesser associations detrimental to the greater one, the will of each of them becomes general in relation to its members and particular in relation to the state. It can then be said that there are no longer as many voters as there are men, but only as many as there are associations. The differences become less numerous and give a less general result. Finally, when one of these associations is so large that it prevails over all the others, the result is no longer a sum of small differences, but a single difference; there is then no longer a general will, and the opinion that prevails is only a particular one.

Therefore, if the general will is to be clearly expressed, it is important that there be no partial societies within the state, and that each citizen form his opinion independently.[8] Such was the unique and sublime system established by the great Lycurgus. When partial societies do exist, they must be made numerous and prevented from being unequal, as was done by Solon, Numa, and Servius. These are the only effective precautions that can be taken to ensure that the general will is always enlightened and the people never mistaken.

CHAPTER IV

Limits of the Sovereign Power

If the state or body politic is only an artificial person whose life is in the union of its members, and if its most important concern is its own preservation, it must have a universal coercive power in order to move and direct each part in the manner most advantageous to the whole. Just as nature gives each man absolute power over the parts of his body, the social pact gives the body politic absolute power over its members, and it is this same power which, under the direction of the general will, bears the name of sovereignty, as I have already said.

But besides this public person, we must also consider the private persons who compose it, and whose life and freedom are naturally independent of it. We must therefore distinguish between the respective rights of the citizens and the sovereign,[9] as well as between the duties which the citizens must fulfill as subjects and the natural rights they should enjoy as men.

It is acknowledged that the social pact requires each individual to relinquish only that part of his power, possessions, and freedom which it is important for the community to control; but it must also be acknowledged that the sovereign is the sole judge of that importance.

If a citizen is able to render certain services to the state, it is his duty to render them as soon as the sovereign requests them. But the sovereign, for its part, cannot place the subjects under any constraint useless to the community; it cannot even will to do so, for under the law of reason, as under the law of nature, nothing can occur without a cause.

The commitments that bind us to the social body are obligatory only because they are mutual, and their nature is such that, in fulfilling them, one cannot work for others without also working for oneself. Why is the general will always well-meaning, and why does everyone constantly will the happiness of each individual, if not because everyone applies the word "each" to himself and thinks of himself when he votes for the good of all? This proves that equality of rights, and the notion of justice it produces, stem from the preference that each man gives to himself, and therefore from the nature of man. It proves that in order to be truly general, the general will must be general in its object as well as in its essence, that it must come from everyone if it is to apply to everyone, and that it loses its natural rectitude when it tends toward a specific individual object, for we are then judging something alien to us, with no true principle of equity to guide us.

As soon as a question of particular fact or right arises on a point that has not been settled by a prior general agreement, the matter becomes contentious. It is a lawsuit in which the individuals concerned are one party and the public is the other, but I do not see which law should be followed, or which judge should hand down the decision. It would be ridiculous to try to resolve the question by an express decision of the general will, which could be only the conclusion of one of the parties, and would consequently be for the other party only an alien, particular will, inclined in this case toward injustice, and subject to error. Thus, just as a particular will cannot represent the general will, the general will in turn changes its nature when it has a particular object, and cannot, in its capacity as the general will, pronounce judgment on either a man or a fact. When the people of Athens, for example, appointed and removed its leaders, bestowed honors on some and inflicted punishment on others, and by multitudes of decrees indiscriminately exercised all functions of government, it no longer had a general will in the true sense of the term; it was no longer acting as a sovereign, but as a magistrate. This will seem contrary to generally accepted ideas, but I must be given time to set forth my own views.

From the above it should be apparent that what makes a will general is not so much the number of individuals involved as the common interest that unites them, for under this system each man necessarily submits to the conditions he imposes on others. This admirable concordance between self-interest and justice gives collective deliberations an equitable character that vanishes in a discussion of any particular matter in which there is no common interest to unite and identify the criteria of the judge with those of the party.

By whatever direction we approach the principle, we always reach the same conclusion, namely, that the social pact establishes such equality among citizens that they all bind themselves under the same conditions and should all enjoy the same rights. Thus by the nature of the pact, any act of sovereignty, that is, any genuine act of the general will, obligates or favors all citizens equally, so that the sovereign recognizes only the nation as a whole and does not distinguish any of the individuals who compose it. What, then, strictly speaking, is an act of sovereignty? It is an agreement not between a superior and an inferior, but between the body politic and each of its members. It is a legitimate agreement because it is based on the social contract; it is equitable because it is common to all; it is useful because it can have no other object than the general good; and it is binding because it is backed by public force and supreme power. As long as the subjects are bound only by such agreements, they obey no one; they obey only their own will, and to ask how far the respective rights of the sovereign and the citizens extend is to ask how far the citizens can go in imposing obligations on themselves, each committing himself to all, and all to each.

From this it can be seen that the power of the sovereign, absolute, sacred, and inviolable though it is, does not and cannot go beyond the bounds of general agreements, and that each man has full control of such goods and freedom as have been left to him by those agreements, so that the sovereign never has a right to burden one subject more than another, because the matter then becomes particular and therefore lies beyond the competency of the sovereign power.

Once these distinctions have been accepted, it becomes obvious that individuals do not really give up anything when they enter into the social contract. Their new situation is genuinely preferable to their old one, before the contract. Rather than depriving themselves of anything, they have made an advantageous exchange: Instead of an uncertain and precarious way of life, they now have one that is better and more secure; instead of natural independence, they now have freedom; instead of the power to harm others, they now have their own security; and instead of their individual strength, which others might overcome, they now have rights which the social union makes invincible. Their lives themselves, which they have devoted to the state, are constantly protected by it, and when they risk them to defend it, are they not simply returning to it what they have received from it? Are they not doing what they would have to do more often and with greater danger in the state of nature, in which they would inevitably have to risk their lives in fights to defend their means of preserving them? It is true that everyone must fight for his country when necessary, but it is also true that no one ever has to fight for himself. Are we not better off in running a risk to defend what gives us our security, rather than running the greater risk that would be imposed on us if we lost that security?

CHAPTER V

The Right of Life and Death

It may be asked how individuals, having no right to dispose of their own lives, can transfer such a right to the sovereign. The question seems difficult to answer only because it is wrongly formulated. Everyone has the right to risk his life in order to preserve it. Has it ever been said that a man who jumps from a window to escape a fire is guilty of suicide? Has that crime ever been imputed to a man who died in a storm at sea, having been aware of the danger when he boarded the ship?

The purpose of the social contract is the preservation of the contracting parties. He who wills the end also wills the means, and in this case the means are inseparable from certain risks, and even certain losses. Anyone who wants to preserve his life at the expense of others must be willing to give it for them when necessary. When the law requires a citizen to expose himself to a danger, he is no longer his own judge of it, and when the government says to him, "It is expedient for the state that you die," he must die, since it is only on that condition that he has so far lived in security, and since his life is no longer merely a gift of nature, but a conditional grant from the state.

The death penalty imposed on criminals can be viewed in much the same light: It is to avoid being a murderer's victim that each man consents to die if he should become a murderer himself. Far from disposing of his life, he thinks only of making it more secure; we may assume that none of the parties to the agreement intends to get himself hanged.

Moreover, every criminal attacks social rights, and by his crimes, becomes a rebel and a traitor to his country. In violating its laws, he ceases to be a member of it, and even wages war against it. The preservation of the state is then incompatible with his, and one of the two must perish. When a criminal is put to death, it is less as a citizen than as an enemy. His trial and judgment prove and declare that he has broken the social contract and is therefore no longer a member of the state. Since he has acknowledged himself to be a member of it, at the very least by living within its boundaries, he must be cut off from it, either by banishment as a violator of the pact, or by death as a public enemy; for such an enemy is not an artificial person, but a man, and in that case the right of war is to kill the vanquished.

But, it will be said, the condemnation of a criminal is a particular act. Granted, and that is why it is outside the competence of the sovereign; it is a right that the sovereign can confer but cannot exercise. My ideas are all consistent, but I cannot expound them all at once.

Frequent executions are always a sign of weakness or laziness on the part of a government. There is no evildoer who could not be made good for something. No man can rightfully be put to death, even as a deterrent example, unless he cannot be spared without danger.

As for the right to grant pardon, to exempt a guilty man from a punishment specified by law and imposed by a judge, it belongs only to what is above judges and the law, that is, the sovereign. But this right is not very clearly defined, and occasions for using it are quite rare. In a well-governed state there are few punishments, not because pardon is granted often, but because there are few criminals. When a state is decaying, crimes are so numerous that most of them go unpunished. Under the Roman Republic, neither the Senate nor the consuls ever tried to grant pardon; the people itself did not do it, although it sometimes revoked its own judgments. Frequent pardons announce that soon criminals will no longer need them, and everyone knows where that leads. But I feel my heart protesting and restraining my pen; let us leave these questions to be discussed by a righteous man who, having never done wrong, has never been in need of pardon for himself.

CHAPTER VI

Law

By the social pact we have given existence and life to the body politic; we must now give it movement and will by legislation, for the original agreement by which it is formed and unified has not yet determined what it must do to preserve itself.

What is proper and in conformity with order is such by the nature of things, independently of human agreements. All justice comes from God, and only from him; but if we were able to receive it directly from that exalted source, we would have no need of either government or laws. There is, no doubt, a universal justice emanating from reason alone, but in order to be accepted among us, this justice must be reciprocal. Looking at things from a human standpoint, it is evident that, lacking natural sanctions, the laws of justice are ineffectual among men; they serve only to reward evil and penalize good when the righteous man always observes them in his dealings with others and others never observe them in their dealings with him. Agreements and laws are therefore needed to join rights to duties and direct justice toward its object. In the state of nature, where everything is held in common, I owe nothing to those to whom I have promised nothing; I recognize as belonging to others only what is useless to me. This is not the case in the civil state, where all rights are fixed by law.

What, then, is a law? Those who content themselves with attaching metaphysical ideas to the word will go on discussing it without ever reaching agreement, and when they have defined a law of nature, they will still have no better understanding of what a law of the state is.

I have already said that there can be no general will with a particular object. Any such object must be either within the state or outside it. If it is outside, a will that is alien to the state is not general with respect to it; if the object is within the state, it is part of it, and there is then a relation between whole and part which makes them two separate entities, of which the part is one and the whole minus that part is the other. But the whole minus a part is not the whole, and as long as that relation subsists there is no longer a whole but two unequal parts. Hence it follows that the will of one is not general with respect to the other.

But when the whole people establishes a rule for the whole people, it considers only itself. If a relation is then formed, it is between the entire object from one viewpoint and the entire object from another viewpoint, with no division of the whole. In this case the matter to which the rule applies is general, like the will that establishes the rule. It is such an act that I call a law.

When I say that the object of a law is always general, I mean that a law always considers the subjects collectively and actions abstractly, never an individual person or a particular action. Thus the law can declare that there will be privileges, but it cannot give them to anyone by name; it can create different classes of citizens, and even stipulate qualifications for membership in them, but it cannot assign specific persons to a given class; it can establish a monarchical government with hereditary succession, but it cannot choose a king or designate a royal family. In short, no function relating to an individual object is within the legislative power.

In this view, it is readily apparent that there is no longer any need to ask who has the power to make laws, since they are acts of the general will; or whether a ruler is above the law, since he is a member of the state; or whether the law can be unjust, since no one is unjust to himself; or how we can be both free and subject to the law, since it is only a declaration of our will.

It can also be seen that since the law combines generality of will with generality of object, no order that any man gives on his own initiative is a law. Even an order given by the sovereign with regard to a particular object is not a law, but a decree, and it is an act not of sovereignty, but of administration.

I therefore give the name of republic to any state controlled by laws, no matter what its form of administration may be, for only in such states does the public interest govern, and only in them is there a genuine "public thing" [res publica]. Every legitimate government is republican;[10] I will later explain what government is.

Laws are, properly speaking, only the terms of the civil

association. A people bound by laws should be the author of them; only those who come together to form a society are entitled to specify the conditions under which they do so. But how are they to specify them? Shall it be by spontaneous assent, by a sudden inspiration? Does the body politic have a voice to declare its will? Who will give it the foresight to formulate and announce its decisions in advance? Or how will it announce them at the moment of need? How can a blind multitude, which often does not know what it wants because it seldom knows what is good for it, accomplish on its own such a great and difficult undertaking as the promulgation of a system of law? Of itself, the people always wills the good, but does not always see it. The general will is always well-meaning, but the judgment that guides it is not always enlightened. It must be made to see things as they are, and sometimes as they ought to appear to it; it must be shown the right path that it is seeking, protected from being led astray by particular wills, made to see places and times in closer relation to one another, taught to weigh the attraction of present and perceptible advantages against remote and hidden evils. Individuals can see a good but reject it; the public can will a good but not see it. Both need guides. Individuals must be made to bring their will into conformity with their reason; the public must be taught to perceive what it wills. Public enlightenment then leads to the union of understanding and will in the social body, which in turn leads to precise coordination among the parts, and finally to maximum strength of the whole. All this is the origin of the need for a lawgiver.

CHAPTER VII

The Lawgiver

To discover the rules of society best suited to nations, a superior intelligence would be required. Such an intelligence would have to see all human passions without feeling any of them; it would have to be completely unrelated to our nature, yet know it thoroughly; it would have to be independent of us for its happiness, yet willing to concern itself with ours; and finally, it would have to seek its glory in the distant reaches of the future, working in one century to enjoy the results in another.[11]

In seeking to define the political or kingly man in his dialogue *The Statesman,* Plato used the same line of reasoning with regard to right as Caligula used with regard to fact; but if it is true that a great ruler is a rare man, what are we to say of a great lawgiver? The lawgiver must draw up a plan; the ruler has only to follow it. The lawgiver is the engineer who invents the machine; the ruler is only the workman who assembles it and keeps it running. When societies are born, says Montesquieu, the leaders of republics establish institutions, and afterward the institutions form the leaders of republics.

Anyone who dares to undertake the task of instituting a nation must feel himself capable of changing human nature, so to speak; of transforming each individual, who by himself is a complete and solitary whole, into a part of a greater whole from which he, in a sense, receives his life and his being; of marring man's constitution in order to strengthen it; of substituting a partial and moral existence for the physical and independent existence that we have all received from nature. He must, in short, take away man's resources to give him others that are foreign to him and cannot be used without the help of other men. The more completely these natural resources are annihilated, the greater and more durable are the acquired ones and the stronger and more perfect are the new institutions. If, then, each citizen is nothing, and can do nothing, without all the others, and if the resources acquired by the whole are equal or superior to the sum of all the individual's natural resources, legislation can be said to have reached its highest possible degree of perfection.

The lawgiver is in every respect an extraordinary man in the state, by the talents he should have, as well as by his function. This function is neither administrative nor sovereign. It institutes the republic but has no place in its institutions. It is a private and superior function which has nothing in common with human dominion, for while it is true that he who controls men must not control laws, it is also true that he who controls laws must not control men; otherwise, his laws would serve his passions, often doing nothing but perpetuating his injustices, and he could never prevent his personal aims from tainting the purity of his work.

When Lycurgus gave laws to his country, he began by abdicating the kingship. Most Greek towns customarily called on outsiders to draw up their laws. The republics of modern Italy often followed that example; Geneva did the same, and found it advantageous.[12] At the height of its glow, Rome suffered a resurgence of all the crimes of tyranny, and was on the verge of perishing, because it had placed legislative authority and sovereign power in the same hands.

The decemvirs themselves, however, never claimed the right to establish any law on their own authority. "Nothing that we propose to you," they said to the people, "can become a law without your consent. Romans, you yourselves must be the authors of the laws that assure your well-being."

He who formulates laws has, or should have, no right to legislate. Even if it should want to do so, the people cannot divest itself of that nontransferrable right, because, according to the fundamental pact, only the general will is binding on individuals, and the only way to determine whether a particular will coincides with the general will is to submit it to a free vote of the people. I have said this before, but it is not useless to repeat it.

Thus in the task of the lawgiver we find two things that seem incompatible: an enterprise beyond human capability, and a lack of authority to put it into execution.

There is another difficulty that deserves attention. If a wise man tries to speak to ordinary people in his own language rather than theirs, he cannot make them understand him. There are all sorts of ideas that cannot be translated into their language. Concepts too general and aims too remote are beyond their comprehension. Each individual, having no inclination toward any plan of government unrelated to his private interest, finds it difficult to see the advantages he is to derive from the constant privations imposed by good laws. In order for a people in the process of formation to value sound political principles and follow the fundamental rules of statecraft, the effect would have to become the cause: The social spirit that is to be produced by the new institutions would have to preside over their creation, and before the laws exist, men would have to be what they are to become by means of those same laws. Therefore, since the lawgiver can use neither force nor reasoning, he must resort to another kind of authority which can lead without compelling and persuade without convincing.

This is what has forced the founders of nations in all ages to appeal to divine intervention and attribute their own wisdom to the gods, so that their peoples, submitting to the laws of the state as to those of nature, and acknowledging the same power in the formation of man as in that of the body politic, will obey with freedom and bear the yoke of public well-being with docility.

The lawgiver puts the demands of this sublime purpose, beyond the grasp of ordinary men, into the mouths of the immortals in order to lead by divine authority those who could not be moved by considerations of human prudence.[13] But it is not given to everyone to make the gods speak, or to be believed when he announces that he is their interpreter. The lawgiver's greatness of soul is the real miracle that must validate his mission. Anyone can carve stone tablets, or bribe an oracle, or pretend to be in secret communication with some divinity, or train a bird to speak in his ear, or find other crude means of beguiling the people. A man whose resources are limited to such things may happen to assemble a band of fools, but he will never found an empire, and his ludicrous creation will soon perish with him. Inane tricks may form a momentary bond; only wisdom can make it last. Judaic law, which has survived to the present, and the law of the child of Ishmael, which has ruled half the world for ten centuries, still bear witness to the greatness of the men who drafted them; and while proud philosophy and blind partisan spirit see those men only as lucky impostors, true political understanding admires in their institutions the great and powerful genius that presides over lasting achievements.

Chapter VIII

The People

Before building a large edifice, an architect studies and tests the ground to determine whether it can bear the weight. Similarly, the wise lawgiver does not begin by drafting laws good in themselves, but first examines the question of whether the people for which they are intended is capable of supporting them. That was why Plato refused to give laws to the Arcadians and the Cyrenians, knowing that those two peoples were rich and could not tolerate equality; and in Crete there were good laws and bad men because Minos had only disciplined a people laden with vices.

There have been a thousand successful nations on earth that could not have tolerated good laws, and even those that could have done so had only a brief period in their whole history when they were capable of it. Most peoples, like most individuals, are malleable only in youth and become incorrigible as they grow older. Once their customs are established and their prejudices have taken root, trying to reform them is a dangerous and futile enterprise; like those foolish and cowardly invalids who tremble at the sight of a doctor, they cannot bear to let anyone touch their infirmities, even to cure them.

It is true that, just as some illnesses unhinge a man's mind and take away his memory of the past, there are sometimes violent periods in the history of a state when revolutions do to the people what certain afflictions do to individuals, when horror of the past corresponds to loss of memory, and when the state, consumed by civil warfare, is reborn from its ashes, so to speak, and regains the vigor of youth in freeing itself from the embrace of death. This was the case with Sparta in the time of Lycurgus, Rome after the Tarquins, and in our own time, Holland and Switzerland after the expulsion of their tyrants.

But such events are rare; they are exceptions whose explanation is always found in the special constitution of the state involved. They cannot even happen twice to the same people, for a people can make itself free as long as it is still uncivilized, but not when its civil energies have been exhausted. It can then be destroyed by upheavals, but cannot be restored by revolutions; as soon as its chains have been broken, it disintegrates and ceases to exist. From that point onward, it needs a master, not a liberator. Free peoples, remember this maxim: Freedom can be acquired, but never regained.

Youth is not childhood. With nations as with individuals, there is a time of youth, or maturity if you prefer, which must be awaited before they are made subject to laws. But a people's maturity is not always easy to recognize, and assuming its existence too soon will result in failure. One people may be amenable to discipline at birth, another may still not be amenable to it after ten centuries. The Russians will never be truly civilized, because the attempt to civilize them was made prematurely. Peter the Great had a genius for imitation; he did not have true genius, which is creative and makes everything from nothing. He did some good things, but most of his efforts were misguided. He saw that his subjects were barbarous, but he did not see that they were not ripe for civilization; he tried to civilize them when they should only have been trained. He first tried to turn them into Germans or Englishmen when he should have begun by turning them into Russians. By persuading them that they were something they were not, he prevented them from ever becoming what they could have been. That is how a French tutor educates his pupil to shine briefly during his childhood, then never do anything worthwhile for the rest of his life. The Russian empire will try to subjugate Europe and will itself be subjugated. The Tartars, its subjects or neighbors, will become its masters, and ours. That revolution seems inevitable to me. All the kings of Europe are working together to hasten it.

CHAPTER IX

The People (*continued*)

Nature has set upper and lower limits to the height of a well-built man, and produces only giants or dwarfs outside them. Similarly, with regard to the best constitution for a state, there are limits to the size it can have if it is to be neither too large to be well governed nor too small to maintain itself. Every body politic has a maximum strength which it cannot exceed. Expansion often makes it fall below this maximum. The more the social bond is stretched, the slacker it becomes, and a small state is usually stronger in proportion to its size than a large one.

There are many reasons for this. First of all, administration becomes more difficult over great distances, as a weight becomes heavier at the end of a long lever. It also becomes more expensive as the number of administrative levels is increased: Each town has an administration which the people pays for; each district has one, also paid for by the people; then each province; then the larger governments, such as satrapies and viceroyalties, each costing more than the one below it, and all paid for by the unfortunate people; and finally the supreme administration, which overwhelms everything. All these accumulated charges are a constant drain on the subjects, and far from being better governed by those different authorities, they are not governed as well as they would be if they were under only one. Meanwhile there are hardly any resources for emergencies, and the state is always on the verge of ruin when it must draw on those that remain.

Nor is that all: Not only is the government less swift and vigorous in enforcing its laws, preventing nuisances, correcting abuses, and forestalling seditious activities that may occur in distant places, but the citizens have less affection for their leaders, whom they never see, for their country, which to them seems to be the whole world, and for their fellow citizens, most of whom are strangers. The same laws cannot suit so many various provinces, which have different customs and contrasting climates and cannot all tolerate the same form of government. But differing laws only give rise to disorder and confusion among peoples which live under the same rulers, are in constant communication, intermarry, and travel freely among one another's territories; forced to accept other customs, they never know if their heritage is really their own. When a multitude of strangers are brought together at the seat of the supreme administration, talents are buried, virtues are unrecognized, and vices go unpunished. The rulers are so busy that they see nothing for themselves, and clerks govern the state. Finally, the measures that must be taken to maintain the general authority, which so many distant officials try to evade or deceive, absorb all governmental concern, so that none is left for the happiness of the people, and scarcely any for its defense, when necessary. It is thus that a body too large for its constitution collapses and perishes, crushed by its own weight.

On the other hand, a state must give itself a certain base if it is to be solid enough to withstand the jolts it is sure to receive and the efforts it will have to make to sustain itself, for all peoples have a kind of centrifugal force by which they continually act against each other and strive to expand at the expense of their neighbors, like Descartes's vortices. The weak are therefore always in danger of being swallowed up, and it is hardly possible for any state to survive unless it forms with others a kind of balance which more or less equalizes the pressure on all of them.

. From this it can be seen that there are some reasons for expansion and others for contraction, and finding the proportion between these two sets of reasons best suited to the preservation of the state is not the least important of political talents. In general it can be said that the reasons for expansion, being only external and relative, must be subordinate to those for contraction, which are internal and absolute. A strong, sound constitution is the first thing to be sought, and the vigor that comes from good government is more likely to create it than the resources provided by a large territory.

There have been states so constituted that a need for conquest was an integral part of their constitution, so that they were forced to expand constantly in order to maintain themselves. They may have been glad to be under that necessity, but it meant that their downfall was inevitable as soon as their greatness came to an end.

CHAPTER X

The People (*continued*)

A body politic can be measured in two ways: by the area of its territory and by the number of its people. The optimum size of a state depends on the relation between these two factors. Men make the state, and land sustains them. The proper relation is therefore achieved when the land is able to feed all its inhabitants and there are as many inhabitants as the land can feed. This proportion ensures the maximum strength of a given number of people, for if there is too much territory, it is expensive to maintain, its cultivation is inadequate, its produce is excessive, and it soon gives rise to defensive wars; but if there is not enough, the state must rely on the willingness of its neighbors to supply it with what it lacks, and this soon leads to offensive wars. Any people in a situation that allows it only a choice between commerce and war is weak in itself: It depends on its neighbors, it depends on events, and its existence can only be uncertain and short. It will either conquer and change its situation, or be conquered and cease to exist. It can remain free only by becoming smaller or larger.

There can be no fixed, mathematically precise ratio between a given area of land and the ideal number of inhabitants for it, because of differences not only in the quality of the soil, its fertility, the nature of its produce, and the influence of climate, but also in the temperaments of its inhabitants, for some people consume little in a fertile region, while others consume much in a barren one. We must also consider the fecundity of the women, the features of the country that are favorable or unfavorable to population growth, and the extent to which the lawgiver can expect to further that growth by his institutions, for he must base his judgment not on what he sees, but on what he foresees, and he must consider not so much the present size of the population as the size it should naturally reach. Finally, there are many situations where special features of the terrain make it necessary or possible to take in more land than might seem to be needed. The population will be more thinly spread in mountainous country, for example, where the natural products, namely, timber and grazing animals, require less work, where experience shows that women are more fecund than in the plains, and where the great area occupied by slopes leaves only a small amount of level ground, which is all that can be relied on for vegetation. Along the seashore, however, population can be denser, even where there are rocks and almost sterile sand, because fishing can to a large extent compensate for the inadequacy of agriculture, because people need to be closer together in order to repulse pirates, and because it is easier to get rid of excess population by means of colonies.

To these conditions for the founding of a people, we must add one which can take the place of no other, but without which all the others would be useless: There must be peace and abundance, for a state is like a battalion, in that the time when it is being formed is the time when it is least capable of offering resistance and easiest to destroy. It could defend itself better in total disorder than in a period of ferment when everyone is concerned with his personal position and not with the common danger. If there is a war, a famine, or a rebellion during that critical time, the state will inevitably be overthrown.

Not that there have not been many governments established during such storms; but then it is the governments themselves that destroy the state. Taking advantage of public panic, usurpers always choose or foment troubled times to enact destructive laws that the people would never adopt in its normal frame of mind. Noting the time chosen for establishing a people's institutions is one of the surest ways to distinguish the work of a lawgiver from that of a tyrant.

What kind of a people, then, is fit to receive laws? One that is already bound together by some tie of origin, interest, or agreement, but has not yet borne the real yoke of law; one that has no deeply rooted customs or superstitions; one that has no fear of being overwhelmed by a sudden invasion, and while remaining aloof from the quarrels of its neighbors, is capable of withstanding any of them alone, or of enlisting the aid of one to repel another; one in which each man can be known to all, and in which there is no need to place a larger burden on anyone than he can bear; one that can do without other peoples, and that all other peoples can do without;[14] one that is neither rich nor poor and can be self-sufficient; and finally, one that combines the stability of an ancient people with the malleability of a new one. What makes the work of the lawgiver difficult is not so much what must be established as what must be destroyed; and what makes success so rare is the impossibility of finding the simplicity of nature together with the needs that arise in society. All these conditions, it is true, cannot easily be combined, which is why there are so few well-constituted states.

There is still one European country capable of receiving laws: the island of Corsica. The valor and steadfastness with which that brave people has recovered and defended its freedom make it deserve to be taught by some wise man how to preserve that freedom. I have a presentiment that some day that little island will astonish Europe.

CHAPTER XI

Various Systems of Law

If we seek to determine precisely what constitutes the greatest good of all, which should be the goal of every system of law, we find that it can be reduced to these two main elements: *freedom* and *equality*. Freedom, because any individual dependence is so much strength taken away from the state; equality, because there can be no freedom without it.

I have already said what civil freedom is. As for equality, the word must not be taken to imply that power and wealth are to be exactly the same for everyone, but rather that power shall not reach the point of violence and shall never be exercised except by virtue of rank and law, and that, so far as wealth is concerned, no citizen shall be rich enough to be able to buy another, and none poor enough to be forced to sell himself. This presupposes moderation with regard to property and influence on the part of those in high positions, and moderation with regard to avarice and covetousness on the part of those in humbler circumstances.[15]

It will be said that such equality is a speculative fancy which cannot exist in reality. But if abuse is inevitable, does it follow that it should not at least be controlled? Precisely because the force of events always tends to destroy equality, the force of law should always tend to uphold it.

But these general objectives of all good institutions must be modified in each country to fit the relations arising from the local situation and the character of the inhabitants, and it is on the basis of these relations that each people must be given the particular system of institutions that will be best, not perhaps in itself, but for the country for which it is intended. For example, is your soil unproductive, or is your territory too small for the number of inhabitants? Then turn to crafts and industry, so that you exchange your products for the foodstuffs you lack. Or, on the other hand, do you live on rich plains and fertile slopes, with good land and too few inhabitants? Then direct all your efforts to agriculture, which increases population, and banish manufacturing, which would further depopulate the countryside by draining off its inhabitants and concentrating them in towns.[16] Do you have a long and accessible coastline? Then cover the sea with vessels, develop trade and shipping; you will have a glorious and short existence. Does the sea along your shores wash against nothing but forbidding rocks. Then remain fish-eating barbarians; you will live more peacefully, perhaps better, and certainly more happily. In short, besides the principles that are common to all, each people has within itself something that orders those principles in a special way and makes its system of law suitable for it alone. Thus long ago the Hebrews, and more recently the Arabs, took religion as their main object; for the Athenians, it was literature; for Carthage and Tyre, commerce; for Rhodes, seafaring; for Sparta, war; and for Rome, virtue. The author of *The Spirit of the Laws* has shown with abundant examples how the art of the lawgiver directs institutions toward each of these objects.

The constitution of a state is truly strong and durable when there is such close observance of what is proper that natural relations are in harmony with law on every point, and law serves only, so to speak, to assure, accompany, and rectify them. But if the lawgiver mistakes his object and adopts a principle different from the one that is called for by circumstances—if one tends toward servitude and the other toward freedom, or one toward wealth and the other toward population growth, or one toward peace and the other toward conquest—then the laws will gradually be weakened, the constitution will deteriorate, and the state will be in constant turmoil until it is either destroyed or changed, and invincible nature regains its dominion.

CHAPTER XII

Classification of Laws

To bring order to the whole, or give the best possible form to the state, various relations must be considered. First, there is the action of the entire body on itself, that is, the relation of the whole to the whole, or of the sovereign to the state, and this relation is composed of relations among intermediate terms, as we shall see later.

The laws governing this relation are known as political laws, and are also called fundamental laws, not without reason if they are wisely conceived. For if there is in each state only one good way of ordering it, the people that has found it should hold to it, but if the established order is bad, why should the laws that prevent it from being good be considered fundamental? In any case, moreover, the people is always free to change its laws, even the best ones, for if it chooses to harm itself, who has a right to prevent it?

The second relation is that of the members among themselves, or with the entire body politic. This relation should be as small as possible in the first case and as great as possible in the second, so that each citizen will be completely independent of all the others and extremely dependent on the state. This is always done by the same means, since only the power of the state makes its members free. It is from this second relation that civil laws arise.

We may consider a third kind of relation between the individual and the law: that of disobedience and punishment. It gives rise to criminal laws, which are actually less a specific type of law than the sanction of all others.

In addition to these three kinds of law, there is a fourth, the most important of all. It is engraved in neither marble nor brass, but in the hearts of the citizens; it forms the true constitution of the state; it renews its vigor every day, and when other laws become obsolete or ineffective, it restores or replaces them; it keeps the people in the spirit of its institutions, and gradually substitutes the force of habit for that of authority. I am referring to morals, customs, and above all, public opinion. This category of laws is unknown to our political theorists, but it is essential to the success of all the others; the great lawgiver concerns himself with it in secret, while seeming to limit himself to specific regulations that are only the sides of the arch, whereas morals, slower to develop, eventually form its unshakable keystone.

Of these various classes, only political laws, which constitute the form of government, are relevant to my subject.

BOOK III

Before speaking of the various forms of government, let us try to determine the precise meaning of that word, which has not yet been very well explained.

CHAPTER I

Government in General

I warn the reader that this chapter must be read carefully, and that I lack the ability to make myself clear to those who will not be attentive.

Every free act is produced by the concurrence of two causes, one mental, namely, the will that determines the act, and the other physical, namely, the force that executes it. If I am to walk to an object, the first condition is that I must will to go to it, and the second is that my feet must take me to it. If a paralytic wills to run and an able-bodied man wills not to, they both stay where they are. The body politic acts by the same two causes, and the same distinction between force and will can be made within it, the latter being known as *legislative power,* the former as *executive power.* Nothing is or should be done in the body politic without the concurrence of both.

We have seen that legislative power belongs only to the people, and can belong only to it. It is clear, however, from the principles I have already established, that executive power cannot belong to the collectivity as legislative or sovereign, because that power is limited to particular acts, which are outside the province of the law and consequently outside the province of the sovereign, all of whose acts are necessarily laws.

The public force therefore needs an agent of its own to

unite it and put it into action under the direction of the general will, to serve as a means of communication between the state and the sovereign, and to do for the collective person more or less what the union of the soul and the body does for the individual. Such is the reason for having a government in the state. The government is sometimes mistakenly identified with the sovereign, but it is only the sovereign's agent.

What, then, is the government? An intermediate body established between the subjects and the sovereign for their mutual communication, charged with the execution of the laws and the maintenance of freedom, both civil and political.

The members of this body are called *magistrates* or *kings*, that is, *governors*, and the whole body is called the *prince*.[17] Those who maintain that the act by which a people submits to rulers is not a contract are therefore quite right. It is nothing more than a commission, an employment. The rulers are mere agents of the sovereign, exercising in its name the power it has placed in their hands. The sovereign can limit, alter, or revoke that power whenever it sees fit; the alienation of its right to do so would be incompatible with the nature of the social body and contrary to the purpose of the association.

I therefore give the name of *government* or supreme administration to the legitimate exercise of executive power, and the name of prince or magistrate to the man or the body charged with that administration.

Within the government are the intermediate forces whose relations compose the relation of the whole to the whole, or of the sovereign to the state. This last relation can be viewed as that between the extremes of a continued proportion, with the government as the geometric mean. The government receives from the sovereign the orders it gives to the people, and if the state is to be properly balanced, there must be, all due allowances being made, equality between the product or power of the government taken in itself and the product or power of the citizens, who are the sovereign in one respect and the subjects in another.

Furthermore, none of the three terms can be varied without immediately breaking the proportion. If the sovereign seeks to govern, or if the magistrate seeks to give laws, or if the subjects refuse to obey, order gives way to chaos, force and will no longer act in harmony, and the state collapses, sinking into either despotism or anarchy. Finally, just as there is only one geometric mean between any two extremes, there is only one good government possible in a state. But since countless events can change the relations of a people, different governments can be good for different peoples, and even for the same people at different times.

To try to give an idea of the various relations that can exist between the two extremes, I shall take the numerical size of the people as an example, since it is a relation that can easily be expressed.

Let us suppose a state composed of ten thousand citizens. The sovereign can be considered only collectively and as a body. But each man, in his capacity as a subject, is considered as an individual. Thus the sovereign is to the subject as ten thousand is to one; that is, each member of the state has as his share of the sovereign authority only one ten-thousandth of it, even though he is totally subordinate to it. If the people's number is increased to a hundred thousand, the status of the subjects remains unchanged; each one is still completely under the dominion of the laws, but his vote is reduced to one hundred-thousandth, and therefore has ten times less influence in determining what the laws will be. Since each subject always remains one individual, the ratio between him and the sovereign increases with the total number of citizens. From this it follows that the larger the state becomes, the more freedom is diminished.

When I say that the ratio increases, I mean that it moves farther away from equality. Hence, taking "ratio" in the mathematical sense and "relation" in the ordinary sense, it can be said that as the ratio grows larger, the relation becomes smaller. The ratio is here considered in terms of quantity and is measured by a quotient, while the relation is considered in terms of identity and is judged by similarity.

The less similarity there is between individual wills and the general will, that is, between morals and laws, the more repressive force must be increased. Therefore if the government is to be good, it must become relatively stronger as the citizens become more numerous.

On the other hand, since the enlargement of the state gives the holders of public authority more temptations to abuse their power, and greater means of doing so, the more strength the government must have to control the people, the more the sovereign must have to control the government. I am not speaking here of absolute strength, but of the relative strength of the different parts of the state.

It follows from this double ratio that the continued proportion between the sovereign, the prince, and the people is not an arbitrary idea, but a necessary consequence of the nature of the body politic. It also follows that since one of the extremes, namely, the people as subjects, is fixed and represented by the number one, whenever the double ratio increases or decreases, the single ratio likewise increases or decreases, and that consequently the middle term is changed. This shows that there is not one unique and absolute form of government, but that there can be as many governments different in nature as there are states different in size.

If, ridiculing this system, someone were to say that to find the geometric mean and form the body of the government, it is only necessary, according to me, to take the square root of the number of people, I would reply that I am here using that number only as an example; that the ratios of which I am speaking are not measured only by the number of men, but in general by the quantity of action, which is produced by a multitude of causes; and that, moreover, if I momentarily borrow geometrical terms in order to express myself in fewer words, I am well aware that geometrical precision cannot be applied to moral quantities.

The government is on a small scale what the body politic, which contains it, is on a large scale. It is an artificial person endowed with certain faculties; it is active like the sovereign, passive like the state, and can be broken down into other similar relations. A new proportion arises from these relations, and within it still another, determined by the order of magistracies, until we reach an indivisible middle term, that is, a single ruler, or supreme magistrate, who may be represented in the middle of this progression as the number one between the series of fractions and the series of whole numbers.

Lest we become entangled in this mass of terms, let us simply consider the government as a new body within the state, distinct from the people and the sovereign, and an intermediary between them.

There is this essential difference between the two bodies: The state exists by itself, while the government exists only through the sovereign. Thus the dominant will of the government is, or should be, only the general will, or the law, and its power is only the public power concentrated in it; as soon as it tries to perform some absolute and independent act on its own authority, the tie that binds the whole together begins to be loosened. If the government finally has a particular will more vigorous than that of the sovereign, and uses the public power vested in it to enforce obedience to that particular will, so that there are two sovereigns, so to speak, one *de jure* and the other *de facto,* the social bond immediately vanishes and the body politic is dissolved.

If, however, the body of the government is to have an existence, a real life that distinguishes it from the body of the state, and if all its members are to be able to act together and serve the purpose for which it was instituted, it must have a particular self, an awareness common to its members, a power, a will of its own that tends toward its preservation. Such a particular existence requires assemblies, councils, the power to deliberate and make decisions, rights, titles, and privileges which belong exclusively to the government and make a magistrate's position honorable in proportion to its arduousness. The difficulty is to order this subordinate whole within the greater whole in such a way as to ensure that it will not impair the general constitution in strengthening its own, that it will always distinguish between its particular power, intended for its own preservation, and the public power, intended for the preservation of the state, and that, in short, it will always be ready to sacrifice the government to the people, rather than the people to the government.

But while the artificial body of the government is the work of another artificial body and has only what might be called a borrowed and subordinate life, it can still act with more or less vigor and speed, and be healthy, so to speak, to a greater or smaller degree. And finally, without moving directly away from its proper purpose, it can deviate from it to a greater or smaller extent, depending on the way in which it is constituted.

Because of these differences, there are different relations

that the government should have with the body of the state, depending on contingent and particular relations by which the state is altered. For the government that is best in itself often becomes the worst when its relations do not change in accordance with the defects of the body politic to which it belongs.

Chapter II

The Constitutive Principle of the Various Forms of Government

To set forth the general cause of these differences, I must here distinguish between the prince and the government, as I have previously distinguished between the state and the sovereign.

The magisterial body may be composed of a smaller or larger number of members. We have said that the ratio between the sovereign and the subjects increases with the number of subjects, and by an obvious analogy we can say the same of the ratio between the government and the magistrates.

Since the total power of the government is always that of the state, it never varies. From this it follows that the more of its power it uses on its own members, the less it has left for acting on the whole people.

Therefore the more numerous the magistrates, the weaker the government. Since this is a fundamental maxim, let us try to make it clearer.

We can distinguish three essentially different wills in each magistrate. The first is his individual will, which tends only toward his private advantage. The second is the collective will of the magistrates, which relates only to the advantage of the prince, and can be called the corporate will; it is general with respect to the government and particular with respect to the state, of which the government is a part. The third is the will of the people, or the sovereign will; it is general with respect both to the state considered as the whole and to the government considered as a part of the whole.

In a perfect system of law, the particular or individual will would be without effect, the corporate will of the government would be extremely subordinate, and consequently the general or sovereign will would always be dominant and the sole guide of the others.

In the natural order, however, these different wills become more vigorous as they are more concentrated. Thus the general will is always the weakest, the corporate will is in second place, and the particular will comes first, so that in the government each member is first himself, then a magistrate, and then a citizen. This sequence is the reverse of what is required by the social order.

With this in mind, let us suppose that the government is in the hands of a single man. The particular will and the corporate will are now perfectly united, and consequently the latter is at its highest possible degree of intensity. Since the exercise of power depends on the degree of will, and since the absolute power of the government is invariable, it follows that the most vigorous of governments is that of one man.

Let us suppose, on the other hand, that the government and the legislative authority are combined, that the sovereign is the prince, and that every citizen is a magistrate. The corporate will and the general will are now merged, neither has any more vigor than the other, and the particular will remains as strong as ever. Thus the government, though still with the same absolute power, has its minimum power or vigor.

These relations are incontestable, and they are further confirmed by other considerations. It is obvious, for example, that each magistrate is more effective within the body to which he belongs than each citizen is in the one to which he belongs, and that consequently the particular will has much more influence on the acts of the government than on those of the sovereign, for each magistrate is nearly always charged with some function of government, while each citizen, taken singly, has no function of sovereignty. Furthermore, the more the state expands, the more its real power increases, though not in proportion to its expansion; when the size of the state does not vary, however, the government cannot increase its real power by increasing the number of its members, because its real power is that of the state, which remains constant. Thus the relative power or vigor of the government diminishes, while its real or absolute power cannot increase.

It is also certain that the handling of public business becomes slower as more people are made responsible for it;

they stress caution at the expense of chance, let opportunities slip past, and often deliberate so long that they lose the fruits of their deliberations.

I have just shown that the government becomes less effective as the number of magistrates is increased, and I have previously shown that the larger the population, the more repressive force there must be. From this it follows that the ratio between the magistrates and the government should vary inversely with the ratio between the subjects and the sovereign; that is, the larger the state becomes, the smaller the government should be, so that the number of magistrates will diminish in proportion to the increase in population.

I am speaking here of the relative power of the government, not of its rectitude, for on the contrary, the more numerous the magistrates are, the more closely the corporate will approaches the general will, whereas under a single magistrate that same corporate will is, as I have said, only a particular will. Thus we lose in one direction what we can gain in another, and the art of the lawgiver is to know how to determine the point where the government's power and will, which always vary inversely, will be combined in the proportion most advantageous to the state.

CHAPTER III

Classification of Governments

We have seen in the preceding chapter why the various kinds or forms of government are distinguished according to the number of members who compose them; in this chapter we shall see how that classification is made.

First, the sovereign may place the government in the hands of the whole people, or most of it, so that there are more citizen magistrates than ordinary private citizens. This form of government is known as *democracy*.

Second, the sovereign may limit the government to a small number of men, so that there are more ordinary citizens than magistrates, and this form is called *aristocracy*.

And finally, the sovereign may concentrate the whole government in the hands of a single magistrate from whom all others derive their power. This third form is the most common, and is known as *monarchy* or royal government.

It should be noted that all these forms, or at least the first two, can exist within a wide numerical range. The range of democracy can go from the entire people to half of it; that of aristocracy from half the people to an extremely small number. Even royal government can be shared to some extent. Sparta always had two kings according to its constitution, and the Roman Empire sometimes had as many as eight emperors at once, without destroying its unity. There is thus a point at which each form of government shades into the next, and although we use only three designations, the government can actually have as many different forms as the state has citizens.

Moreover, since a government can, in some respects, be subdivided into different parts, each administered in a different way, various combinations of the three forms can produce a multitude of mixed forms, each of which can be multiplied by all the unmixed forms.

All through the ages, men have argued about the best form of government, without realizing that each form is the best in some cases and the worst in others.

If in each state the number of supreme magistrates should be in inverse ratio to the number of citizens, it follows that, in general, democracy is best suited to small states, aristocracy to medium-sized ones, and monarchy to large ones. This rule is directly derived from the principle we have established; but how are we to reckon the multitude of circumstances that may provide exceptions to it?

CHAPTER IV

Democracy

He who makes the law knows better than anyone else how it should be executed and interpreted. It might therefore seem that there could be no better constitution than one in which the executive and legislative powers are combined. But that very combination is what makes such a government inadequate in certain respects, for things that ought to be separate are united, and since the prince and the sovereign are one, they form, so to speak, a government without government.

It is not desirable for the maker of laws to execute them, or for the people as a body to divert its attention from general objectives and turn it to particular ones. Nothing is more dangerous than the influence of private interests on public affairs, and abuse of the laws by the government is a lesser evil than corruption of the legislator, which is the inevitable result of pursuing particular objectives. When such corruption exists, the very substance of the state deteriorates, and all reform becomes impossible. A people that never misused governmental power would never misuse independence either; a people that always governed well would have no need to be governed.

Taking the term in its strictest sense, no genuine democracy has ever existed, and none ever will exist. It is contrary to the natural order for the majority to govern and the minority to be governed. It is unimaginable that the people should remain constantly assembled to deal with public affairs, and it obviously cannot establish agencies for that purpose without changing the form of administration.

I believe it can be stated as an axiom that when the functions of government are divided among several agencies, those with the fewest members eventually acquire the greatest authority, if only because they are naturally led to it by the ease with which they can dispatch business.

A democratic government, furthermore, presupposes a number of things that are difficult to unite. First, a very small state in which the people can easily be assembled and each citizen can easily know all the others. Second, a great simplicity of customs and morals, to prevent public affairs from becoming too numerous, and thorny discussions from arising. Third, a high degree of equality in rank and wealth, without which equality in rights and authority could not last long. And finally, little or no luxury, for luxury is either the effect of wealth or makes wealth necessary; it corrupts both the rich and the poor: the former by possessiveness, the latter by covetousness; it sells the country to indolence and vanity; it deprives the state of all its citizens by enslaving some to others, and all to public opinion.

That is why a famous author made virtue the basic principle of a republic; for all those conditions cannot exist without virtue. But because he did not make the necessary distinctions, that great genius was often inaccurate and sometimes unclear, and he did not see that since sovereign authority is everywhere the same, the same principle should be observed in every well-constituted state, though to a greater or lesser degree, depending on the form of government.

We may add that a democratic or popular government is more subject than any other to civil wars and internal disturbances, because no other has such a strong and constant tendency to change its form, or requires such vigilance and courage to maintain it in the form it has. It is above all in a democracy that the citizen must arm himself with strength and steadfastness, and repeat every day of his life, in the depths of his heart, what a virtuous palatine[18] once said in the Polish Diet: "I prefer freedom with danger to peace with slavery."

If there were a people of gods, it would govern itself democratically. Such a perfect government is not suited to men.

Chapter V

Aristocracy

We have here two quite distinct artificial persons, namely, the government and the sovereign, and consequently two general wills, one general with respect to all the citizens, the other only with respect to the members of the administration. Thus, although the government can regulate its internal affairs as it sees fit, it can speak to the people only in the name of the sovereign, that is, in the name of the people itself. This must never be forgotten.

The first societies were governed aristocratically. The heads of families deliberated on public affairs among themselves. The young men readily yielded to the authority of experience. Hence the terms "priests," "elders," "senate," "gerontocracy." The savages of North America still govern themselves in that way, and they are very well governed.

But as artificial inequality came to prevail over natural inequality, wealth or power[19] was preferred to age, and aristocracy became elective. Finally, when fathers began bequeathing power as well as property to their children, certain families became patrician; this made government hereditary, and there were sometimes twenty-year-old senators.

There are thus three kinds of aristocracy: natural, elective, and hereditary. The first is suitable only for simple peoples; the third is the worst of all governments. The second is the best: it is aristocracy in the proper sense of the word.

Besides the advantage of separating the two powers, it also has the advantage of selective membership. In a democracy, all citizens are born magistrates, but this kind of aristocracy limits magistrates to a small number, and they attain their position only by election,[20] a method by which integrity, enlightenment, experience, and all the other qualities that win public preference and esteem become so many further guarantees of wise government.

Moreover, assemblies are more easily held, business is discussed better and handled in a more orderly and diligent manner, and the prestige of the state is better maintained abroad by venerable senators than it would be by an unknown or despised multitude.

In short, it is the best and most natural arrangement for the wisest to govern the multitude, when one can be sure that they govern it for its advantage and not for their own; there is no need to multiply jurisdictions uselessly, or to employ twenty thousand men to do something that a hundred selected men could do even better. But it must be noted that corporate interest here begins to direct public power less in accordance with the general will, and that there is also an inevitable tendency for part of the executive power to be taken away from the laws.

As for specific requirements, the state should not be so small, or the people so simple and straightforward, that execution of the laws follows immediately from the public will, as it does in a good democracy. Nor should the nation be so large that its magistrates, widely scattered in order to govern it, can assume the role of the sovereign, each in his own area, and make themselves independent, then finally become masters.

But while aristocracy does not demand all the same virtues as democracy, it demands others that are peculiar to it, such as moderation on the part of the rich and contentment on the part of the poor, for it seems that rigorous equality would be out of place in an aristocracy; it did not exist even in Sparta.

If, however, this form of government involves a certain inequality of wealth, it is so that, in general, the administration of public affairs can be entrusted to those best able to devote all their time to it, and not, as Aristotle maintained, so that the rich should always be given preference. On the contrary, it is important that a man who is not rich should sometimes be chosen, to teach the people that merit is a sounder reason for preference than wealth.

CHAPTER VI

Monarchy

So far, we have considered the prince as an artificial and collective person, unified by the force of the law, and entrusted with the executive power in the state. We must now consider that power concentrated in the hands of a natural person, a real man, who is exclusively entitled to wield it in accordance with the law. Such a man is known as a monarch, or a king.

Contrary to the other forms of government, in which a collective being represents an individual, in this one an individual represents a collective being, so that the artificial unity which constitutes the prince is at the same time a physical unity, and all the faculties united by the law with such great effort, in the first case, are here united naturally.

Thus the will of the people, the will of the prince, the public power of the state, and the particular power of the government all respond to the same prime mover; all the controls of the machine are in the same hand, everything works toward the same goal, and there are no conflicting, mutually destructive movements. It is impossible to imagine any other kind of constitution in which such great effects are produced by so little effort. To me, Archimedes sitting quietly on the shore and easily pulling a great ship afloat represents an able monarch governing a vast state from his study, moving everything while he himself appears to be motionless.

But if there is no form of government more vigorous than monarchy, there is also none in which a particular will is more dominant and controls other wills more easily. It is true that everything works toward the same goal, but that goal is not the happiness of the people, and the very strength of the administration is constantly detrimental to the state.

Kings want to be absolute rulers, and men cry out to them from afar that the best means to that end is to make their subjects love them. This is a fine maxim, and in some respects it is even quite true. Unfortunately it will always be ridiculed at courts. The power that comes from the people's love is no doubt the greatest, but it is precarious and conditional, and kings will never be content with it. Even the best of kings want to keep the possibility of being malicious whenever they are so inclined, without losing their power. It will do no good for a political sermonizer to tell them that since their strength is the same as the people's, it is to their greatest advantage that the people be prosperous, numerous, and formidable; kings know that this is not true. Their personal interest is primarily that the people be weak, impoverished, and never able to resist them. I grant that if a king's subjects were always perfectly obedient, it would be to his interest that they be strong, so that their strength, being his also, would make him formidable to his neighbors; but since that interest is only secondary and subordinate, and since strength and perfect obedience are incompatible, it is natural that kings always prefer the guiding principle that is most immediately useful to them. Samuel expressed this forcefully to the Hebrews, and Machiavelli demonstrated it clearly. While pretending to instruct kings, Machiavelli was actually teaching great lessons to peoples. His *Prince* is a handbook for republicans.[21]

We have already seen, from an examination of general relations, that monarchy is suited only to large states, and an examination of monarchy in itself leads to the same conclusion. The larger the number of public administrators, the more the ratio between the prince and the subjects diminishes and approaches equality, so that in a democracy it is one to one, or exactly equal. This ratio increases as the government becomes smaller, and reaches its maximum when the government is in the hands of one man. There is then too great a distance between the prince and the people, and the state lacks cohesion, which can be gained only by establishing intermediate positions, with princes, lords, and noblemen to occupy them. All this is unsuitable for a small state, which would be ruined by such an elaborate hierarchy.

But if it is difficult for a large state to be well governed, it is much more difficult for it to be well governed by one man, and everyone knows what happens when a king gives himself deputies.

Monarchical government has one essential and inevitable defect that will always make it inferior to republican government. In a republic, the voice of the people nearly always raises enlightened and able men to the highest positions, men who fulfill their duties with honor, whereas those who rise in a monarchy are usually nothing but petty troublemakers, scoundrels, and schemers, small men with small talents that enable them to succeed at court, but serve only to demonstrate their incompetence to the public when they have been placed in important posts. Bad choices of men for high office are much more likely to be made by kings than by peoples, and a man of real merit in a royal ministry is almost as rare as a fool at the head of a republican government. So when by some fortunate accident a man born to govern takes charge of public affairs in a monarchy that has nearly been wrecked by hordes of opportunistic administrators, everyone is amazed at the resources he finds, and his rise to power is an epoch-making event in the history of the country.

In order for a monarchical state to be well governed, the abilities of the man who governs it would have to be proportionate to the size of its population and territory. It is easier to conquer than to rule. If he had a long enough lever, any man could shake the world with one finger, but to support it he would need to have the shoulders of Hercules. Whatever the size of a state, the king is nearly always too small for it. If, however, a state is too small for its king, which is very rare, it is still badly governed because, always absorbed in the pursuit of his lofty goals, he forgets the interests of the people, so that by misusing his overabundant abilities he makes his subjects as unhappy as they would be under a mediocre ruler whose abilities were inadequate. It can be said that a kingdom ought to expand or contract with each reign, according to the capacity of the king; but with a senate, whose abilities remain more constant, the state can maintain a fixed size without detriment to its administration.

The most palpable disadvantage of one-man government is lack of that continuity of succession which provides an unbroken bond in the other two forms of government. When a king dies, another is needed; elections leave a dangerous interval; they are stormy, and unless the citizens have more disinterestedness and integrity than a monarchical government usually produces, there will be intrigue and corruption. When the state has been sold to a man, it is likely that he will also sell it, and take money from the weak to make up for what he has had to pay to the strong. Sooner or later everything becomes venal under such an administration, and then the peace assured by the king is worse than the turbulence of the interregnum.

What has been done to prevent these evils? Thrones have been made hereditary within certain families, and an order of succession has been established to forestall dispute when a king dies. That is, the disadvantage of regencies have been substituted for those of elections, apparent tranquillity has been placed before wise administration, and the risk of having children, monsters, or imbeciles for rulers has been deemed preferable to the conflicts involved in choosing a good king. What has been overlooked is that when we thus expose ourselves to the risks of these alternatives, the odds are overwhelmingly against us. Dionysius the Younger made a shrewd reply to his father when the latter, reproaching him for some shameful act, asked him, "Have I ever set you such an example?" "No," his son answered, "but your father was not a king!"

When a man has been brought up to command others, everything combines to deprive him of justice and reason. Great pains are taken, we are told, to teach young princes the art of ruling; this training does not seem to be effective. It would be better to begin by teaching them the art of obeying. The greatest kings acclaimed by history were not brought up to rule; ruling is a skill that is mastered least when it has been taught too much, and it is better acquired by obeying than by commanding. "For the best and quickest way of deciding what is good and what is bad is to consider what you would or would not have wanted if someone other than you had been king" (Tacitus, *History*, Book I).

One result of the lack of continuity in royal government

is instability. Following first one plan and then another, depending on the character of the ruling monarch, or of those who rule for him, the government cannot maintain a fixed objective or a consistent policy for very long. This fluctuation, which causes the state to be always shifting from policy to policy and from project to project, does not occur in the other forms of government, in which the prince is always the same. Thus we see that, in general, while there is more cunning in a court, there is more wisdom in a senate, and that republics move toward their objectives by means of more stable and consistently followed plans, whereas every upheaval in a royal ministry produces an upheaval in the state, since all ministers and most kings make it a rule to reverse their predecessors' policies in everything.

This same lack of continuity provides a rebuttal to a sophism often used by royalist political theorists. It consists not only in comparing civil government to household government and the king to the head of a family, an error that has already been refuted, but also in generously attributing to the king all the virtues he should have, and in always assuming that he is what he ought to be. On this assumption, royal government is obviously preferable to any other, because it is undeniably the strongest, and to be the best it needs only a corporate will more in conformity with the general will.

But if, as Plato says in *The Statesman*, the born king is a very rare man, how often do nature and fortune combine to crown him? And if royal education necessarily corrupts those who receive it, what are we to expect of a succession of men brought up to rule? It is thus deliberate self-deception to confuse royal government with government by a good king. To see what royal government actually is, we must consider it under incompetent or evil kings, for if they are not already incompetent or evil when they ascend the throne, they will be made so by occupying it.

Our theorists are aware of these difficulties, but they are not troubled by them. The remedy, they tell us, is to obey without a murmur. God gives us bad kings in his wrath, and they must be endured as a divine punishment. This is no doubt an edifying argument, but I believe it might be less out of place in a pulpit than in a political treatise. What would we say of a doctor who promised miracles, but whose entire skill lay in exhorting the sick to be patient? Everyone knows that we must put up with a bad government when that is what we have; the problem is to find a good one.

CHAPTER VII

Mixed Governments

Strictly speaking, no government can exist in an unmixed form. A single ruler must have subordinate magistrates; a democracy must have a leader. Thus in the division of executive power there is always a gradation from the greater to the smaller number, though sometimes the greater number is dependent on the smaller, and sometimes the smaller on the greater.

Sometimes there is an equal division, either when the constituent parts are mutually dependent, as in the government of England, or when the authority of each part is independent but imperfect, as in Poland. This latter form is bad, because there is no unity in the government and because the state lacks cohesion.

Which is better, a mixed or an unmixed government? To this question, which has been vigorously debated by political theorists, I must give the same answer as I gave earlier with regard to all forms of government.

In itself, unmixed government is better because it is simpler. But when the executive power is insufficiently dependent on the legislative power, that is, when the ratio of the prince to the sovereign is greater than that of the people to the prince, this faulty proportion must be remedied by dividing the government. All its parts will then have the same authority over the subjects, but their separation will make them less powerful with respect to the sovereign.

Sometimes there is an equal division, either when the constituent parts are mutually dependent, as in the government of England, or when the authority of each part is independent but imperfect, as in Poland. This latter form is bad, because there is no unity in the government and because the state lacks cohesion.

Which is better, a mixed or an unmixed government?

To this question, which has been vigorously debated by political theorists, I must give the same answer as I gave earlier with regard to all forms of government.

In itself, unmixed government is better because it is simpler. But when the executive power is insufficiently dependent on the legislative power, that is, when the ratio of the prince to the sovereign is greater than that of the people to the prince, this faulty proportion must be remedied by dividing the government. All its parts will then have the same authority over the subjects, but their separation will make them less powerful with respect to the sovereign.

The same faulty proportion can also be corrected by establishing intermediate magistrates who, leaving the government undivided, serve only to balance the two powers and maintain their respective rights. The government is then not mixed, but moderated.

Similar means can be used to remedy the opposite kind of disproportion: When the government is too loosely organized, agencies can be created to draw it more tightly together. This is done in all democracies. In the first case, the government is divided to weaken it; in the second, to strengthen it. Maximum strength and maximum weakness are both found in unmixed forms of government, while mixed forms have a moderate degree of strength.

CHAPTER VIII

All Forms of Government Do Not Suit All Countries

Since freedom is not a fruit that grows in all climates, it is not within the reach of all peoples. The more one reflects on this principle put forward by Montesquieu, the more its truth becomes apparent; and the more one disputes it, the more opportunities one gives for confirming it with new proofs.

In every government in the world, the public person consumes but does not produce anything. What, then, is the source of what it consumes? The work of its members. Public necessities are provided by the surpluses of individuals. From this it follows that the civil state can subsist only if men's work produces more than they need.

This surplus is not the same in all parts of the world. It is large in some and moderate in others; in still others, production either meets the level of need, with no surplus, or falls below it. The relation depends on the fertility of the region, the kind of work required by its soil, the nature of its products, the strength of its inhabitants, the level of consumption they require, and various other similar relations of which the overall relation is composed.

Moreover, not all governments are of the same nature; some are more voracious than others, and their differences are based on another principle, namely, that the farther taxes are removed from their source, the more burdensome they are. The burden should not be measured by the amount of the taxes, but by the distance they must cover before returning to the hands that paid them. When this circulation is rapid and well established, it does not matter whether payments are large or small: The people will always be rich and the state will always be in sound financial condition. On the other hand, however little the people gives, when that little does not return to it, its resources are soon exhausted by continued payments; the state is never rich, and the people is always impoverished.

It follows that taxation is burdensome in proportion to the distance between the people and the government, so that the weight of taxation borne by the people is lightest in a democracy, heavier in an aristocracy, and heaviest in a monarchy. Monarchy is therefore suited only to rich states, aristocracy to those of moderate wealth and size, and democracy to those that are small and poor.

The more we reflect on it, the more difference we find in this respect between free states and monarchies: In the former, everything is used for the common welfare; in the latter, public resources are in inverse proportion to private resources, and one is increased by decreasing the other. And finally, instead of governing the subjects to make them happy, despotism impoverishes them to govern them.

In each region there are natural conditions which enable us to determine the form of government that will be most favored by its climate, and even the kind of inhabitants it should have.

Unfruitful regions where the products of the land necessitate more work than they are worth should either remain uncultivated and uninhabited or be inhabited only by savages. Regions where work yields no more than what is strictly necessary for human life should be inhabited by barbaric peoples; no political society is possible in such places. Regions where work yields a moderate surplus over and above the necessities of life are suited to free peoples. Those with abundant and fertile land which produces plentifully in return for a small amount of labor should be governed monarchically, so that the subjects' excessive surplus will be consumed by the luxuries of the prince, because it is better for it to be absorbed by the government than dissipated by individuals. There are exceptions, I know, but those very exceptions confirm the rule, in that sooner or later they cause upheavals which bring things back to the natural order.

We must always distinguish general laws from particular causes that may modify their effects. If the entire South were covered with republics and the entire North with despotic states, it would still be true that, considering only the effect of climate, despotism is suited to hot countries, barbarism to cold countries, and good polity to temperate regions. I realize that this principle may be accepted and its application contested: It may be pointed out that there are fertile cold countries and barren southern ones. But this is a difficulty only for those who do not consider all aspects of the matter. As I have already said, one must take into account such factors as work, strength, consumption, etc.

Let us suppose two territories of equal size, one yielding five units, the other ten. If the inhabitants of the former consume four units and those of the latter nine, the surplus of the former will be one-fifth and that of the latter one-tenth. Since the surpluses of the two territories are in inverse ratio to their yields, the territory that yields only five units will give a surplus double that of the one that yields ten.

But there is no question of a double yield, and I do not think that anyone will venture to equate the productivity of cold countries, in general, with that of hot countries. Let us suppose such equality nevertheless; let us say, for example, that England is in balance with Sicily, and Poland with Egypt. Farther south we have Africa and India; farther north we have nothing. What differences in agricultural methods are involved in achieving that equality of production? In Sicily, one has only to scratch the soil, while in England, what effort is required to till it! But where more men are needed to produce the same amount, the surplus is necessarily smaller.

We must also consider the fact that a given number of men consume much less in hot countries. Because of the climate, one must eat sparingly to remain healthy. Europeans who try to live in hot countries as they do at home die of dysentery and indigestion. "We are," says Chardin,

> carnivorous beasts, wolves, compared to the Asians. Some attribute the moderation of the Persians to the fact that their land is less cultivated, but I believe that their land produces less food because the inhabitants need less. If their frugality were the result of scarcity, only the poor would eat little, whereas, in general, everyone does so; and the amount that people eat would vary from province to province, according to the fertility of the soil, whereas one finds the same frugality throughout the whole kingdom. They are perfectly satisfied with their way of life, and say that one has only to look at their complexions to see how much better their way is than that of the Christians. The Persians do indeed have smooth complexions; their skin is attractive, finely textured and lustrous, while the Armenians, their subjects, who live in the European manner, have rough, blotchy complexions and fat, coarse bodies.

The closer men live to the equator, the less they eat. They eat almost no meat; their usual foods are rice, corn, couscous, millet, and manioc. In India there are millions of people whose food costs less than one sou a day. Even in Europe there are sharp differences in appetite between northern and southern peoples. A Spaniard could live for a week on a German's dinner. In countries where people are more voracious, luxury is conceived in terms of what they consume. In England it is shown by a table laden with meats; in Italy one is regaled with sugar and flowers.

Luxury in clothing shows similar differences. In regions where the changes of season are abrupt and violent, people have better and simpler garments; in regions where they dress only for ornamentation, they care more for appearance than utility, and clothes themselves are a luxury. Every day in the Posillipo quarter of Naples one can see men strolling in gold-embroidered jackets and no stockings. It is the same with buildings: Magnificence is the only consideration where there is nothing to fear from the weather. In Paris and London, people want to be housed warmly and comfortably. In Madrid they have superb drawing rooms, but no windows that close, and their bedrooms are like rats' nests.

Foods are tastier and more substantial in hot countries; this is a third difference which cannot fail to influence the second. Why are so many vegetables eaten in Italy? Because they are good, nourishing, and flavorful. In France, where they are made up mostly of water, they are not nourishing, and almost no value is placed on them at table. Yet it takes as much land and at least as much labor to raise them. It is a proven fact that Barbary wheat, otherwise inferior to that of France, yields much more flour, and that French wheat in turn yields more than wheat grown in the North. From this we may infer that, generally speaking, there is a similar gradation from the equator to the pole. Is it not an obvious disadvantage to obtain less food from an equal amount of produce?

To all these different considerations I may add another which follows from them and strengthens them: that hot countries have less need of inhabitants than cold countries, and could feed more; this produces a double surplus that is always to the advantage of despotism. The larger the area occupied by a given number of people, the more difficult it is for them to rebel, because they cannot conspire quickly or secretly, and it is always easy for the government to discover their plans and cut off their communications. But the more closely a large population lives together, the less the government is able to encroach on the sovereign; the people's leaders can deliberate as safely in their houses as the government in its council chamber, and crowds can assemble as quickly in public squares as troops in their quarters. It is thus to the advantage of a tyrannical government to act over great distances. Each of the strongpoints it provides for itself acts as the fulcrum of a lever, making its power increase with distance.[22] The power of the people, however, is effective only when it is concentrated; when it is spread out, it evaporates and is lost, just as gunpowder scattered on the ground ignites only grain by grain. The most thinly populated countries are therefore most suited to tyranny; ferocious beasts reign only in a wilderness.

CHAPTER IX

The Signs of a Good Government

When, therefore, the question "What is the best government?" is asked in absolute terms, it is unanswerable because it is indeterminate; or rather, it has as many right answers as there are possible combinations in the absolute and relative positions of peoples.

But if we ask by what sign we can recognize whether a people is well or badly governed, that is another matter; it is a question of fact that can be answered.

It is not answered, however, because everyone wants to answer it in his own way. The subject extols public tranquillity, the citizen individual freedom; one prefers security of possessions, the other security of persons; one maintains that the best government is the most severe, the other that it is the most lenient; one wants crime to be punished, the other wants it to be prevented; one likes his country to be feared by its neighbors, the other prefers it to be ignored; one is happy when money circulates, the other demands that the people have enough food. But even if there were agreement on these and other similar points, would the problem be any closer to solution? If we were all to accept a criterion, how could we agree on its application, since moral quantities cannot be measured precisely?

For my part, I am always astonished that one simple criterion either goes unrecognized or is rejected with deliberate insincerity. What is the purpose of a political association? The preservation and prosperity of its members. What is the surest sign that they are preserving themselves and prospering? Their number and the rate of its growth. We need look no further for the much-debated criterion. All other things being equal, the best government is unquestionably the one whose citizens increase and multiply most, without extraneous means such as naturalizations and colonies. The worst government is one under which the people diminishes and wastes away. Calculators, it is now your affair: count, measure, compare.[23]

CHAPTER X

The Abuse of Government and Its Tendency to Degenerate

Just as the particular will acts unceasingly against the general will, the government makes a constant effort against the sovereign. The more that effort increases, the more the constitution deteriorates, and since there is here no other corporate will to oppose that of the prince and balance it, it is inevitable that sooner or later the prince will finally oppress the sovereign and break the social treaty. This is the inherent and unavoidable defect which, from the birth of the body politic, works incessantly to destroy it, just as old age and death destroy the human body.

There are two general ways in which a government degenerates: by contracting, and by dissolution of the state.

A government contracts when it passes from the larger number to the smaller, that is, from democracy to aristocracy, and from aristocracy to monarchy. That is its natural tendency.[24] If it were to pass from the smaller number to the larger, it could be said to expand, but a progression in that direction is impossible.

A government never takes on a new form unless the exhaustion of its energies leaves it too weak to maintain the form it has. If it slackened still more by expanding, its strength would be reduced to nothing, and it would be even less able to preserve itself. It must therefore wind up and tighten its mechanism to prevent it from running down; otherwise the state it supports will fall into ruin.

The dissolution of the state can take place in two ways.

First, it occurs when the prince no longer administers the state in accordance with the law, and usurps the sovereign power. There is then a remarkable change: It is not the government that contracts, but the state; I mean that the state as a whole dissolves and another is formed inside it, composed only of the members of the government. To the rest of the people, this new state is nothing but a master and a tyrant. Therefore as soon as the government usurps sovereignty, the social pact is broken and all the ordinary citizens, rightfully resuming their natural freedom, are forced but not obligated to obey.

The same thing happens when the members of the government separately usurp the power that they should exercise only as a body. This is no less an infraction of the law, and it produces even greater disorder. There are, so to speak, as many princes as magistrates, and the state, no less divided than the government, either perishes or changes its form.

When the state is dissolved, the abuse of government, whatever its form, takes the general name of *anarchy*. More precisely, democracy degenerates into *mob rule*, aristocracy into *oligarchy*, and I would add that monarchy degenerates into *tyranny* if it were not for the fact that this word is ambiguous and requires explanation.

In ordinary usage, a tyrant is a king who rules violently and without regard for justice and law. In the exact sense, a tyrant is an individual who arrogates royal authority to himself without having any right to it. This was how the Greeks used the word "tyrant." They applied it indiscriminately to good or bad kings whose authority was not legitimate.[25] Thus "tyrant" and "usurper" are exact synonyms.

To give different names to different things, I apply the word "tyrant" to a usurper of royal authority, and the word "despot" to a usurper of sovereign power. A tyrant thrusts himself forward, contrary to the law, to govern in accordance with the law; a despot places himself above the law itself. Thus a tyrant may not be a despot, but a despot is always a tyrant.

CHAPTER XI

The Death of the Body Politic

Such is the natural and inevitable tendency of even the best-constituted governments. If Sparta and Rome perished, what state can hope to last forever? If, then, we wish to form a durable state, let us not dream of making it eternal. To succeed, we must avoid attempting the impossible and foolishly believing that we can give any work of man a permanence that nothing human can have.

The body politic, like a man's body, begins dying as soon as it is born, and bears the causes of its destruction within itself. But either kind of body can have a stronger or weaker constitution which will tend to preserve it a longer or shorter time. A man's constitution is produced by nature, a state's by art. Men cannot prolong their own lives, but they can prolong the life of the state as far as possible by giving it the best constitution it can have. The best-constituted state will eventually come to an end, but it will last longer than others if some unforeseen accident does not destroy it prematurely.

The essence of political life is in the sovereign authority. The legislative power is the heart of the state; the executive power is the brain which sets all the parts in motion. A man may go on living after his brain has become paralyzed. He will be imbecilic, but still alive. As soon as the heart ceases to function, however, the body dies.

It is not by the law that the state remains alive, but by the legislative power. Yesterday's law is not binding today, but silence is taken as tacit consent, and the sovereign is presumed to give continued affirmation to all laws which it does not repeal when it is able to do so. Whatever it has once declared to be its will is still its will, unless it revokes the declaration.

Why, then, are old laws held in such respect? Precisely because they are old, for we may assume that they owe their long survival only to their excellence: If the sovereign had not always considered them to be sound, it would long since have repealed them. Thus, far from weakening, the laws of a well-constituted state constantly gain new strength; the prestige of antiquity makes them more venerable every day. But where laws weaken with age, this shows that the legislative power has become inoperative, and that the state is no longer alive.

CHAPTER XII

How the Sovereign Authority Maintains Itself

The sovereign, having no other force than the legislative power, acts only through the laws, and since the laws are nothing other than authentic acts of the general will, the sovereign can act only when the people is assembled. "The people assembled?" it may be said. "What an idle fancy!"

It *is* an idle fancy today, but two thousand years ago it was not. Have men changed their nature?

The limits of possibility in the moral realm are less narrow than we think. It is our weaknesses, vices, and prejudices that constrict them. Base souls do not believe in great men; abject slaves smile mockingly at the word "freedom."

Let us consider what can be done in the light of what has been done. I shall not speak of the republics of ancient Greece, but the Roman Republic was, it seems to me, a large state, and the city of Rome a large city. The last census of the city showed four hundred thousand arms-bearing citizens, and the last census of the empire showed more than four million citizens, not counting subjects, foreigners, women, children, or slaves.

It is easy to imagine the difficulties that must have been involved in holding frequent assemblies of the immense people of the capital and its environs. Yet few weeks passed without an assembly of the Roman people, and sometimes there were even several in a single week. The people exercised not only the rights of sovereignty, but also some of the rights of government. It transacted certain business, it tried certain cases, and in its public gatherings this whole people performed the functions of magistracy almost as often as those of citizenship.

Going back to the earliest history of nations, we see that most ancient governments, even monarchical ones, such as those of the Macedonians and Franks, had similar councils. In any case, this one incontestable fact answers all objections. It seems to me that it is sound reasoning to deduce the possible from the actual.

CHAPTER XIII

How the Sovereign Authority Maintains Itself (*continued*)

It is not enough that the people has assembled once to determine the constitution of the state by giving sanction to a body of law; it is not enough that it has established a permanent government or made definitive provisions for the election of magistrates. In addition to any special assemblies that unforeseen events may make necessary, there must be regularly scheduled assemblies that nothing can abolish or postpone, so that on each specified day the people will automatically be called together by law, with no need of any other formal convocation.

But aside from these assemblies, which are lawful simply by virtue of their date, any assembly of the people that has not been convened by magistrates authorized to do so, and in accordance with the prescribed procedures, must be regarded as unlawful, and all its acts as invalid, because the order to assemble must emanate from the law.

As for the frequency with which lawful assemblies should be held, it depends on so many considerations that no precise rules for it can be given. We can only say that, in general, the stronger the government is, the more often the sovereign should show itself.

This, it will be said, may be good for a single town, but what is to be done when the state includes several towns? Shall the sovereign authority be divided, or shall it be concentrated in one town, with all the others subordinate to it?

I answer that neither should be done. First, the sovereign authority is a single whole and cannot be divided without being destroyed. Second, towns are like nations, in that none can be legitimately subordinated to another, because the essence of the body politic lies in the union of obedience and freedom, and the words "subject" and "sovereign" are exact correlatives whose meanings are combined in the single word "citizen."

I also answer that it is always disadvantageous to unite several towns in one state, and that anyone who wants to form such a union should not delude himself into believing that he can avoid its natural drawbacks. The abuses of large states cannot be used as objections against someone who wants only small ones. But how can small states be given enough strength to resist large ones, as the Greek towns resisted a great king in ancient times, and as Holland and Switzerland, more recently, resisted the House of Austria?

If, however, the state cannot be limited to a reasonable size, there remains another possibility: to have no capital, to move the seat of government from town to town in rotation, and to have the estates of the realm assemble in each town in turn.

Populate the territory evenly, extend the same rights to

all parts of it, bring abundance and life everywhere, and the state will become as strong and as well governed as possible. Remember that the walls of towns are made only from the debris of rural houses. Whenever I see a palace being built in the capital, I feel as if I were watching the homes of an entire countryside being reduced to rubble.

CHAPTER XIV

How the Sovereign Authority Maintains Itself (*continued*)

The moment the people is lawfully assembled as a sovereign body, all jurisdiction of the government ceases, the executive power is suspended, and the person of the humblest citizen is as sacred and inviolable as that of the nighest magistrate, because there can be no representatives in the presence of those they represent. Most of the disturbances that broke out in the Roman public assemblies resulted from ignorance or neglect of this rule. The consuls were then only the people's chairmen, the tribunes were only speakers,[26] and the Senate was nothing at all.

The government always dreads these intervals of suspension, when it recognizes, or should recognize, a present superior; and such assemblies of the people, which are the shield of the body politic and the brake on the government, have always been the terror of magistrates, who therefore spare no pains in raising objections, making difficulties, and giving promises to discourage the citizens from assembling. When the citizens are avaricious, lethargic, cowardly, or fonder of tranquillity than of freedom, they do not hold out long against the redoubled efforts of the government. It is thus that, as the opposing force constantly increases, the sovereign authority finally vanishes, and most republics fall and perish before their time.

But between the sovereign authority and arbitrary government there is sometimes an intermediate power, of which we must now speak.

CHAPTER XV

Deputies or Representatives

Once public service ceases to be the main concern of the
citizens and they prefer to serve with their purses rather
than their persons, the state is already close to ruin. If soldiers are needed for war, the citizens pay mercenaries and
stay at home; if an assembly is to be held, they appoint
deputies and stay at home. By being lazy and spending
money, they eventually acquire soldiers to enslave the
country and representatives to sell it.

It is the cares of commerce and industry, avid pursuit
of gain, softness, and love of comfort that change personal
service into money. The citizen gives up part of his income to have more time to increase it. Give money and
you will soon have chains. The word "Treasury" is a term
of slavery; it has no place in a republic. In a truly free
state, the citizens do everything with their own hands and
nothing with money. Far from paying for exemption from
their duties, they would pay to fulfill them in person. My
ideas are quite different from those commonly accepted; I
believe that forced labor is less contrary to freedom than
taxes.

The better the state is constituted, the more public affairs take precedence over private business in the minds of
the citizens. There is, in fact, much less private business,
because the sum of public happiness, so that he has less
portion of each individual's happiness, so that he has less
of it to seek by private means. In a well-governed republic, everyone hurries to assemblies; under a bad government, no one likes to take a step to go to them, because
no one has any interest in what takes place in them, because everyone assumes that the general will has no
chance of prevailing in them, and finally, because everyone is completely absorbed in his own domestic concerns.
Good laws cause better ones to be made; bad laws bring
on worse ones. A state must be considered lost as soon as
someone says, with regard to its affairs, "What does it matter to me?"

The decline of love of one's country, the vigorous pursuit of private interest, the vastness of states, conquests, and the abuse of government have led to the invention of sending deputies or representatives of the people to the assemblies of the nation. Some countries dare to call them the representatives of the "third estate," thus giving first and second priority to the private interests of two classes, with the public interest only in third place.

Sovereignty cannot be represented, for the same reason that it cannot be alienated. Its essence is the general will, and a will cannot be represented: It is either itself or not itself; there is no middle ground. The deputies of the people therefore are not and cannot be its representatives; they are only its agents and cannot decide anything definitively. Any law that the people has not ratified in person is invalid; it is not a law. The English believe themselves to be free; they are seriously mistaken, for they are free only during elections of members of Parliament, and in the time between those elections the people is in slavery, it is nothing. In the brief moments of their freedom, the English use it in such a way that they deserve to lose it.

The idea of representatives is modern: It comes to us from feudal government, that iniquitous and absurd government in which the human race is degraded and the name of man is dishonored. In the republics and even the monarchies of antiquity, the people never had representatives; the word was unknown. It is remarkable that in Rome, where the tribunes were so sacred, the idea of their usurping the functions of the people never even occurred to anyone, and that in the midst of such a great multitude they never tried to put through a *plebiscitum* [people's decree] on their own authority. Yet the difficulties that were sometimes presented by the size of the assemblies can be judged from what happened in the time of the Gracchi, when some of the citizens cast their votes from rooftops.

Where law and freedom are everything, difficulties are nothing. Those wise citizens never let anything go beyond its proper bounds: They allowed their lictors to do what their tribunes would not have dared to do; they were not afraid that their lictors would try to represent them.

To explain how the tribunes did sometimes represent them, however, we have only to understand how the government represents the sovereign. Since the law is only the declaration of the general will, it is clear that the people cannot be represented in its legislative power; but it can and should be represented in its executive power, which is only force applied to the law. This shows that if one looked closely one would see that very few nations have laws. Be that as it may, it is certain that the tribunes, having no part of the executive power, were never able to represent the Roman people by the rights of their office, but only by encroaching on the rights of the Senate.

In Greece, everything the people had to do it did for itself; it was constantly assembled outdoors. The Greeks lived in a mild climate, they were not avaricious, their work was done for them by slaves, and freedom was their primary concern. Without the same advantages, how can the same rights be preserved? Our harsher climates increase our needs,[27] our outdoor public places are unusable six months of the year, our muted languages cannot be understood in the open air, we devote more effort to gain than to freedom, and we fear slavery less than poverty.

What! Freedom can be maintained only with the support of slavery? Perhaps. The two extremes meet. Everything that is not in nature has its disadvantages, civil society more than all the rest. There are unfortunate situations in which one man can preserve his freedom only at the expense of another's, in which the citizen can be perfectly free only if the slave is in extreme servitude. Such was the situation of Sparta. As for you, modern peoples, you have no slaves, but you yourselves are enslaved; you pay for their freedom with your own. You may boast of your preference, but I see more baseness than humanity in it.

I do not mean by all this that slavery is necessary, or that the right of enslavement is legitimate, for I have proved the contrary. I am only stating the reasons why modern peoples, who consider themselves free, have representatives, and why ancient peoples had none. In any case, as soon as a people gives itself representatives, it is no longer free; it no longer exists.

All things considered, I do not see how the sovereign can continue to exercise its rights in our modern world, except in very small republics. But if a republic is very small, will it not be subjugated? No. I will show later[28] how it is possible to combine the external power of a large people with the easy administration and good order of a small state.

CHAPTER XVI

The Institution of the Government Is Not a Contract

Once the legislative power has been well established, the next task is to establish the executive power, for the latter, which operates only through particular acts, is essentially different from the former and is therefore naturally separate from it. If it were possible for the sovereign, considered as such, to have the executive power, the *de jure* and the *de facto* would be so intermingled that no one would know what was law and what was not, and the body politic, thus perverted, would soon fall prey to the violence it was instituted to prevent.

Since the citizens are all equal by the social contract, all can prescribe what all must do, whereas none has the right to demand that another do anything that he himself does not do. It is precisely this right, indispensable for imparting life and movement to the body politic, that the sovereign gives to the prince in instituting the government.

Some writers have claimed that the act of instituting a government is a contract between the people and the leaders it chooses for itself, a contract that stipulates the conditions under which one party obligates itself to command and the other to obey. It will be acknowledged, I am sure, that this is a strange way of contracting. But let us see whether or not the view is tenable.

First, the supreme authority can no more be modified than alienated; to limit it is to destroy it. It is absurd and contradictory that the sovereign should give itself a superior; in assuming the obligation to obey a master, the people would be reverting to its original freedom.

Furthermore, it is obvious that such a contract between the people and certain individuals would be a particular act. From this it follows that the contract could not be a law or an act of sovereignty, and that consequently it would be illegitimate.

It can also be seen that the contracting parties, between themselves, would be only under the law of nature and without any guarantee of their reciprocal commitments, which is thoroughly contrary to the civil state. Since the party that had all force at its disposal could always decide what was to be done, the term "contract" could equally well be applied to the act of one man who said to another, "I give you everything I have, on condition that you will give me back as much of it as you please."

There is only one contract in the state: that of the association; and it excludes all others. It is impossible to imagine any other public contract that would not violate the original one.

Chapter XVII

The Institution of the Government

In what terms, then, shall we conceive the act by which the government is instituted? First let me point out that this act is complex, that is, composed of two others: the establishment of the law and the execution of the law.

By the first, the sovereign ordains that there shall be a governing body with a certain form; and it is clear that this act is a law.

By the second, the people appoints the magistrates who will be charged with the government that has been established. Since this appointment is a particular act, it is not a second law, but only a consequence of the first, and an act of government.

The difficulty is to understand how there can be an act of government before the government exists, and how the people, being only the sovereign or the subjects, can become the prince or a magistrate in certain circumstances.

Here again we see one of those astonishing properties of the body politic by which it reconciles seemingly contradictory operations. For this operation is accomplished by a sudden conversion of sovereignty into democracy, so that without any perceptible change, simply by virtue of a new relation of all to all, the citizens become magistrates and pass from general acts to particular acts, and from the law to its execution.

This change of relation is not a theoretical subtlety that has no practical exemplification. It occurs every day in the English Parliament, where the House of Commons occasionally turns itself into a "committee of the whole house" to discuss certain matters better, thus ceasing to be a sovereign court and becoming a mere commissioner; it later reports to itself, as the House of Commons, what it has decided as a "committee of the whole house" and reconsiders under one name what it has already settled under another.

Such is the exclusive advantage of a democratic government: It can be called into existence by a single act of the general will. Afterward, this provisional government either remains in effect, if such is the form adopted, or establishes in the name of the sovereign the government prescribed by law, and everything is thus in order. It is not possible to institute the government legitimately in any other manner, without abandoning the principles I have previously established.

CHAPTER XVIII

The Means of Preventing Usurpation of the Government

From these explanations it follows, in confirmation of Chapter XVI, that the act which institutes the government is not a contract, but a law; that the holders of the executive power are not the people's masters, but its agents; that the people can appoint and dismiss them whenever it sees fit; that they are required only to obey, not to make a contract; and that in assuming the responsibilities imposed on them by the state, they are only fulfilling their duty as citizens and have no right whatever to question the conditions involved.

Thus when it happens that the people institutes a hereditary government, whether monarchical within one family or aristocratic within one class of citizens, it does not assume an obligation: It simply adopts one form of administration provisionally, until it chooses to adopt another.

It is true that such changes are always hazardous, and that the established government should be left as it is unless it has become incompatible with the public welfare; but this caution is a precept of politics, not a rule of law, and the state is no more obligated to leave civil authority in the hands of any given magistrate than it is to leave military authority in the hands of any given general.

It is also true that in such cases one cannot be too careful in observing all the requisite formalities for distinguishing a proper and legitimate act from seditious agitation, and the will of a whole people from the clamor of a faction. It is here above all that nothing more must be conceded to dangerous demands than what is strictly required by law. This obligation gives a great advantage to a government that wants to remain in power against the people's wishes without incurring the charge of usurpation, for it can easily extend its rights while appearing only to exercise them, and on the pretext of preserving public tranquillity it can prevent public assemblies designed to correct abuses. The silence it has thus imposed is then used as a justification for claiming the support of those who are afraid to speak, and the irregularities it has caused to occur become the ostensible reason for punishing those who dare to protest. It was thus that the decemvirs, having first been elected for one year, then kept on for another, tried to make their power permanent by not allowing the Roman public assemblies to be held; and it is by this easy means that all governments in the world, once the public force has been vested in them, sooner or later usurp the sovereign authority.

The periodic assemblies of which I spoke earlier are the best means of preventing or postponing this evil, especially when they have no need of a formal convocation, for then the government cannot prevent them without openly declaring itself a violator of the law and an enemy of the state.

These assemblies, whose only purpose is the maintenance of the social treaty, should always be opened with a vote on two questions. Each should be voted on separately, and neither should ever be omitted.

The first: "Does it please the sovereign to keep the present form of government?"

The second: "Does it please the people to leave the administration in the hands of those now responsible for it?"

I am here assuming what I believe I have demonstrated, namely, that there is no fundamental law in the state that cannot be repealed, not even the social pact itself, for if all the citizens were to assemble to break that pact by common consent, there can be no doubt that it would be quite lawfully broken. Grotius even believes that any man can renounce his membership in the state, and recover his natural freedom and possessions, by leaving the country.[29] It would be absurd to maintain that all the citizens cannot do collectively what each can do individually.

BOOK IV

CHAPTER I

The General Will Is Indestructible

As long as a number of men, having joined together, consider themselves a single body, they have only one will, which is directed toward the common security and well-being. The forces that move the state are then simple and vigorous; its principles are clear and illuminating; there are no tangled, conflicting interests; the common good is always so obvious that it can be seen by anyone with common sense. Peace, unity, and equality are enemies of political guile. Simple, straightforward men are difficult to deceive because of their very simplicity. They are not taken in by blandishments and devious arguments; they are too unsophisticated to be dupes. When, in the world's happiest nation, one sees groups of peasants conducting the affairs of the state under an oak tree and always acting wisely, how can one help despising the refinements of other nations, which make themselves illustrious and wretched by such artful and mysterious means?

A state so governed requires very few laws, and whenever there is a need to promulgate new ones, that need is apparent to all. The first man who proposes them is only saying what everyone else already feels, and neither intrigue nor eloquence plays any part in enacting into law what each has already resolved to do as soon as he is sure that others will do the same.

What misleads glib theorizers is that, seeing only states which were badly constituted from the start, they are struck by the impossibility of conducting the affairs of such states in the way I have described. They laugh when they imagine all the foolish acts into which a clever scoundrel of an ingratiating orator could lead the people of Paris or London. They do not know that Cromwell would have been put to forced labor by the people of Berne, and the Duc de Beaufort imprisoned by the Genevans.

But when the social bond begins to loosen and the state to weaken, when private interests make themselves felt and smaller associations begin to influence the whole society, then the common interest becomes distorted and encounters opposition, voting is no longer unanimous, the general will is no longer the will of all, conflicts and debates arise, and even the wisest opinions are disputed.

Finally, when the state is close to ruin and exists only in an empty, illusory form, when the social bond has been broken in all hearts, when the vilest self-interest brazenly adorns itself with the sacred name of the public good, then the general will becomes mute, each man is guided by secret motives, the opinions he expresses are no more those of a citizen than if the state had never existed, and unjust decrees that have no other object than private interest are falsely presented as laws.

Does it follow from all this that the general will is annihilated or corrupted? No: It is still changeless, incorruptible, and pure; but it is subordinated to other wills that prevail over it. In detaching his interest from the common interest, each man clearly sees that he cannot separate the two completely, but his share of the public evil seems negligible to him, compared with the exclusive good that he intends to obtain for himself, Except where this private good is concerned, he wills the general good, in his own interest, as strongly as anyone else. Even if he sells his vote for money, he does not extinguish the general will in himself; he evades it. The transgression he commits is to change the formulation of the question, so that his answer concerns something other than what he was asked to decide; that is, instead of saying by his vote, "It is advantageous to the state," he says, "It is advantageous to a certain man or a certain faction that such and such a measure be adopted." Therefore the purpose of rules for regulating public assemblies is less to uphold the general will in them than to make sure that it is always questioned and always replies.

There are many observations that I could make here about the simple right of voting in every act of sovereignty, a right which nothing can take away from the citizens, and about the right of expressing opinions, making proposals, analyzing, and discussing, which the government always makes great efforts to reserve only for its members; but that important subject would require a separate treatise, and I cannot say everything in this one.

Chapter II

Voting

From what has been said in the preceding chapter it can be seen that the manner in which public affairs are conducted is a reliable indication of the current state of public morality and the health of the body politic. The more agreement there is in the assemblies, that is, the closer opinions come to being unanimous, the more the general will is dominant; but long debates, dissension, and tumult herald the ascendancy of private interests and the decline of the state.

This seems less obvious when two or more orders enter into the constitution of the state. In Rome, for example, the assemblies were often disturbed by quarrels between the patricians and the plebeians, even in the finest days of the Republic. But this exception is more apparent than real, for in such cases, because of an inherent defect in the body politic, there are, so to speak, two states in one, and what is not true of both together is true of each separately. Even in the stormiest times, the decrees of the Roman people, when the Senate did not interfere, were always promulgated peacefully and by a large majority of votes. Since the citizens had only one interest, the people had only one will.

Unanimity returns at the opposite extreme, when the citizens have fallen into servitude and no longer have either freedom or will. Fear and obsequiousness then change voting into acclamation; there is no longer deliberation, but only worship or damnation. Such was the vile way in which the Roman Senate expressed itself under the emperors. It was sometimes done with ridiculous precautions: Tacitus writes that, during the reign of Otho, when the senators heaped abuse on Vitellius they made a great uproar at the same time, so that if he should happen to gain control of the empire he would not be able to learn what each of them had said.

These various considerations give rise to the principles by which the counting of votes and the comparing of opinions should be conducted, depending on the ease with which the general will can be recognized, and the extent to which the state is declining.

There is only one law which by its nature requires unanimous assent: the social pact. For civil association is the most voluntary act in the world; since each man is born free and his own master, no one can bind him to anything, on any pretext whatever, without his consent. To decide that the son of a slave woman is born a slave is to decide that he is not born human.

If, then, there are those who oppose the social pact at the time when it is made, their opposition does not invalidate the contract: It only excludes them from it. They are foreigners among the citizens. When the state is instituted, residence indicates consent; to live in its territory is to acknowledge the authority of its sovereign.[30]

Apart from this original contract, the decision of the majority is always binding on the minority. This is a consequence of the contract itself. But it may be asked how a man can be free, and at the same time be forced to conform to wills that are not his own. How can dissenters be both free and subject to laws to which they have not consented?

I answer that the question is wrongly formulated. The citizen consents to all the laws, even those that are passed against his opposition, and even those that punish him if he dares to violate one of them. The unequivocal will of all the members of the state is the general will; it is through it that they are citizens and free.[31] When a law is proposed in their assembly, what is asked of them is not precisely whether they accept or reject the proposal, but whether it is in conformity with the general will that is theirs. In voting, each man gives his opinion on this question, and the declaration of the general will is drawn from the count of the votes. When, therefore, the opinion contrary to mine prevails, it proves only that I was mistaken, that what I thought was the general will was not. If my private opinion had prevailed, I would have done something other than what I had willed, and then I would not have been free.

This presupposes, it is true, that all the characteristics of the general will are still present in the majority; when they cease to be there, no matter what decision is made, there is no longer any freedom.

When I showed earlier how particular wills were substituted for the general will in public decisions, I spoke at some length about the practical means of preventing that abuse, and I shall return to them later. As for the proportion of votes needed to declare the general will, I have also given the principles by which it can be determined. A difference of one vote breaks a tie, and one dissenting vote breaks unanimity; but between a tie and unanimity there are many unequal divisions, any one of which may be made the required proportion, depending on the condition and needs of the body politic.

Two general maxims may be used to determine the proportion. The first is that the more serious and important the decision is, the closer the prevailing opinion should approach unanimity. The second is that the shorter the time in which the decision must be made, the more the required majority should be reduced; in matters that must be decided without delay, a difference of one vote should be enough. The first of these maxims seems better suited to enacting laws, the second to conducting public affairs. In any case, it is by a combination of both that the best proportion to require for a decisive majority can be determined.

Chapter III

Elections

Elections of the prince and the magistrates—which are, as I have said, complex acts—can be carried out in two ways: by voting, or by drawing lots. Each has been used in various republics, and a very complicated mixture of both is now used in the election of the Doge of Venice.

"Election by drawing lots," says Montesquieu, "is characteristic of democracy." I agree, but why is it so? "Drawing lots," he continues, "is a method of election which distresses no one; it gives each citizen a reasonable hope of serving his country." That explains nothing.

If we bear in mind that the election of leaders is a function of government and not of sovereignty, we can see why drawing lots is more in the nature of democracy, in which administration is better in proportion as its acts are fewer.

In a genuine democracy, public office is not an advantage but a heavy burden which no one can justly impose on one man rather than another. Only the law can impose it on a man who has been selected by chance, for in that case, since the condition is equal for all, and since the selection does not depend on any human will, the law is not given a particular application that would adulterate its universality.

In an aristocracy, the prince chooses the prince, the government assures its own continuity, and it is here that election by voting is the right method.

The example of the election of the Doge of Venice confirms this distinction, rather than destroying it. That mixed form is proper for a mixed government. For it is a mistake to regard the government of Venice as a genuine aristocracy: Although the people has no part in it, the nobility itself is a people. A multitude of "Barnabites" [poor noblemen] have never come close to any public office, and their nobility gives them only the empty title of "Excellency" and the right to attend the Grand Council. Since that Grand Council is as large as our General Council in Geneva, its illustrious members have no more privileges than our ordinary citizens. It is certain that, apart from the extreme disparity between the two republics, the bourgeoisie of Geneva is the exact counterpart of the Venetian patriciate, our natives and inhabitants correspond to the townsmen and people of Venice, and our peasants to the Venetian subjects on the mainland. In short, no matter how that republic is considered, disregarding its size, its government is no more aristocratic than ours. The only difference is that, having no lifetime leader, we do not have the same need for election by drawing lots.

Such elections would have few disadvantages in a genuine democracy, for if all men were equal, in character and ability as well as in principles and wealth, it would matter little who was chosen. But as I have already said, there are no genuine democracies.

When election by voting and election by lot occur together, the first should be used to fill offices that require specific abilities, such as military commands, and the second for those in which common sense, fairness, and integrity are sufficient, such as administrative posts, for in a well-constituted state these qualities are common to all citizens.

Neither election by voting nor election by lot has any place in a monarchical government. Since the monarch alone is the prince and the sole magistrate, the choice of his subordinates is his exclusive prerogative. When the Abbé de Saint-Pierre proposed increasing the Councils of the King of France and electing their members by ballot, he did not see that he was proposing to change the form of government.

At this point I ought to speak of the way in which votes should be cast and counted in the people's assembly, but perhaps the history of the Roman procedure will provide a more vivid explanation of all the principles I could establish. It will be worth a judicious reader's time to see in some detail how public and private affairs were conducted in a council of two hundred thousand men.

CHAPTER IV

The Roman Public Assemblies

We have no really reliable records concerning the earliest history of Rome, and it is quite likely that most of what is said about it consists of fables.[32] As a general rule, the most instructive part of the annals of a people, namely, the story of its origin as a people, is the part we know least about. The causes that bring about the rise and fall of empires are still demonstrated to us every day by experience, but since no peoples are being formed in our time, we have little more than conjectures to explain how they were formed in the past.

From the practices we find established, we can at least conclude that they had an origin. Of the traditions that deal with those origins, those that are supported by the greatest authorities and the strongest reasons must be regarded as the most reliable. Such are the principles I have tried to follow in examining the question of how the world's freest and most powerful people exercised its supreme power.

After the founding of Rome, the nascent Republic— that is, the founder's army, composed of Albans, Sabines, and foreigners—was divided into three classes, which because of that triple division were known as tribes. Each tribe was subdivided into ten curiae, and each curia into decuriae, with leaders called curiones and decuriones.

In addition, a body of one hundred equites, or knights, known as a century, was drawn from each tribe. Since there was little need for these subdivisions in a town, we may assume that their original purpose was purely military. But it seems that an instinct for greatness made the little town of Rome adopt an organizational system suited to the capital of the world.

This first division soon presented a problem. The tribes of the Albans (Ramnes) and Sabines (Tities) remained the same, while the tribe of the foreigners (Luceres) grew steadily as more foreigners arrived, and soon surpassed the two others. Servius's solution to this dangerous problem was to change the division: He abolished the racial division and substituted one that was based on the part of the town occupied by each tribe. In place of the three tribes, he established four, each of which occupied one of the hills of Rome and bore its name. Thus, in correcting the existing inequality, he also forestalled the development of any future inequality; and to make the division one of people as well as places, he forbade the inhabitants of one district to move to another, which prevented the races from becoming mingled.

He also doubled the three original centuries of equites and added twelve more, but he organized them all under the old names, a simple and astute device by which he accentuated the distinction between the knights and the people without making the latter complain.

To these four urban tribes, Servius added fifteen others, called rural tribes because they were composed of inhabitants of the countryside, each with its own district. New tribes were later formed, until finally the Roman people was divided into thirty-five tribes, a number that remained constant until the end of the Republic.

This distinction between town tribes and country tribes had one result that is worth noting because there is no other instance of it, and because it was responsible for both the preservation of Rome's morals and the growth of her empire. One might have thought that the urban tribes would soon monopolize power and honors and reduce the rural tribes to degradation, but what happened was just the opposite. The early Romans' taste for country life is well known. It came to them from the wise founder who associated freedom with rural work and military service, and banished to the city, so to speak, the arts and crafts, intrigue, wealth, and slavery.

Thus, since all the illustrious Romans lived in the country and cultivated the land, it became customary to seek the mainstays of the Republic only in the country. Everyone honored the rural life because the noblest patricians lived on farms, and the simple, hard-working life of the villager was preferred to the soft, indolent life of the Roman townsman. A man who would have been only a wretched proletarian in the city could become a respected citizen by working on a farm. "It was not without reason," said Varro, "that our noble ancestors chose the village as the place in which to breed those robust and valiant men who defended them in time of war and fed them in time of peace." Pliny states plainly that the rural tribes were honored because of the men who composed them, and that cowards were stigmatized by the disgrace of being transferred to one of the urban tribes. When Appius Claudius, the Sabine, came to live in Rome, honors were heaped on him and he was made a member of a rural tribe which later took the name of his family. Finally, all freedmen were incorporated into the urban tribes, never into the rural ones, and all through the history of the Republic there was not one example of a freedman who attained public office, even though he had become a citizen.

This was an excellent principle, but it was carried so far that it finally brought about a change, and certainly an abuse in the government.

First, the censors, having long since arrogated to themselves the right of arbitrarily transferring citizens from one tribe to another, allowed most of them to enter any tribe they chose, a practice that assuredly did no good and deprived the censorship of one of its main resources. Furthermore, since the great and powerful all had themselves inscribed in the rural tribes, while the freedman, having become citizens, remained with the populace in the urban tribes, the tribes in general were no longer associated with any specific place; they all became so intermingled that their members could be identified only by means of the registers, so that the word "tribe" lost all territorial reference and took on a purely personal meaning, or rather became almost void of any meaning whatever.

Another result was that the city tribes, now composed

of riffraff, and often outnumbering members of the rural tribes in the assemblies because it was easier for them to attend, sold the state to anyone willing to buy their votes.

As for the curiae, the founder had created ten of them in each tribe; the whole Roman people, therefore, at the time when it lived entirely within the walls of the town, was divided into thirty curiae, each of which had its own temples, gods, officials, and priests, as well as its own festivals, called *compitalia*, which resembled the *paganalia* later celebrated by the rural tribes.

When Servius made his new division, the thirty curiae could not be evenly distributed among the four tribes, and since he did not want to change the number, curiae that were independent of the tribes became another of the categories into which the inhabitants of Rome were divided. But there were no curiae among the rural tribes or the people who composed them, for when the tribes had become a purely civil institution and another system of raising troops had been adopted, Romulus's military divisions no longer had any function. Thus, although every citizen was a member of a tribe, there were many who did not belong to a curia.

Servius also made a third division, which had no relation to the other two, and by its consequences became the most important of all. He divided the entire Roman people into six classes that were based on property, rather than personal or territorial distinctions, so that the first classes were filled by the rich, the last by the poor, and those in the middle by men of moderate means. These six classes were subdivided into one hundred ninety-three other bodies known as centuries, which were distributed in such a way that the first class alone contained more than half of them, while the last class contained only one. Thus the class with the fewest members had the most centuries, and the whole last class counted as only one subdivision, even though more than half the inhabitants of Rome belonged to it.

To make the implications of this arrangement less clear to the people, Servius gave it a military appearance. He placed two centuries of armorers in the second class, and two of makers of instruments of war in the fourth. In each class except the last, he distinguished between young and old, that is, between those who were obliged to bear arms and those who were exempt by law because of their age; this distinction, more than that of wealth, made frequent censuses necessary. Finally, he ordained that the assembly was to be held on the Campus Martius, and that all men of military age were to come to it with their weapons.

The reason he did not make the distinction between young and old in the last class was that the common people who composed it were not granted the honor of bearing arms for the fatherland; a man had to own a home to acquire the right to defend it, and of the countless derelicts who adorn the armies of kings today, there is perhaps not one who would not have been scornfully turned away from a Roman cohort in the days when soldiers were defenders of freedom.

In the last class, however, a distinction was made between proletarians and those who were called *capite censi*. The former, who were not complete paupers, at least gave citizens to the state, and even soldiers when the need was urgent. As for those who had nothing at all, and could be counted only by their heads, they were considered worthless, and Marius was the first who deigned to enroll them.

Without deciding here whether this third classification was good or bad in itself, I believe I can say that it could have been made practicable only by the early Romans' simple ways, their disinterestedness, their taste for agriculture, and their contempt for commerce and avid pursuit of gain. Where is the modern people whose devouring greed, restlessness, incessant movements, and constant reversals of fortune would allow such a system to last twenty years without overturning the whole state? It should also be noted that morals and censorship were stronger than the system and corrected its vices; a rich man could be relegated to the class of the poor for having displayed his wealth too ostentatiously.

From all this is is easy to understand why only five classes were usually mentioned, even though there were actually six. The sixth, which provided no soldiers for the army, sent no voters to the Campus Martius,[33] and had almost no function in the Republic, was seldom considered significant.

Such were the different divisions of the Roman people. Let us now examine the effect that they had in the assemblies. Lawfully convened assemblies, called comitia, were usually held in the Forum or the Campus Martius. They were of three kinds: curial, centurial, and tribal, depending on whether they were organized by curiae, centuries, or tribes. The curial assemblies were founded by Romulus, the centurial assemblies by Servius, and the tribal assemblies by the tribunes of the people. Only in these assemblies were laws sanctioned and magistrates elected, and since there was no citizen who was not a member of a curia, a century, or a tribe, it follows that no citizen was excluded from the right to vote, and that the Roman people was truly sovereign by law and in fact.

In order for the assemblies to be lawfully convened and for their acts to have the force of law, there were three conditions: First, the body or the magistrate convening them had to be vested with the required authority; second, each assembly had to be held on the days permitted by law; and third, the auguries had to be favorable.

The reason for the first rule needs no explanation. The second was a procedural matter; no assembly could be held on a holiday, for example, or on a market day, when the country people who came to Rome for business did not have time to spend the day in the Forum. By the third, the Senate was able to keep the proud, restless people in check, and when necessary, to temper the ardor of seditious tribunes, although the latter found more than one way of evading that restraint.

Laws and the election of leaders were not the only matters submitted to the judgment of the assemblies. Since the Roman people had usurped the most important functions of government, it can be said that the fate of Europe was decided in those assemblies. The variety of business transacted gave rise to the different forms taken by the assemblies, according to the questions that had to be decided.

To judge these various forms, it is enough to compare them. In creating the curiae, Romulus's aim was to have the people control the Senate and the Senate control the people, while he dominated both. By this arrangement, therefore, he gave the people all the authority of number to balance the authority of power and wealth which he left to the patricians. Following the spirit of monarchy, however, he allowed the patricians to hold the advantage through the influence of their clients in voting majorities. This admirable institution of patrons and clients was a masterpiece of politics and humanity; without it, the patriciate, so contrary to the spirit of the Republic, could not have existed. Only Rome has had the honor of giving the world that fine example, which has never been followed, even though no abuses ever resulted from it.

Since the curiae continued in the same form under all the kings down to Servius (the reign of the last Tarquin was not considered legitimate), royal laws were generally known as *leges curiatae*.

Under the Republic, the curiae, still limited to the four urban tribes and now containing only the common people of Rome, suited neither the Senate, which led the patricians, nor the tribunes, who, although they were plebeians, led the well-to-do citizens. They therefore fell into disrepute, and their degradation was such that their thirty lictors assembled to do what the curial assemblies should have done.

The division by centuries was so favorable to the aristocracy that at first sight it is not easy to understand why the Senate did not always dominate the centurial assemblies, in which the consuls, censors, and other curule magistrates were elected. For of the one hundred ninety-three centuries that formed the six classes of the whole Roman people, the first class contained ninety-eight, and since votes were counted only by centuries, this one class had more votes than all the others together. When all its centuries were in agreement, the rest of the votes were not even counted; what the smallest minority had decided was held to be the decision of the multitude, and it can be said that matters were settled in the centurial assemblies more by weight of money than by number of votes.

But that great power was tempered in two ways. First, the tribunes usually belonged to the class of the rich, and there were always many plebeians in it; their influence counterbalanced that of the patricians in the first class.

Second, the order in which the centuries began voting was not determined by rank, which would have meant that the first class would always have cast its votes before the others. Instead, one century was chosen by lot, and it carried out the election by itself;[34] then, on another day, all the other centuries were summoned to repeat the same election, which they usually confirmed. Thus the authority of example was taken away from rank and given to chance, in accordance with the principle of democracy.

This procedure had still another advantage: Citizens living in the country had time between the two elections to inquire about the merit of the provisionally elected candidate, so that they would not be voting blindly. But on the pretext of saving time the procedure was finally abolished and both elections were held on the same day.

The tribal assemblies were the true council of the Roman people. They were convened only by the tribunes; in them, the tribunes were elected and had their decrees adopted. Not only did the Senate have no rank in them, but senators did not even have the right to attend them; forced to obey laws on which they had not been able to vote, the senators were, in this respect, less free than the humblest citizens. This unjust rule was thoroughly ill-conceived, and was enough in itself to invalidate the decrees of a body that did not allow all its members to be present. If all the patricians had attended those assemblies in accordance with their rights as citizens, they would have done so as ordinary private persons and would therefore have had little influence on the decisions made, since votes were counted on an individual basis and the head of the Senate could have done no more than the lowest proletarian.

It can be seen, then, that aside from the order which resulted from these various systems of gathering the votes of such a large people, the forms that arose from them were not inconsequential in themselves, for each one had effects related to the intentions that caused it to be chosen.

Without going into further details, we may conclude from the foregoing explanations that the tribal assemblies were the most favorable to popular government, and the centurial assemblies to aristocracy. As for the curial assemblies, they were suited to favoring only tyranny and evil designs, and therefore fell into disrepute; they were not used even by those bent on sedition, because they would have forced them to reveal their plans too openly. It is certain that the whole majesty of the Roman people was found only in the centurial assemblies. They were the only complete assemblies, since the rural tribes were absent from the curial assemblies, and the Senate and patricians from the tribal assemblies.

The method of voting used by the early Romans was as simple as their morals and customs, though less simple than that of Sparta. Each man cast his vote by announcing it aloud, and it was recorded by a clerk. The majority within each tribe determined its vote, the majority among the tribes determined the vote of the people, and the same was true of the curiae and the centuries. This practice was good as long as honesty reigned among the citizens and everyone would have been ashamed to vote publicly for an unjust measure or an unworthy candidate, but when the people became corrupt and votes were bought and sold, it was preferable to cast them in secret, so that buyers would be restrained by mistrust and sellers would have a chance to be scoundrels without being traitors.

I know that Cicero condemned this change and held it partly responsible for the ruin of the Republic. But although I am aware of the weight that must be given to Cicero's authority here, I cannot share his opinion. I believe, on the contrary, that the downfall of the state was hastened because such changes were too rare. Just as a healthy man's diet is not right for an invalid, laws that are proper for an upright people should not be used for governing a people that has become corrupt. Nothing confirms this maxim better than the duration of the Venetian Republic, which still retains a semblance of existence only because its laws are suited solely to evil men.

Each Roman citizen was given a tablet by means of which he could cast his vote without having it known to others. New procedures were also established for gathering the tablets, counting the votes, comparing numbers, etc. This did not prevent the officials charged with these functons[35] from often being suspected of corruption. And finally there were edicts intended to prevent intrigue and the buying of votes; their multiplicity shows how ineffective they were.

Toward the end of the Republic it was often necessary to resort to extraordinary expedients to make up for the inadequacy of the laws. Sometimes miracles were proclaimed, but although the citizens may have been taken in by this, those who governed them were not; sometimes assemblies were called abruptly, before the candidate had time to buy votes; sometimes a whole session was taken up with talk, when it was seen that the people had been suborned and was ready to make a bad decision. But in the end, ambition eluded everything; and the incredible part of it is that amid all those abuses that immense people, by means of its ancient regulations, continued to elect magistrates, pass laws, try cases, and transact public and private business with an aptitude that the Senate itself could scarcely have surpassed.

Chapter v

The Tribunate

When an exact proportion cannot be established among the constituent parts of the state, or when their relations are constantly changed by uncontrollable causes, a special governmental agency, separate from the others, can be instituted to restore each element to its proper relation and serve as a link or middle term between the prince and the people, or the prince and the sovereign, or both if necessary.

This body, which I shall call the *tribunate,* is the guardian of the laws and the legislative power. It serves sometimes to protect the sovereign against the government, as the tribunes of the people did in Rome, sometimes to uphold the government against the people, as the Council of Ten now does in Venice, and sometimes to maintain a balance between the two sides, as the ephors did in Sparta.

The tribunate is not a constituent part of the republic and should have no share in either the legislative or the executive power, but for that very reason its own power is all the greater, for although it can do nothing, it can prevent anything. It is more sacred and revered as the defender of the laws than the prince that executes them or the sovereign that enacts them. This was seen quite clearly in Rome when the proud patricians, who always despised the whole people, were forced to bow to one of its ordinary officers who had neither patronage nor jurisdiction.

A wisely tempered tribunate is the strongest support of a good constitution; but if it has even a little more power than it should have, it will disrupt everything. Weakness is not in its nature, and as long as it is something, it is never less than it ought to be.

It degenerates into tyranny when it usurps the executive power, which it should only moderate, and tries to make laws, which it should only protect. The enormous power of the ephors, without danger as long as Sparta kept its morals intact, accelerated their corruption once it had begun. The blood of Agis, murdered by those tyrants, was avenged by his successor. Both the crime and the punishment of the ephors hastened the downfall of the Republic; after Cleomenes, Sparta was nothing. Rome also perished in the same way: The excessive power which the tribunes usurped by degrees finally served, with the aid of laws made for freedom, as a safeguard for emperors who destroyed freedom. As for the Council of Ten in Venice, it is a tribunal of blood, abhorred by patricians and commoners alike; far from nobly protecting the laws, now that they have been debased, it is nothing but a means of striking underhanded blows that no one dares to acknowledge.

Like a government, a tribunate is weakened by the multiplication of its members. When the tribunes of the Roman people, of whom there were originally two, then five, sought to double their number, the Senate consented, confident that it could use some of them to control the others, and that was precisely what happened.

Although no government has yet discovered it, the best means of preventing such a formidable body from usurping power would be to give it only a periodic existence, with specified intervals during which it would be dissolved. These intervals, which should not be long enough to give abuses time to take root, could be fixed by law in such a way that it would be easy to shorten them by a special order when necessary.

It seems to me that this arrangement would have no disadvantages, for as I have said, the tribunate is not part of the constitution and could therefore be suspended without detriment to it. It also seems to me that the arrangement would be effective, because a newly installed magistrate does not begin with the power his predecessor had, but with the power given to him by the law.

CHAPTER VI

Dictatorship

The inflexibility of the laws, which prevents them from yielding to events, can in some cases make them pernicious, and cause the downfall of the state in a time of crisis. The order and deliberateness of legal procedures require an amount of time that circumstances do not always allow. There can be countless situations for which the lawgiver has made no provision; knowing that one cannot foresee everything is an essential part of foresight.

Political institutions should therefore not be made so strong that their operation cannot be suspended. Even Sparta sometimes put its laws to sleep.

But only a very great danger can outweigh that of disarranging the public order, and the sacred power of the laws should be suspended only when the survival of the country is at stake. In such rare and obvious cases, public safety is provided for by a special act which places responsibility for it in the hands of the worthiest men. This responsibility can be delegated in two ways, depending on the nature of the danger.

If increasing the activity of the government is enough to meet the danger, the government can be concentrated in one or two of its members. Thus it is not the authority of the laws that is changed, but only the form of their administration. But if the peril is such that the apparatus of the laws is an obstacle to effective action, a supreme leader should be appointed who can silence all the laws and temporarily suspend the sovereign authority; in such a case the general will is quite clear, and it is obvious that the people's primary intention is to prevent the state from perishing. Therefore the suspension of the legislative authority does not abolish it; the magistrate who silences it cannot make it speak; he dominates it without being able to represent it; he can do anything except make laws.

The first means was used by the Roman Senate when, by an established procedure, it gave the consuls the duty of providing for the safety of the Republic; the second was used when one of the two consuls appointed a dictator,[36] a practice whose example had been given to Rome by Alba Longa.

In the early days of the Republic the Romans often resorted to dictatorship because the state was not yet firmly enough established to be able to maintain itself by the strength of its constitution. The morality which prevailed during this period made unnecessary many of the precautions that would have been required in later times, and there was no fear that a dictator might abuse his authority or try to keep it beyond the time limit set for it. On the contrary, that great power seemed to be a burden for those who had it, because they hastened to relinquish it, as if the task of taking the place of the laws were too difficult and perilous for them.

The injudicious use of this supreme office at the beginning of the Republic was therefore blameworthy not because of any risk that the power it involved might be abused, but because of the danger that the office itself might be degraded. For when it was lavished on elections, dedications, and purely formal matters, there was reason to fear that it would command less respect in time of need, and that its title, associated only with insignificant ceremonies, would come to be regarded as equally insignificant.

Toward the end of the Republic, the Romans became more cautious and used dictatorship sparingly with as little reason as they had used it lavishly in the past. It was easy to see that their fears were ill-founded, that the weakness of the capital was then its protection against the magistrates within it, that in some cases a dictator could defend public freedom without ever being able to attempt to destroy it, and that Rome's chains would not be forged in Rome itself, but in its armies; the weak resistance that Marius offered to Sulla, and Pompey to Caesar, showed clearly what could be expected of internal authority opposed by external force.

This misunderstanding led the Romans to make great mistakes, such as, for example, not appointing a dictator in the Catiline affair; for since it involved only the city itself and, at most, a province of Italy, a dictator, with the boundless authority given to him by the law, could easily have quelled the conspiracy, whereas it was in fact suppressed only by a combination of lucky accidents that human prudence should never have expected.

Instead of appointing a dictator, the Senate merely transferred all its power to the consuls. As a result, Cicero had to exceed that power on a crucial point in order to act effectively, and while his conduct was approved in the first outburst of joy, he was later rightfully called to account for the blood of citizens that had been shed in violation of the law, a reproach which could not have been made against a dictator. But the consul's eloquence swept aside all opposition; and he himself, although he was a

Roman, loved glory more than his country and was less concerned with finding the surest and most legitimate means of saving the state than with making sure that he would be given all honor in the situation.[37] Thus he was justly honored as the liberator of Rome, and justly punished as a violator of the law. However triumphant his recall from exile may have been, there can be no doubt that it was a pardon.

But no matter how that powerful office is conferred, it is important that it be limited to a very short duration which can never be extended. In the crises that cause it to be instituted, the state is soon either destroyed or saved, and when the emergency is over, dictatorship becomes either tyrannical or useless. In Rome, dictators were allowed to remain in office for only six months, and most of them resigned before the end of that time. If the term had been longer, they might have been tempted to extend it, like the decemvirs, who had a one-year term. The dictator was in power only long enough to deal with the crisis that had brought about his appointment; he had no time to think of other plans.

Chapter VII

Censorship

Just as the general will is declared by the law, public judgment is declared by the office of the censor; public opinion is a form of law whose minister is the censor, and like the prince, he only applies it to particular cases.

For from being the arbiter of the people's opinion, therefore, the censorial tribunal is merely its spokesman, and as soon as it departs from that opinion, its decisions are vain and ineffectual.

It is useless to distinguish a nation's morals from the objects of its esteem, for they both stem from the same principle and are necessarily intermingled. Among all the peoples of the world, it is not nature but opinion that determines their choice of pleasures. Rectify men's opinions and their morals will automatically be purified. Men always love what is admirable, or what they regard as such, but since it is in judging what is admirable that they are subject to error, it is this judgment that must be regulated. He who judges morals judges honor, and he who judges honor takes his rule from opinion.

A people's opinions arise from its constitution; although the law does not regulate morals, it is legislation that gives birth to them; when legislation weakens, morals degenerate, but then the judgment of the censors will not do what the force of the law has not done.

From this it follows that censorship can be useful for preserving morals, but never for restoring them. Establish censors while the laws still have their vigor, for as soon as that vigor is gone, everything is hopeless; nothing lawful has any force when the laws themselves no longer have any.

Censorship maintains morals by preventing opinions from being corrupted, by preserving their rectitude with wise applications, and sometimes even by fixing them when they are still uncertain. The use of seconds in duels, once a raging fad in the kingdom of France, was abolished there by these words in a royal edict: "As for those who are cowardly enough to have seconds. . . ." This judgment anticipated that of the public and immediately determined it. But when the same edicts tried to establish the idea that it was also cowardly to fight a duel—which is quite true, but contrary to common opinion—the public derided that pronouncement because it had already formed its judgment on the matter.

I have said elsewhere[38] that since public opinion is not subject to constraint, there should be no trace of constraint in the tribunal established to represent it. We cannot too greatly admire the skill with which that institution, entirely lost in the modern world, was put into operation by the Romans, and even better by the Spartans.

Once when an immoral man made a good proposal to the council of Sparta, the ephors ignored him and had the same proposal put forward by a virtuous citizen. What an honor for one, and what a humiliation for the other, without praise or blame being given to either! Some drunkards from Samos[39] once defiled the tribunal of the ephors; the next day a public edict gave the Samians permission to be slovenly boors. Actual punishment would have been less severe than such impunity. When Sparta had pronounced on what was or was not proper, Greece did not appeal its judgments.

CHAPTER VIII

Civil Religion

Men originally had no kings but the gods, and no other government than theocracy. They reasoned like Caligula, and at the time they reasoned rightly. Only after a long deterioration of feelings and ideas can men bring themselves to accept one of their fellow men as their master, and persuade themselves that it will be to their advantage.

From the single fact that God was placed at the head of each political society, it followed that there were as many gods as peoples. Two peoples foreign to each other, and nearly always enemies, could not long acknowledge the same master: Two armies fighting each other could not obey the same leader. Thus national divisions gave rise to polytheism, and hence to theological and civil intolerance, which are naturally the same, as will be shown later.

The Greeks' fantasy of finding their own gods among barbarian peoples came from another of their fantasies: regarding themselves as the natural rulers of those peoples. But in our time it is a ridiculous form of scholarship to seek identity among the gods of various nations; as though Moloch, Saturn, and Chronos could be the same god; as though the Baal of the Phoenicians, the Zeus of the Greeks, and the Jupiter of the Latins could be the same; as though there could be anything in common among imaginary beings bearing different names!

It may be asked why in the days of paganism, when each state had its own cult and gods, there were no wars of religion. I answer that it was because of the very fact that each state, having its own religion as well as its own government, did not distinguish its gods from its laws. Political war was also theological: The provinces of the gods were marked off, so to speak, by the boundaries of nations. One people's god had no rights over other peoples. The gods of the pagans were not jealous gods; they shared command of the world among themselves. Even Moses and the Hebrew people sometimes acquiesced in this idea by speaking of the God of Israel. It is true that they did not recognize the gods of the Canaanites, a proscribed people, doomed to destruction, whose land they were to occupy; but consider how they spoke of the gods of neighboring peoples that they were forbidden to attack! "It is for you to possess whatever Kemosh your god gives you," Jephthah said to the Ammonites; "and all that the Lord our God gave us as we advanced is ours."[40] This, it seems to me, clearly recognizes parity between the rights of Kemosh and those of the God of Israel.

But when the Jews, subject to the kings of Babylon and later to the kings of Syria, stubbornly refused to recognize any other god than their own, their refusal, regarded as a rebellion against the conqueror, brought on the persecutions of them that we read about in their history, and of which we find no other example before Christianity.[41]

Since each religion was attached solely to the laws of the state that prescribed it, a people could be converted only by subjugation, and conquerors were the only missionaries; and since the obligation to change religions was imposed by conquest, a people had to conquer before it could consider converting anyone. Men did not fight for the gods; on the contrary, it was the gods who fought for men, as in Homer. Everyone asked his god for victory, and paid for it with new shrines. Before capturing a city, the Romans called on its gods to abandon it. When they let the Tarentines keep their angry gods, it was because they regarded those gods as subject to their own and forced to pay homage to them; they let the vanquished keep their gods as well as their laws. A wreath dedicated to Jupiter Capitolinus was often the only tribute they demanded.

Finally, when the Romans had spread their religion and their gods along with their empire, and had often adopted those of the vanquished, giving freedom of the city to both the peoples and their gods, the inhabitants of that vast empire gradually came to have multitudes of gods and religions that were more or less the same everywhere, and that was how paganism eventually became a single religion throughout the known world.

It was in these circumstances that Jesus came to establish a spiritual kingdom on earth. By separating the theological system from the political system, this destroyed the unity of the state, and caused the internal divisions that have never ceased to agitate Christian peoples. Since this new idea of an otherworldly kingdom was incomprehensible to the pagans, they always regarded the Christians as real rebels who, behind a mask of hypocritical submission, were looking only for an opportunity to seize independence and power, and cleverly usurp the authority they pretended to respect while they were weak. Such was the cause of the persecutions.

What the pagans feared finally happened. Everything then became different; the humble Christians changed their tone, and the supposedly otherworldly kingdom, under a visible ruler, soon became the most violent despotism in this world.

But since there have always been princes and civil laws, that dual power has resulted in a ceaseless conflict of jurisdiction which has made good administration impossible in Christian states, and no one has ever succeeded in determining whether he is obliged to obey the civil authorities or the clergy.

Several peoples, however, even in Europe and nearby regions, have tried to preserve or restore the old system, but without success; the spirit of Christianity has completely prevailed. The holy religion has always kept or regained its independence of the sovereign, with no necessary connection to the body of the state. Mohammed had very sound views: He bound his political system tightly together; as long as his government continued to exist under the caliphs, his successors, it was a single whole and, to that extent, good. But when the Arabs became prosperous, literate, polished, soft, and fainthearted, they were subjugated by barbarians, and then there was again a division between the two powers. Although it is less apparent among the Moslems than among the Christians, it is still there, especially in the sect of Ali, and there are some states, such as Persia, where it constantly makes itself felt.

Among us, the kings of England have established themselves as heads of the Church, and the czars have done the same; but by that title they have made themselves less the masters of the Church than its agents; they have acquired not so much the right to change it as the power to maintain it. They are not legislators in it, but only princes. Wherever the clergy forms a body,[42] it is both master and legislator in its own domain. There are thus two powers, two sovereigns, in England and in Russia, the same as elsewhere.

Of all Christian authors, the philosopher Hobbes is the only one who has clearly seen the evil and its remedy, and who has dared to proposed renuniting the two heads of the eagle and bringing everything back to political unity, without which no state or government will ever be well constituted. But he must have seen that the domineering spirit of Christianity was incompatible with his system, and that the interest of the priest would always be stronger than that of the state. His political philosophy has been execrated less because of its horrible and false aspects than because of those parts of it that are just and true.[43]

I believe that by presenting the historical facts from this standpoint, one could easily refute the opposing views of Bayle and Warburton, one of whom states that no religion is useful to the body politic, while the other maintains, on the contrary, that Christianity is its strongest support. It could be proved to the first that no state has ever been founded without a religious basis, and to the second that Christian law is ultimately more harmful than beneficial to the strength of a state's constitution. To finish making myself clear, I need only give a little more precision to the overly vague ideas of religion that are relevant to my subject.

Religion considered in relation to society—either human society in general or a particular political society—can be divided into two types: the religion of man and that of the citizen. The first, without temples, altars, or rites, limited to purely inward reverence for the Supreme God and the eternal duties of morality, is the pure and simple religion of the Gospel, the true theism, and what can be called divine natural law. The second, established in a single country, gives it its gods, its own tutelary deities; it has its dogmas, its rites, its external worship prscribed by laws; outside the one nation that follows it, everything is faithless, alien, and barbarous to it; it extends the duties and rights of- man only as far as its altars. Such were the religions of all the first peoples. They can be given the name of civil or formal divine law.

There is a third and stranger type of religion which, by giving men two sets of laws, two rulers, and two homelands, subjects them to contradictory duties and prevents them from ever being both citizens and devoutly religious. Such is the religion of the lamas, such is that of the Japanese, such is Roman Christianity. It can be called the religion of the priest. It produces a kind of mixed and antisocial system of law that has no name.

Considered politically, each of these three types of religion has its defects. The third is so obviously bad that amusing myself by demonstrating its drawbacks would be a waste of time. Anything that breaks social unity is worthless. All institutions that place man in contradiction with himself are worthless.

The second is good in that it joins divine worship to love of the law, and by making the fatherland an object of worship for the citizens, teaches them that to serve the state is to serve its tutelary god. It is a kind of theocracy in which there should be no other pontiff than the prince, and no other priests than the magistrates. To die for one's country is then to become a martyr, to violate the law is to be impious, and to subject a guilty man to public execration is to submit him to the wrath of the gods; *sacer estod*.

But it is bad in that, being founded on error and falsehood, it deceives men, makes them credulous and superstitious, and drowns true worship of the Divinity in vain ceremonies. It is also bad when, becoming exclusive and tyrannical, it makes a people bloodthirsty and intolerant, so that its members breathe only murder and slaughter, and believe that they commit a holy act when they kill anyone who does not accept their gods. This places the people in a natural state of war with all others, which is very harmful to its own security.

There remains the religion of man, or Christianity—not the Christianity of today, but that of the Gospel, which is completely different. By that holy, sublime, and genuine religion, men, as children of the same God, recognize all others as their brothers, and the society that unites them is not dissolved even by death.

But this religion, having no specific relation to the body politic, leaves the law with only the force it draws from itself, without adding any other force to it, and hence one of the great bonds of particular society remains ineffective. Still worse, far from attaching the hearts of the citizens to the state, it detaches them from it, as from all other earthly things. I know of nothing more contrary to the social spirit.

We are told that a people of true Christians would form

the most perfect society imaginable. I see in this supposition only one great difficulty: that a society of true Christians would no longer be a society of men.

I will even say that this hypothetical society, with all its perfection, would be neither the strongest nor the most durable. It would be so perfect that it would lack cohesion; its very perfection would be its destructive defect.

Everyone would fulfill his duty; the people would obey the law, the rulers would be just and moderate, the magistrates would be honest and incorruptible, the soldiers would despise death, and there would be neither vanity nor luxury. All that is admirable, but let us look further.

Christianity is a wholly spiritual religion, concerned only with heavenly things: The Christian's homeland is not of this world. He does his duty, it is true, but he does it with deep indifference to the success or failure of his efforts. As long as he has no reason for self-reproach, he cares little whether things go well or badly here below. If the state prospers, he scarcely dares to enjoy the public happiness, for fear that he may be made proud by his country's glory; if the state declines, he blesses the hand of God which weighs down on his people.

If peace and harmony are to be maintained in the society we are assuming, all its citizens without exception will have to be equally good Christians. But if unfortunately there is among them one ambitious man, one hypocrite—a Catiline, for example, or a Cromwell—he will inevitably make short work of his pious compatriots, whose Christian charity enjoins them from readily thinking ill of others. As soon as he has found some ruse that enables him to deceive them and seize part of the public authority, he becomes a dignitary, and it is God's will that he be respected; before long he is a man who wields power, and it is God's will that he be obeyed; and if he abuses that power, he is the scourge by which God punishes his children. The citizens will be reluctant to make any attempt to evict the usurper: It would require disturbing the public peace, using violence, and shedding blood, all of which is scarcely in keeping with Christian meekness. And after all, what does it matter whether one is free or enslaved in this vale of tears? The essential thing is to go to heaven, and resignation is a surer means to that end.

If a foreign war breaks out, the citizens will readily march into battle, and none will have any thought of fleeing. They will do their duty, but without any passion for victory; they know how to die, but not how to conquer. What does it matter whether they win or lose? Does not Providence know better than they what is best for them? Imagine the advantage that a proud, spirited, and impassioned enemy could draw from their stoicism! Pit them against one of those great-hearted peoples that were consumed with an ardent love of glory and their country; suppose your Christian republic to be at war with Sparta or Rome: The pious Christians will either be beaten, crushed, and destroyed before they have time to realize what is happening to them, or they will owe their salvation only to the contempt they have aroused in their enemy. Fabius's soldiers took an oath that I find excellent: They did not swear to conquer or die, but to return victorious, and they kept their word. Christians would never have taken such an oath; they would have felt that it would be tempting God.

But I am wrong to speak of a Christian republic: Those two words exclude each other. Christianity preaches only servitude and dependence. Its spirit is too favorable to tyranny for tyranny not always to take advantage of it. True Christians are made to be slaves; they know it and hardly care; this short life has too little value in their eyes.

Christian troops are excellent, we are told. I deny it. Let such troops be shown to me. For my part, I know of no Christian troops. The Crusades will be cited as an example. Without disputing the valor of the crusaders, I will point out that, far from being Christians, they were soldiers of the priests, citizens of the Church; they were fighting for its spiritual homeland, which in some unknown way it had made temporal. Properly considered, this amounts to paganism; since the Gospel does not establish a national religion, all holy war is impossible among Christians.

Under the pagan emperors, Christian soldiers were brave; all Christian authors say so, and I believe them: It was a matter of competing for honor among pagan troops. As soon as the emperors became Christians this competition ceased, and when the cross had driven away the eagle, all Roman valor disappeared.

But putting aside political considerations, let us return to the question of right and set forth principles on this important point. The right that the social pact gives the sovereign over the subjects does not go beyond the bounds of public utility,[44] as I have already said. The subjects are therefore accountable to the sovereign for their opinions only insofar as those opinions are important to the community. Now it is quite important to the state that each citizen have a religion that will make him love his duties; but the dogmas of that religion concern neither the state nor its members except insofar as those dogmas are related to morality and the duties toward others that are imposed on all who profess the religion. Aside from that, everyone may have whatever opinions he chooses, and the sovereign has no right to know what they are. The sovereign has no jurisdiction in the next world; therefore, whatever may be the subjects' fate in the life to come, it is not the sovereign's affair, as long as they are good citizens in this life.

There is thus a purely civil creed whose tenets the sovereign is entitled to determine, not precisely as dogmas of religion, but as sentiments of sociability, without which it is impossible to be a good citizen or a loyal subject.[45] Though unable to oblige anyone to believe in them, the sovereign can banish from the state anyone who does not; it can banish him not for impiety, but for being antisocial, for being incapable of sincerely loving law and justice and of sacrificing himself to his duty is necessary. If, after having publicly acknowledged those tenets, anyone behaves as though he did not believe in them, let him be put to death; he has committed the greatest of all crimes: He has lied before the law.

The tenets of the civil religion should be simple, few in number, and enunciated precisely, without explanations or commentaries. The existence of a powerful, intelligent, benevolent, foreseeing, and provident Divinity, the life to come, the happiness of the righteous, the punishment of the wicked, the sanctity of the social contract and the law—these are the positive tenets. As for negative tenets, I limit them to a single injunction: There shall be no intolerance, which is part of the religions we have excluded.

Those who distinguish civil intolerance from theological intolerance are mistaken, in my opinion. Those two intolerances are inseparable. It is impossible to live in peace with people whom one believes to be damned; to love them would be to hate the God who punishes them; it is imperative that they be either redeemed or tormented.

Wherever theological intolerance is accepted, it is impossible for it not to have some civil consequences,[46] and as soon as it does so, the sovereign is no longer sovereign, even in the temporal realm. From then on, priests are the real masters, and kings are only their agents.

Now that there is no longer, and can no longer be, an exclusive national religion, all religions that tolerate others must be tolerated, insofar as there is nothing in their dogmas contrary to the duties of the citizen. But anyone who dares to say, "There is no salvation outside the Church," should be expelled from the state, unless the state is the Church and the prince is the pontiff. Such a dogma is good only in a theocratic government; in any other, it is pernicious. The reason for which Henry IV is said to have embraced the Roman religion should cause it to be abandoned by any man of integrity, and especially by any ruler who knows how to reason.

Chapter ix

Conclusion

After laying down the true principles of political right and trying to establish the state on its foundation, I might have gone on to support it by its external relations, which would include the law of nations, commerce, the right of war and conquest, public law, leagues, negotiations, treaties, etc. But all that would form a new subject too vast for my limited vision; I would have to keep my eyes fixed on matters closer to me.

NOTES

1. "Learned inquiries into public law are often only a history of past abuses, and anyone who persists in making the effort of studying them too closely is misguided" (Marquis d'Argenson, *Traité des intérêts de la France avec ses voisins*). That is precisely what Grotius does.

2. See a short treatise by Plutarch entitled *That Animals Use Reason.*

3. The Romans, who understood and respected the law of war better than any other nation in the world, were so scrupulous on this point that no citizen was allowed to serve as a volunteer unless he had expressly engaged himself against the enemy, and against a specifically named enemy. When the legion in which Cato the Younger fought his first campaign under Popilius was re-formed, Cato the Elder wrote to Popilius that if he wanted his son to continue serving under him, he would have to administer a new military oath to him, for now that his first oath was annulled he could no longer bear arms against the enemy. And Cato also wrote to his son to be sure not to go into battle until he had sworn a new oath. I know that the siege of Clusium and other individual episodes can be cited against me, but I am speaking of laws and customs. The Romans broke their own laws less often than any other nation, and no other nation has ever had such excellent laws.

4. The true meaning of this word has become almost entirely lost in modern times. Most people now take a town for a city* and a burgher for a citizen. They do not

---

*The French words translated here as "town" and "city" are *ville* and *cité*. (*Cité* can have the general meaning of "political community.") In other passages, however, I have translated *ville* as "city" to conform to normal English usage; Rome, for example, is a *ville*, but could hardly be called a town. (Translator's note.)

know that houses make a town, but citizens make a city. The Carthaginians once paid dearly for that same mistake. I have never read that the title of *cives* was given to the subjects of any monarch, not even to the Macedonians in the past, or to the English in our time, though they are closer to freedom than any other nation. Only the French commonly take the name of "citizens," because they have no true idea of its meaning, as can be seen in their dictionaries; otherwise, in usurping it, they would fall into the crime of lèse-majesté. With them, the word expresses a virtue and not a right. When Bodin spoke of our citizens and burghers, he made a gross error by confusing the two. Monsieur d'Alembert is not guilty of that error: in his article on Geneva he distinguishes the four orders of men (five, in fact, if ordinary foreigners are counted) that are in our town. No other French author, to my knowledge, has understood the true meaning of the word "citizen."

5. Under a bad government, this equality is only apparent and illusory; it serves only to keep the poor in their poverty and the rich in their usurpation. In reality, laws are always useful to those with possessions and harmful to those who have nothing. From this it follows that the social state is advantageous to men only insofar as they all have something and none has too much.

6. In order for a will to be general it is not always necessary for it to be unanimous, but it is necessary that all the votes be counted; any formal exclusion destroys generality.

7. "Every interest," says the Marquis d'Argenson, "has different principles. Harmony between two particular interests is formed by opposition to that of a third party." He might have added that harmony among all interests is formed by opposition to that of each party. If there were no different interests, one would scarcely be aware of the common interest, which would never encounter any obstacles: Everything would go smoothly of its own accord, and politics would cease to be an art.

8. "True it is," says Machiavelli, "that some divisions injure republics, while others are beneficial to them. When accompanied by factions and parties they are injurious; but when maintained without them they contribute to their prosperity. The legislator of a republic, since it is impossible to prevent the existence of dissensions, must at least

take care to prevent the growth of faction" (*History of Florence*, Book VII).

9. Attentive readers, please do not be hasty in accusing me of contradiction here. I have not been able to avoid it in my terms, because of the poverty of the language; but wait.

10. By this word I understand not only an aristocracy or a democracy, but in general any government guided by the general will, which is law. If it is to be legitimate, the government must not be merged with the sovereign, but must be its agent; in such a case, even a monarchy is a republic. This will be clarified in the following book.

11. A people does not become famous until its system of law begins to decline. We do not know for how many centuries Lycurgus's system gave happiness to the Spartans before there was talk of them in the rest of Greece.

12. Those who regarded Calvin only as a theologian do not know the extent of his genius. The drafting of our wise edicts, in which he played a large part, does him as much honor as his *Institutes of the Christian Religion*. Whatever revolutions time may bring to our religion, as long as love of country and of freedom is still alive among us, the memory of that great man will never cease to be a blessing to us.

13. "In truth," says Machiavelli, "there never was any remarkable lawgiver amongst any people who did not resort to divine authority, as otherwise his laws would not have been accepted by the people; for there are many good laws, the importance of which is known to the sagacious lawgiver, but the reasons for which are not sufficiently evident to enable him to persuade others to submit to them" (*Discourses on the First Ten Books of Titus Livius*, Book I, Chapter XI).

14. If one of two neighboring peoples cannot do without the other, the situation is very harsh for the first and very dangerous for the second. In such a case, any wise nation will hasten to deliver the other from its dependence. The Republic of Thlascala, an enclave in the Mexican Empire, preferred to do without salt rather than buy it from the Mexicans, or even accept it as a gift. The wise Thlascalans saw the trap hidden in that generosity. They kept their freedom, and that small state, enclosed within a great empire, was finally the instrument of the empire's ruin.

15. Do you want to give cohesion to the state? Then bring the extreme ranks as close together as possible: See to it that there is neither great wealth nor utter poverty. These two conditions, naturally inseparable, are equally harmful to the common good. Supporters of tyranny come from one, and tyrants from the other. The trade in freedom always takes place between them: One sells it and the other buys it.

16. Any branch of foreign trade, says the Marquis d'Argenson, brings little more than illusory advantages to a kingdom as a whole; it may enrich a few individuals, or even a few cities, but the entire nation gains nothing from it, and the people is no better off.

17. Thus in Venice the ruling body is given the name "Most Serene Prince" even when the Doge is not present.

18. The Palatine of Poznan, father of the King of Poland, Duke of Lorraine.

19. It is clear that to the ancients the word *Optimates* did not mean "the best," but "the most powerful."

20. It is very important that the procedure for electing magistrates be specified by law, for if it is left to the will of the prince, the state cannot avoid falling into hereditary aristocracy, as happened to the republics of Venice and Berne. The former has long been a dissolved state, but the latter still maintains itself by the extreme wisdom of its senate; it is a very honorable and very dangerous exception.

21. Machiavelli was an upright man and a good citizen; but, being attached to the house of Medici, he was forced during the oppression of his country to disguise his love of freedom. The choice of his execrable hero is enough in itself to show his secret intention, and the opposition between the maxims in his book *The Prince* and those in his *Discourses on Titus Livius* and *History of Florence* demonstrates that this profound political philosopher has so far had only superficial or corrupted readers. The court of Rome strictly prohibited his book, as it quite understandable, since it is that court which it depicts most clearly.

22. This does not contradict what I have said earlier, in Book II, Chapter IX, about the disadvantages of large states, for I was there considering the government's authority over its members, and I am here considering its strength against its subjects. Its scattered members serve

as fulcrums by means of which it acts on the people at a distance, but it has no fulcrum by which to act on those members themselves. Thus the length of the lever is its weakness in one case and its strength in the other.

23. The same principle should be used in judging which centuries deserve to be given preference with regard to the prosperity of the human race. People have been too much inclined to admire those in which there was a flowering of arts and letters, without discerning the secret object of their culture or considering its harmful effects. "The ignorant gave the name of culture to what was part of slavery." Shall we never see in the maxims of books the crude self-interest that makes their authors speak? No, whatever they may say, when despite its brilliance a country loses population, it is not true that all is going well; the fact that a poet has an income of a hundred thousand francs is not enough to make his century the best of all. We should consider not so much apparent peace, and the tranquillity of leaders, as the well-being of entire nations, and especially of the most populous states. Hailstorms may ravage a few districts, but they seldom cause a famine. Riots and civil wars may throw rulers into panic, but they do not cause the real misfortunes of peoples, who may even enjoy a respite while leaders are fighting to determine who will tyrannize them. It is their permanent condition that gives rise to their real prosperity or adversity; when everything remains crushed beneath the yoke, it is then that everything wastes away, it is then that leaders can destroy them with ease. "Where they create desolation, they call it peace." When the kingdom of France was convulsed by quarrels among those in high places and the Coadjutor of Paris went to Parliament with a dagger in his pocket, this did not prevent the French people from being happy and numerous, and living in free and honest affluence. In ancient times, Greece flourished in the midst of the cruelest wars; blood flowed in torrents, yet the whole country was covered with men. "It seemed," says Machiavelli, "that amid murders, proscriptions, and civil wars, our republic became all the more powerful; its citizens' virtue, morals, and independence were more effective in strengthening it than all its dissensions were in weakening it." A little agitation gives resilience to the soul, and what really makes the species prosper is less peace than freedom.

24. The slow formation and progress of the Republic of

Venice in its lagoons offers a notable example of this process; and it is amazing that after more than twelve hundred years the Venetians still seem to be only at the second stage, which began with the *Serrar di Consiglio* in 1198. As for the ancient dukes for whom they have been reproached, it has been proved, no matter what the *Squitinio della Libertà Veneta* may say about it, that they were not their sovereigns.

Someone will be sure to cite the Roman Republic as an objection against me, saying that it went through a reverse sequence, passing from monarchy to aristocracy, and from aristocracy to democracy. I am very far from sharing that opinion.

The first government instituted by Romulus was a mixed one that quickly degenerated into despotism. For special reasons, the state perished before its time, as some children die before reaching adulthood. The expulsion of the Tarquins marked the real birth of the Republic. But at first it did not take on a stable form, because failure to abolish the patriciate meant that the work was only half done. Since hereditary aristocracy, which is the worst of all legitimate administrations, thus remained in conflict with democracy, the shifting, uncertain form of the government did not become fixed, as Machiavelli has demonstrated, until the establishment of the tribunes; only then was there a real government and a true democracy, for the people was not only sovereign, but also magistrate and judge, the Senate was only a subordinate agency for tempering or concentrating the government, and the consuls themselves, even though they were patricians, chief magistrates, and absolute commanders in war, were in Rome only the chairmen of the people.

And it was during this period that the government began to follow its natural inclination by tending strongly toward aristocracy. When the patriciate had abolished itself, as it were, the aristocracy was no longer within the body of the patricians, as it is in Venice and Genoa, but within the body of the Senate, which was composed of both patricians and plebeians, and even within the body of the tribunes when they began to usurp active power; for words have no effect on things, and when the people has leaders who govern for it, they form an aristocracy, no matter what name they may bear.

The abuse of aristocracy gave rise to civil wars the triumvirate. Sulla, Julius Caesar, and Augustus became *de facto* monarchs, and finally, under the despotism of Tiberius, the state was dissolved. Roman history therefore does not disprove my principle; it confirms it.

25. "All those who hold permanent power in a state accustomed to freedom are called and considered tyrants" (Cornelius Nepos, *Mitiades*). It is true that Aristotle, in his *Nichomachean Ethics,* Book VIII, Chapter 10, distinguishes the tyrant from the king on the basis that the former governs for his own advantage and the latter only for the advantage of his subjects; but aside from the fact that in general all the Greek authors used the word "tyrant" with a different meaning, as is especially clear in Xenophon's *Hiero,* it would follow from Aristotle's distinction that there has never been a single king since the beginning of the world.

26. In more or less the same sense as is given to the word in the English Parliament. The resemblance between these functions would have placed the consuls and the tribunes in conflict, even if all jurisdiction had been suspended.

27. To adopt in a cold country the luxury and softness of the Orientals is to will to give oneself their chains and be bound by them even more inevitably than the Orientals themselves.

28. That is what I had intended to do in the latter part of this work when, in dealing with external relations, I came to the subject of confederations. It is an unexplored subject whose principles have yet to be established.

29. With the understanding that no man may leave in order to shirk his duty and avoid serving his country when it needs him. Flight would then be criminal and punishable, it would not be a withdrawal, but a desertion.

30. This must always be understood as referring to a free state, for otherwise family, property, lack of asylum, need, or violence may keep an inhabitant in the country against his will, and then his residence no longer implies his consent either to the contract or to violation of it.

31. In Genoa the word *Libertas* appears in front of prisons and on the fetters of convicts. This use of the motto is admirable and just, for it is only evildoers of all classes who prevent the citizen from being free. In a country where all such people were kept in prison, the most perfect freedom would be enjoyed.

32. The name "Rome," which is said to come from "Romulus," is Greek, and means "strength." The name "Numa" is also Greek, and means "law." How likely is it that the two first kings of that city should have borne, in advance, names so clearly related to what they did?

33. I say "to the Campus Martius" because that was where the centurial assemblies were held; in the two other forms, the people gathered in the Forum or elsewhere, and even the *capite censi* had as much influence and authority as the leading citizens.

34. The century thus chosen by lot was called *prae rogativa* because it was the first that was asked to vote, and that is the origin of the word "prerogative."

35. *Custodes, Diribitores, Rogatores suffragiorum.*

36. This appointment was made at night and in secret, as if they were ashamed of placing a man above the law.

37. He could not have been sure of this if he had proposed appointing a dictator, for he would not have dared to appoint himself, and he would have had no guarantee that his colleague would appoint him.

38. In this chapter I have only indicated what I discussed at greater length in my *Letter to Monsieur d'Alembert.*

39. They were from another island, which the delicacy of our language forbids me to name here.*

40. *Nonne ea quae possidet Chamos deus tuus tibi jure debentur?* That is the text of the Vulgate. Here is Father de Carrière's translation: "Do you not believe that you have a right to possess what belongs to Chamos, your God?" I do not know the purport of the Hebrew text, but I see that in the Vulgate, Jephthah positively recognizes the right of the god Kemosh, and that the French translator weakens that recognition by the idea of "according to you," which is not in the Latin.

41. It is perfectly obvious that the Phocian War, called the "Sacred War," was not a war of religion. Its object was to punish sacrilege, not to impose submission on unbelievers.

42. It should be noted that the clergy is bound together in a body less by formal assemblies, like those of France, than by the communion of churches. Communion and ex-

---

*The island was Chios. Rousseau declined to write its real name because of its resemblance to the indecent French word *chier*, "to shit." (Translator's note.)

communication are the social pact of the clergy, the pact through which it will always be master of peoples and kings. All priests who commune together are fellow citizens, even if they are at opposite ends of the earth. This invention is a political masterpiece. There was nothing like it among pagan priests, and they therefore never formed a body of clergy.

43. See, among other things, in a letter from Grotius to his brother, dated April 11, 1643, what that learned man approved and condemned in *De Cive*. It is true that, being inclined toward indulgence, he seems to feel that the evil in Hobbes's book makes him deserve to be forgiven for the good in it, but not everyone is so clement.

44. "In a republic," says the Marquis d'Argenson, "everyone is perfectly free to do anything that does not harm others." There is the immutable boundary marker; it cannot be described more precisely. I have not been able to deny myself the pleasure of occasionally quoting from this manuscript, although it is unknown to the public, to honor the memory of an illustrious and estimable man who, even as a minister of state, kept the true heart of a citizen and always had just and sound views concerning the government of his country.

45. In pleading for Catiline, Caesar tried to establish the dogma of the mortality of the soul; to refute him, Cato and Cicero did not waste time philosophizing; they simply showed that Caesar was speaking as a bad citizen and advancing a doctrine harmful to the state. It was indeed this issue, and not a question of theology, on which the Senate had to pass judgment.

46. Marriage, for example, being a civil contract, has civil effects without which society cannot even exist. Let us suppose that a certain clergy has succeeded in giving itself the exclusive right to perform marriages, a right that it must necessarily usurp in any intolerant religion. It is not then clear that by judiciously asserting the authority of the Church it will vitiate that of the prince, and that, once this has happened, the prince will have only those subjects whom the clergy is willing to give him? If the Church can marry or refuse to marry people according to whether or not they hold a certain doctrine, whether they accept or reject a certain ceremony, or whether they are more or less devout, is it not clear that if the clergy acts prudently and holds firm, it will eventually gain full control of inher-

itances, public offices, the citizens, and even the state it-self, which could not subsist if it were composed only of bastards? But, it may be said, there will be appeals against such abuse, there will be summonses, decrees, seizures of Church property. How pitiful! If the clergy has the slightest amount, I will not say of courage, but of com-mon sense, it will continue to go about its affairs without offering any resistance; it will calmly accept the appeals, summonses, decrees, and seizures, and in the end it will re-gain all its power. Giving up a part is no great sacrifice, it seems to me, when one is sure of getting the whole.

Discourse On the Origin and Basis of Inequality Among Men

By

Jean-Jacques Rousseau,
Citizen of Geneva

But then we must look for the
intentions of nature in things
which retain their nature, and not
in things which are corrupted.

—ARISTOTLE
(*Politics*, Bk. I, Ch. 5)

The footnotes to the *Discourse on Inequality* have
been omitted for reasons best expressed by Rousseau himself in his "Notice Concerning the

Notes": "I have added a few notes to this work, according to my lazy habit of working unmethodically. They are sometimes so far removed from the subject that they should not be read with the text. I have therefore relegated them to the end of the Discourse, in which I have done my best to follow the straightest path. Those who have the courage to begin again may try to read through the notes, amusing themselves by seeking out what little remains to be gleaned; there will be no great loss if others do not read them at all." (Translator's note.)

DEDICATION

To the Republic of Geneva

MAGNIFICENT, MOST HONORED, AND SOVEREIGN LORDS:* Convinced that only a virtuous citizen can bestow honors on his country which it can acknowledge, I have been working for thirty years to make myself worthy of offering you a public tribute, and since this fortunate opportunity compensates for what my efforts have failed to achieve, I feel that it is now permissible for me to follow the zeal that animates me, rather than the right that ought to be my authorization. Having had the good fortune to be born among you, how could I have meditated on the equality that nature has placed among men, and on the inequality that they have instituted, without thinking of the profound wisdom with which both, happily combined in your republic, work together in the manner closest to natural law, and most favorable to society, to maintain public order and assure the happiness of individuals? In seeking the best principles that common sense can dictate with regard to the constitution of a government, I have been so struck at finding them all exemplified in yours that, even if I had not been born within your walls, I would still have considered it indispensable to offer this picture of human society to the people which more than any other, it seems to me, possesses the greatest advantages of that society and has best succeeded in preventing its abuses.

If I could have chosen my birthplace, I would have chosen a society limited by the extent of human faculties, that is, by the possibility of being well governed; one in which, since everyone is capable of fulfilling his responsibilities, no one is forced to entrust them to others; a state in which all individuals are acquainted with each other, so

---

*Rousseau is addressing the General Council of Geneva, which included all citizens. (Translator's note.)

that neither the stealthy machinations of vice nor the modesty of virtue can escape public notice and judgment, and in which the pleasant habit of seeing and knowing one another makes love of one's country take the form of love of its citizens, rather than of its soil.

I would have chosen to be born in a country where the sovereign and the people can have only one and the same interest, so that all the movements of the mechanism never tend toward anything but the common happiness; and since this can be true only if the people and the sovereign are the same being, it follows that I would have chosen to be born under a wisely tempered democratic government.

I would have chosen to live and die free; that is, so thoroughly subject to law that neither I nor anyone else could shake off its honorable yoke, that light and salutary yoke which the proudest heads bear with all the more docility because they are made to bear no other.

I would have wished, then, that no one in the state could say that he was above the law, and that no one outside it could impose a law that the state would be obliged to recognize; for whatever the constitution of a government may be, if there is a national ruler and a foreign ruler as well, it is impossible, no matter how they may share authority, for both of them to be properly obeyed, or for the state to be well governed.

I would not have chosen to live in a recently instituted republic, however good its laws might be, for fear that the government might not be constituted as it ought to be at that time, so that it might not suit the new sitizens, or they it, and the state would therefore be in danger of being overthrown and destroyed almost at birth. For freedom is like those solid, succulent foods or rich wines which are capable of nourishing and fortifying robust constitutions that are used to them, but overwhelm, injure, or intoxicate weak and delicate constitutions that are not used to them. Peoples once accustomed to masters are no longer in condition to do without them. If they try to shake off the yoke, they move still farther away from freedom, because they confuse it with an unbridled license that is opposed to it, and their revolutions nearly always deliver them into the hands of seducers who only make their chains heavier than before. Even the Roman people, that model of all free peoples, was not in condition to govern itself immediately after escaping from the oppression of the Tarquins. Degraded by slavery and the ignominious work imposed on it, it was at first only a witless mob that had to be treated cautiously and governed with great wisdom, to allow time for its soul, enervated, or rather brutalized, by tyranny, to become gradually accustomed to breathing the healthy air of freedom, and acquire by degrees the stern morality and proud courage that finally made the Romans the most admirable of all peoples. I would therefore have chosen as my country a happy and peaceful republic whose origins were lost in the mists of the past, so to speak; a republic which had experienced only stresses that brought out and strengthened its inhabitants' courage and partiotism, and in which the citizens, long accustomed to wise independence, were not only free, but worthy of freedom.

I would have chosen a country diverted from fierce love of conquest by a fortunate lack of power, and secured against fear of becoming the conquest of another state by a still more fortunate position; a free city situated among several different nations, none with any interest in invading it, and each with an interest in preventing it from being invaded by the others; a republic, in short, which would not tempt its neighbors' ambitions, and could reasonably count on their aid in case of need. It follows that, being in such a fortunate position, it would have nothing to fear except from itself, and that if its citizens were trained in the use of weapons, it would be in order to maintain that warlike ardor and proud courage which suit freedom so well and sustain men's love of it, rather than because they had to be prepared to defend themselves.

I would have sought a country where the right of legislation was common to all citizens; for who can know better than they under which conditions it suits them to live together in a single society? But I would not have approved of *plebiscita* like those of the Romans, in which the leaders of the state, and those most interested in its preservation, were excluded from deliberations on which its security often depended, and by an absurd inconsistency, the magistrates were deprived of rights enjoyed by the ordinary citizens.

On the contrary, I would have wished that, in order to curb self-interested, ill-conceived plans and dangerous innovations like those that finally brought on the downfall of the Athenians, no one should have the power to propose new laws capriciously; that the right to propose laws should belong only to the magistrates; that they should make use of it so cautiously, that the people, for its part, should be so reserved in consenting to new laws, and that their promulgation should be attended by such solemnity that, before the constitution could be impaired, everyone would have time to realize that it is above all the great antiquity of laws that makes them sacred and venerable, that the people soon despises laws which change every day, and that by becoming accustomed to neglecting ancient ways on the pretext of making improvements, we often introduced great evils to correct lesser ones.

I would have especially avoided, as being necessarily ill-governed, a republic in which the people, believing that it could either do without its magistrates or leave them with only a precarious authority, had imprudently reserved for itself the administration of civil affairs and the execution of its own laws; this must have been the crude constitution of the earliest governments, immediately after emerging from the state of nature, and it was also one of the vices that ruined the Republic of Athens.

But I would have chosen a republic in which the individuals, content with sanctioning the laws and making collective decisions concerning the most important public affairs, on the basis of reports by their leaders, had established respected tribunals, carefully defined the jurisdiction of each one, and elected year by year their most capable and righteous fellow citizens to administer justice and govern the state. In such a republic, since the virtue of the magistrates bears witness to the wisdom of the people, each honors the others, so that if the public peace is disturbed by harmful misunderstandings, even those periods of blindness and error will be marked by manifestations of moderation, mutual esteem, and common respect for the law which foreshadow and guarantee a sincere and lasting reconciliation.

Such are the advantages, Magnificent, Most Honored, and Sovereign Lords, which I would have sought in the country I had chosen for myself. If Providence had added to them a charming situation, a temperate climate, fertile soil, and the most delightful landscape under the sun, then, to fill my measure of happiness to overflowing, I would have desired only to enjoy all those blessings in the bosom

of that fortunate country, living peacefully in the pleasant
society of my fellow citizens, practicing toward them,
from their example, humanity, friendship, and all virtues,
and leaving behind me the honorable memory of a good
man and an upright, virtuous patriot.

If, less fortunate or having become wise too late, I had
been forced to end a feeble and languishing life under other skies, vainly longing for the peace and tranquillity of which an imprudent youth had deprived me, I
would at least have harbored those same feelings in my
soul, without being able to put them into practice in my
country; and, filled with tender and disinterested affection
for my distant fellow citizens, I would have addressed to
them, from the depths of my heart, a discourse like the
following:

"My dear fellow citizens, or rather my brothers, since
the bonds of blood, as well as the laws, unite nearly all of
us, it pleases me to be unable to think of you without
thinking at the same time of the blessings you enjoy. None
of you, perhaps is better aware of their value than I, who
have lost them. The more I reflect on your political and
civil situation, the less I am able to imagine that the
nature of human affairs would allow a better one. In all
other governments, when there is a question of assuring
the greatest good of the state, nothing ever goes beyond
hypothetical plans or, at most, mere possibilities. As for
you, your happiness is already a reality; you have only to
enjoy it, and in order to be perfectly happy, you need only
the ability to content yourselves with being so. Your sovereignty, acquired or recovered by the sword, and
preserved for two centuries by valor and wisdom, is at last
fully and universally recognized. Honorable treaties fix
your boundaries, guarantee your rights, and assure your
tranquillity. Your constitution is excellent, dictated by the
most sublime reason and protected by friendly and respectable powers; your state is peaceful; you have neither wars
nor conquerors to fear; you have no other masters than
the wise laws you have made, administered by honest
magistrates whom you have chosen. You are neither rich
enough to be enervated by indolence and to lost in frivolous pleasures the taste for true happiness and solid virtues,
nor poor enough to need more foreign assistance than
your industry procures for you. And that precious free-

dom, which in large nations is maintained only by exorbitant taxes, costs you almost nothing to preserve.

"May your wisely and happily constituted republic last forever, for the well-being of its citizens and as an example to other peoples! That is the only wish which remains for you to make, and the only precaution which remains for you to take. It now depends on you alone, not to create your happiness, since your ancestors have spared you that effort, but to make it durable by using it wisely. Your preservation depends on your permanent unity, your obedience to law, and your respect for its administrators. If there remains among you the smallest seed of bitterness or mistrust, hasten to destroy it as a baneful leaven which would sooner or later bring you misfortune and ruin the state. I entreat each of you to look into his heart and consult the secret voice of his conscience. Is there anyone among you who knows, anywhere in the world, a more upright, enlightened, and estimable body than your magistracy? Do not all its members set you an example of moderation, simplicity of living habits, respect for law, and the most sincere spirit of reconciliation? Give those wise leaders the salutary confidence which reason owes to virtue; remember that you have chosen them, that they justify your choice, and that the honors owed to those whom you have placed in high positions necessarily fall back on you. None of you is so unenlightened as not to know that when the laws lose their vigor and their defenders cease to have any authority, there can be no security or freedom for anyone. It is not, then, simply a matter of doing wholeheartedly and with legitimate confidence what you would in any case be obliged to do by genuine self-interest, duty, and reason? Never let criminal and pernicious indifference to the maintenance of the constitution make you neglect, in case of need, the wise counsel of those among you who are most enlightened and zealous; but let equity, moderation, and the most respectful firmness continue to guide all your actions and provide the whole world, through you, with an example of a proud and modest people as jealous of its glory as of its freedom. Above all, refrain— and this will be my last recommendation to you—from listening to sinister interpretations and envenomed speeches whose secret motives are often more dangerous than the acts to which they are directed. A whole household awakens and takes alarm at the first sound from a good and faithful watchdog that barks only at the approach of thieves; but everyone hates the importunity of those noisy animals which constantly disturb the public peace, and whose incessant warnings are so often unwarranted that no one heeds them when they are necessary."

And you, Magnificent and Most Honored Lords, worthy and estimable magistrates of a free people, allow me to offer you in particular my homage and respect. If there is anywhere in the world a position capable of glorifying those who occupy it, it is undoubtedly that which is bestowed by ability and virtue, the position of which you have made yourselves worthy, and to which your fellow citizens have elevated you. Their own merit adds new luster to yours; and since men capable of governing others have chosen you to govern them, I consider that you are as far above other magistrates as a free people, and especially the one you have the honor of leading, is, by its enlightenment and reason, above the populace of other states.

Permit me to cite an example of which better traces ought to remain, and which will always be present in my heart. I never recall without tender emotion the virtuous citizen to whom I owe the gift of life, and who during my childhood often spoke of the respect that was your due. I can still see him, living by the work of his hands and nourishing his soul with the most sublime truths. I see the books of Tacitus, Plutarch, and Grotius mingled before him with the tools of his trade. I see beside him a cherished son, receiving with too little profit the tender instructions of the best of fathers. But if the errors of a wanton youth made me forget those wise lessons for a time, I now have the happiness of having finally realized that, whatever inclination one may have toward vice, when one has had an unbringing in which the heart was involved, it is unlikely to be lost forever.

Such, Magnificent and Most Honored Lords, are the citizens and even the ordinary inhabitants born in the state you govern; such are those educated and sensible men concerning whom, under the name of workers and the people, such base and false ideas are held in other nations. My father, I gladly acknowledge, was in no way distinguished among his fellow citizens; he was only what they all are, and such as he was, there is no country in which his acquaintance would not have been sought and culti-

vated, and profitably, too, by the most respectable people.
It does not behoove me—and, thank Heaven, it is not
necessary—to speak to you of the consideration which
men of that stamp can expect from you. They are your
equals by upbringing as well as by the rights of nature and
birth; they are your inferiors by thier own will, by the preference which they owe and have granted to your merit,
and for which you in turn owe them a debt of gratitude.
It gives me keen satisfaction to know how well, in your
dealings with them, you temper with gentleness and gra-
ciousness the gravity that befits ministers of the law, and
how you repay in esteem and attention the obedience and
respect that they rightfully give to you. Your conduct is
full of justice and wisdom, and well suited to further effac-
ing the memory of unhappy events that must be forgotten
to prevent them from ever recurring; it is all the more
judicious because that equitable and generous people takes
pleasure in doing its duty, because it naturally loves to
honor you, and because those most ardent in upholding
their own rights are most inclined to respect yours.

It should not be surprising when the leaders of a civil
society love its glory and happiness; but unfortunately for
the peace of mankind, it is all too unusual for those who
regard themselves as the magistrates, or rather the masters, of a holier and more sublime country to show some
love for the earthly country that feeds them. It is gratifying for me to be able to make a rare exception in our case
by placing in the rank of our best citizens those zealous
depositaries of sacred dogmas, authorized by the law,
those venerable shepherds of souls whose forceful yet
gentle eloquence is all the better able to instill the maxims
of the Gospel into their hearers' hearts because they always begin by practicing them themselves. Everyone
knows how successfully the great art of the pulpit is cultivated in Geneva. But saying one thing and doing another
is such a common practice that few people are aware of
the extent to which the spirit of Christianity, holy morality, severity toward oneself, and kindness toward others
reign within the whole body of our ministers. It is perhaps
given to the city of Geneva alone to show an example of
such perfect unity in a society of theologians and men of
letters. It is largely on their acknowledged wisdom and
moderation, and on their zeal for the prosperity of the
state, that I base my hopes for its everlasting tranquillity;

and I note, with pleasure mingled with astonishment and respect, how greatly they abhor the frightful maxims of those sacred and barbarous men of whom history provides us with more than one example: men who, to uphold the supposed rights of God—that is, their own interests—were all the less sparing of human blood because they had persuaded themselves that their own would always be respected.

Could I forget that precious half of the Republic which makes the happiness of the other, and whose sweetness and wisdom maintain its peace and good morals? Gracious and virtuous women citizens, it will always be the lot of your sex to govern ours. And that is fortunate for us when your chaste power, exercised only within the conjugal union, makes its influence felt only in furthering public happiness and the glory of the state. It was thus that women commanded in Sparta, and it is thus that you deserve to command in Geneva. Is there any man so barbarous that he could resist the voice of honor and reason from the lips of a loving wife? And who would not despise vain luxury on seeing your simple and modest attire, which, because of the luster it derives from you, seems most favorable to your beauty? It is your function always to maintain, by your amiable and innocent dominion and your ingratiating ways, love of the law within the state and harmony among its citizens; to reunite divided families by happy marriages; and above all to correct, by the gentle persuasion of your lessons and the modest grace of your conversation, the failings that our young men acquire in other countries, from which, instead of all the useful things that might benefit them, they bring back only a puerile tone and ridiculous airs taken from lost women, and an admiration of various kinds of so-called grandeur, frivolous compensations for servitude which will never approach the lofty value of freedom. Never cease to be what you are: the chaste guardians of morality and of the gentle bonds of peace; and continue to assert on every occasion the rights of the heart and of nature, in the interest of duty and wisdom.

I flatter myself that events will not prove me wrong in taking such guarantees to support my hopes for the glory of the Republic and the common happiness of its citizens. I admit that with all those advantages it will not shine with the kind of brilliance that dazzles most eyes. A puerile and pernicious taste for that brilliance is the deadliest enemy of happiness and freedom. Let dissolute youth seek elsewhere for easy pleasures and long repentances; let self-styled people of good taste go to other places to admire the grandeur of palaces, the beauty of carriages, superb furniture, the pomp of public spectacles, and all the refinements of indolence and luxury. In Geneva one finds only men; but such a sight has a value of its own, and those who seek it out are well worth the admirers of other things.

May you all deign to accept with equal kindness, Magnificent, Most Honored, and Sovereign Lords, my respectful manifestation of the interest I take in your common prosperity. If I have been unfortunate enough to be guilty of some indiscreet transport in this fervent outpouring of my heart, I beg you to excuse it in favor of the tender affection of a true patriot, and the ardent and legitimate zeal of a man who can envisage no greater happiness for himself than that of seeing you all happy.

I am, with the deepest respect, Magnificent, Most Honored, and Sovereign Lords, your most humble and most obedient servant and fellow citizen.

JEAN-JACQUES ROUSSEAU

Chambéry
June 12, 1754

PREFACE

Of all branches of human knowledge, it appears to me that the study of man is the most useful and the least advanced, and I venture to say that the brief inscription on the temple at Delphi ["Know thyself"] contained a more important and difficult precept than all the thick volumes ever written by moralists. I regard the subject of this discourse as one of the most interesting questions that philosophy can propose, and unfortunately for us, as one of the thorniest that philosophers can undertake to resolve. For how can we know the source of inequality among men if we do not begin by knowing men themselves? And how shall man succeed in seeing himself as nature formed him, through all the changes that the passing of time and events must have produced in his original constitution? Like the statue of Glaucus which was so disfigured by time, storms, and the sea that it looked more like a wild beast than a god, the human soul, modified in society by countless constantly recurring causes—by the acquisition of a mass of knowledge and errors, by changes in the constitution of the body, by the unceasing onslaught of passions—has changed its appearance, so to speak, to the point where it is almost unrecognizable. And instead of a being always acting in accordance with certain and invariable principles, instead of the majestic, celestial simplicity imparted to him by his Maker, we now find only the grotesque contrast of passions mistaken for reason, and intelligence in the grip of delirium.

What is still more grievous is that, since all the progress of the human race continues to move it farther away from its original state, the more new knowledge we amass, the more we deprive ourselves of the means of acquiring the most important knowledge of all, and in a sense, it is by studying man that we have made ourselves unable to know him.

It is easy to see that if we are to discover the origin of the differences that now exist among men, we must seek it in those successive changes in the human constitution. It is commonly accepted that men are naturally as equal among themselves as were the animals of each species before physical causes had brought about the variations that we now observe in some of them, for it is inconceivable that those first changes, however they may have occurred, should have altered the individual of the species all at once and in the same way. While some improved or deteriorated and acquired various qualities, good or bad, others continued to remain in their original state. Such was the first source of inequality among men. It is easier to demonstrate it thus in general than to specify its true causes with precision.

Let my readers not imagine, then, that I am claiming to have seen what appears to me so difficult to see. I have begun a few lines of reasoning and ventured a few conjectures, less in the hope of resolving the question than with the intention of casting some light on it and reducing it to its proper terms. Others will easily be able to go farther along the same path, though no one can easily reach its end, for it is no simple matter to distinguish what is original from what is artificial in the present nature of man, to gain genuine knowledge of a state that no longer exists, or may never have existed, and will probably never exist in the future; yet we must have accurate ideas of it if we are to form a sound judgment of our present state. If anyone even undertakes to determine precisely what precautions must be taken in order to make valid observations on this subject, he will need more philosophy than one might think; and it seems to me that a good solution of the following problem would not be unworthy of the Aristotles and Plinys of our century: "By means of what experiments could we come to know natural man, and how could those experiments be carried out in society?" Far be it from me to attempt a solution to that problem, for I believe I have meditated on the subject enough to justify me in venturing to state in advance that the greatest philosophers would be none too good to direct those experiments, nor the most powerful sovereigns to carry them out, and it is scarcely reasonable to expect such a combination, especially in view of the perseverance, or rather the unfailing understanding and good will, that would be required on both sides in order to achieve success.

Little thought has so far been given to this difficult research, yet it is our only remaining means of overcoming the many difficulties that prevent us from knowing the real foundations of human society. It is because of our ignorance of the nature of man that the true definition of natural right is still surrounded by such obscurity and uncertainty; for, as Burlamaqui says, the idea of right, and still more the idea of natural right, are obviously related to the nature of man. Thus the principles of right, he continues, must be deduced from that nature itself, from man's constitution and condition.

It is surprising and appalling to observe how little agreement there is among the various authors who have dealt with this important subject. It is rare to find the same opinion shared by even two of the most serious writers. The Roman jurists—not to speak of the ancient philosophers, who seem to have deliberately made it a rule to contradict each other on the most fundamental principles—indiscriminately subjected man and all other animals to the same natural law, because they took the term to mean not the law that nature prescribes, but the law that nature imposes on itself, or rather because of the special sense in which they used the word "law"; in this context they seem to have understood by it only the general relations established by nature among all living creatures, for their common preservation. To the moderns, the word "law" designates only a rule prescribed to a moral being, that is, one who is intelligent, free, and considered in terms of his relations with others. They therefore limit the application of natural law to the only animal endowed with reason: man. But since each of them defines natural law in his own way, they all establish it on such metaphysical principles that there are very few people, even among us, capable of understanding those principles, much less of discovering them for themselves. The definitions of those learned men, otherwise in perpetual contradiction, have only one thing in common: They all support the conclusion that it is impossible to understand the law of nature, and consequently to obey it, without being a powerful reasoner and a profound metaphysician, which necessarily implies that in order to establish society, men had to make use of intellectual achievements that are developed only with great effort, and by a very small number of people, within society itself.

With so little knowledge of nature and so much discord concerning the meaning of the word "law," it would be very difficult to agree on a good definition of natural law. Aside from not being uniform, all the definitions of it that we find in books have the defect of being drawn from various kinds of knowledge which men do not possess naturally, and from advantages which they cannot even imagine until after they have emerged from the state of nature. The authors of such definitions begin by deciding which rules men ought to accept for their common welfare, and then they give the name of natural law to this collection of rules, with no other proof than the good that would presumably result from them if they were universally observed. This is surely a very convenient way of composing definitions, and of explaining the nature of things by almost arbitrary ideas of what is proper.

But as long as we are ignorant of natural man, it will be futile for us to try to determine which law he received, or which is best suited to his constitution. All we can see clearly with regard to that law is that in order for it to be a law, those who are bound by it must knowingly submit their wills to it, and that furthermore, in order for it to be natural, it must speak directly by the voice of nature.

Leaving aside, then, all scientific books that teach us only to see men as they have made themselves, and meditating on the first and simplest operations of the human soul, I believe I perceive in it two principles prior to reason, one of which makes us ardently interested in our own well-being and self-preservation, while the other gives us a natural repugnance to seeing any sentient creature, especially our fellow man, perish or suffer. It seems to me that the way in which the human mind is able to combine and coordinate those two principles, with no need to introduce the principle of sociability, is the source of all the rules of natural right—rules which reason is later forced to establish on other foundations, when, by its successive developments, it has succeeded in smothering nature.

On this view, we are not obliged to make man a philosopher before making him a man. His duties toward others are not dictated to him solely by the belated lessons of wisdom; and as long as he does not resist the inner impulse of compassion, he will never harm another man, or even any other sentient creature, except in those legitimate cases where, since his own preservation is involved, he is obliged to give preference to himself. This view also enables us to end the ancient dispute concerning the participation of animals in natural law, for it is clear that, lacking understanding and freedom, they cannot recognize that law, but since they share our nature to some extent because of the sensitivity with which they are endowed, it follows that they must participate in natural right, and that man is bound by a certain kind of duty toward them. It appears, in fact, that if I am obliged to do no harm to my fellow man, it is less because he is an intelligent being than because he is a sentient creature, and since that quality is common to both men and animals, it should at least give the latter the right not to be needlessly mistreated by the former.

This same study of original man, of his true needs and the fundamental principles of his duties, is also the only means that can be used to overcome the many difficulties that arise with regard to the origin of moral inequality, the true foundations of the body politic, the reciprocal rights of its members, and countless other similar matters whose importance is equaled only by their obscurity.

If we look upon human society with a calm and disinterested gaze, it seems at first to show us only violence on the part of powerful men and oppression of the weak; the mind rebels against the harshness of the former, or is moved to lament the blindness of the latter. And since nothing is less stable among men than those external relations which are produced more often by chance than by wisdom, and which are known as weakness or power, wealth or poverty, human institutions appear at first glance to be heaps of shifting sand. It is only on closer examination, after having cleared away the dust and sand surrounding the edifice, that we perceive the unshakable base on which it stands, and learn to respect its foundations. But without a serious study of man, of his natural faculties and their successive developments, we shall never succeed in making these distinctions and separating, in the present constitution of things, what has been done by the divine will and what human art has claimed to have done. The political and moral investigations necessitated by the important question I am examining are therefore useful in all respects, and the hypothetical history of governments provides a lesson instructive to man in every way. In considering what would have become of us if we had been left to ourselves, we should learn to bless Him whose benevolent hand, correcting our institutions and giving them a firm basis, has forestalled the disorders that would have resulted from them, and brought forth our happiness from what seemed destined to overwhelm us with misery.

"Learn what the Diety has commanded you to be, and your place in the human world."

DISCOURSE

On this question proposed by the Academy of Dijon:

*What is the origin of inequality among men,
and is it authorized by natural law?*

It is of man that I have to speak, and the question I am examining shows me that I shall be speaking to men, for such questions are not proposed by those who are afraid to honor the truth. I shall therefore confidently defend the cause of humanity before the wise men who have invited me to do so, and I shall not be dissatisfied with myself if I make myself worthy of my subject and my judges.

I see two kinds of inequality in the human race. One, which I call natural or physical inequality because it is established by nature, consists in differences of age, health, bodily strength, and qualities of the mind or the soul. The other can be called moral or political inequality because it depends on a kind of agreement and is established, or at least authorized, by the consent of men. It consists in the various privileges which some men enjoy to the detriment of others, such as being richer, more honored, more powerful than they, or even being able to make them obey.

It would be pointless to ask what the source of natural inequality is, because the mere definition of the term supplies the answer. It would be still more pointless to ask whether there is any essential connection between the two kinds of inequality, for that would amount to asking whether those who command are necessarily better than those who obey, and whether strength of body or mind, wisdom or virtue, are always present in the same individuals in proportion to power or wealth. This may be a good question for slaves to discuss within the hearing of their masters, but it is unfit for rational and free men in search of truth.

Precisely what, then, is the purpose of this discourse? To distinguish, in the course of events, the time when violence was succeeded by right and nature became subject to law; to explain the sequence of wonders by which the strong consented to serve the weak, and the people to buy imaginary tranquillity at the price of real happiness.

Philosophers who have examined the foundations of society have all felt the necessity of going back to the state of nature, but none of them has ever reached it. Some have not hesitated to attribute to man, in that state, the idea of justice and injustice, without bothering to show that he had to have that idea, or even that it was useful to him. Others have spoken of man's natural right to keep what belongs to him, without explaining what they meant by "belongs." Others have given the strong authority over the weak and then immediately postulated the birth of government, without thinking of the time that had to pass before the meaning of the words "authority" and "government" could exist among men. And all of them, constantly speaking of need, avidity, oppression, desires, and pride, have transferred to the state of nature ideas which they acquired in society; they have spoken of savage man, but depicted social man. It has not even occurred to most of our authors to doubt that the state of nature ever existed, whereas it is clear from the Scriptures that the first man, having received understanding and precepts immediately from God, was not himself in that state; and if we give credence to the writings of Moess, as every Christian philosopher must do, we are obliged to deny that, even before the Deluge, men were ever in the pure state of nature, unless they had fallen back into it as the result of some extraordinary event, a paradox that would be very difficult to defend and completely impossible to prove.

Let us begin, then, by setting aside all the facts, for they are irrelevant to the problem. The investigations that may be made concerning this subject should not be taken as historical truths, but only as hypothetical and conditional reasonings, better suited to casting light on the nature of things than to showing their real origin, like those that our physicists put forward every day with regard to the formation of the world. Religion commands us to believe that since God himself drew men out of the state of nature immediately after the Creation, they are unequal because he wanted them to be so; but it does not forbid us to form conjectures, based solely on the nature of man and the creatures around him, concerning what the human race might have become if it had been left to itself. That is the question which I have been asked, and which I propose to examine in this discourse. Since my subject concerns mankind in general, I shall try to speak in terms applicable to all nations; or rather, forgetting time and place, and thinking only of the men to whom I am speaking, I shall suppose myself to be in the Lyceum of Athens, reciting the lessons of my masters, with men like Plato and Xenocrates as my judges, and the human race as my audience.

O man, whatever may be your country, and whatever opinions you may hold, listen to me: Here is your history, as I believe I have read it, not in books by your fellow men, who are liars, but in Nature, who never lies. Everything that comes from her will be true; if there is falsehood, it will be mine, added unintentionally. The times of which I am going to speak are very remote: How greatly you have changed from what you once were! It is, so to speak, the life of your species that I shall describe to you, on the basis of the qualities that you have received. Your upbringing, education, and habits may have corrupted those qualities, but they have not been able to destroy them. There is, I feel, an age at which each individual man would like to stop; you will seek the age at which you would have liked your species to stop. Dissatisfied with your present state, for reasons that portend even greater dissatisfactions for your unfortunate descendants, you may wish that you could go backward in time; that feeling must be interpreted as praise of your early ancestors, criticism of your contemporaries, and a fearful omen for those who will have the misfortune of living after you.

PART ONE

However important it may be, in order to form sound judgments of man's natural state, to consider him from his origin and to examine him, so to speak, in the first embryo of the species, I shall not follow his formation through his successive developments; I shall not delve into the animal realm in search of what he may have been at the beginning, before finally becoming what he is. I shall not inquire whether, as Aristotle believed, his long nails were at first hooked claws, whether he was covered with fur, like a bear, or whether he walked on all fours, with his gaze, directed toward the earth and confined to a horizon of a few paces, marking both the character and the limits of his ideas. I could do nothing but make vague and almost imaginary conjectures on that subject. Comparative anatomy has still made so little progress, and the observations of naturalists are still so uncertain, that no solid structure of reasoning can be built on such foundations. Thus, without resorting to the supernatural knowledge that we have on the matter, and without taking into account all the changes that must have occurred in man's inner and outer conformation as he applied his members to new uses and began eating new foods, I shall assume that he has always been made as I see him today: walking upright, using his hands as we use ours, casting his gaze over all of nature, and measuring with his eyes the vast expanse of the sky.

When I strip that being, thus constituted, of all the supernatural gifts he may have received, and of all the artificial faculties that he could have acquired only by long progress; when I consider him, in short, as he must have come from the hands of nature, I see an animal less strong than some, less agile than others, but on the whole, the most advantageously constituted of all. I see him sitting under an oak tree, quenching his thirst at the nearest stream, finding his bed at the foot of the same tree that supplied him with his meal; and thus all his needs are satisfied.

The earth, left to its natural fertility and covered with immense forests that have never been mutilated by an axe, offers abundant food and shelter to animals of every species. Men, scattered among them, observe and imitate their industry, and thereby attain the instincts of beasts, with the advantage that, whereas each of the other species has only its own instincts, man, who may never have had any peculiar to himself, appropriates all of them, eats most of the different foods that the other animals divide among themselves, and consequently finds his sustenance more easily than any of them.

Accustomed from childhood to inclement weather and the rigors of the seasons, inured to fatigue, and forced to defend, naked and unarmed, their lives and their prey against other ferocious animals, or to escape from them by fleeing, men form a robust and almost indestructible constitution. Children come into the world with the excellent constitution of their parents and strengthen it by the same exercises that produced it, thus acquiring all the vigor that the human race is capable of having. Nature deals with them exactly as the law of Sparta dealt with the children of citizens: She gives strength and health to those who are robust, and destroys the others, differing in this respect from our societies, in which, by making children a burden on their fathers, the state kills them indiscriminately before they are born.

Since a savage man's body is the only instrument he knows, he uses it for various purposes that ours are incapable of serving, for lack of practice. Our industry deprives us of the strength and agility that necessity obliges him to acquire. If he had an axe, would his arm be able to break such thick branches? If he had a sling, could he throw a stone with such force? If he had a ladder, could he climb a tree so nimbly? If he had a horse, would he be such a swift runner? Give a civilized man time to gather all his machines around him, and there will be no doubt that he can easily overcome a savage; but if you want to see an even more unequal combat, pit them against each other naked and unarmed. You will soon see the advantage of always having one's resources available, of always being ready for any event, and of always carrying one's entire self, so to speak, with one.

Hobbes maintains that man is naturally intrepid, and intent only on attacking and fighting. A famous philosopher believes, on the contrary—and Cumberland and Pufendorf hold the same view—that nothing is more timid than man in the state of nature, that he is always trembling and ready to flee at the slightest sound he hears or the slightest movement he sees. This may be true when he encounters things that are unfamiliar to him. I do not doubt that he is frightened by any new sight that presents itself to him, when he does not know whether to expect physical good or evil from it and cannot measure his strength against the danger that may lie before him; such cases, however, are rare in the state of nature, where things take place in a uniform manner and the face of the earth is not subject to the abrupt and continual changes that are caused in it by the passions and inconstancies of people living in society. But since savage man lives among animals and finds himself obliged to contend with them at an early age, he soon makes a comparison between them and himself, and seeing that he surpasses them more in adroitness than they surpass him in strength, he learns to cease being afraid of them. Put a bear or a wolf in combat against a savage who is robust, agile, and brave, as all savages are, and armed with stones and a stout club; you will soon see that the danger is at least equal on both sides, and that after several such encounters, ferocious beasts, which do not like to attack each other, will be reluctant to attack man, having found him to be as ferocious as themselves. With regard to animals that unquestionably have more strength than he has adroitness, he is in the same situation as other weaker species, which are nevertheless able to subsist. He does, however, have one advantage: Since he is an equally good runner and can take almost certain refuge in trees, he is able to decline or accept any encounter, and always has a choice between fleeing and fighting. Furthermore, it seems that no animal naturally attacks man, except in cases of self-defense or extreme hunger, or shows toward him that violent antipathy which appears to indicate that nature intends one species to be food for another.

That is no doubt why Negroes and savages have so little anxiety about the ferocious beasts they may encounter in the forest. The Caribs of Venezuela, among others, live without the slightest apprehension or difficulty in this respect. Although they are nearly naked, says Francisco Coreal, they boldly expose themselves in the forest, armed only with bows and arrows; but no one has ever heard of one of them being devoured by an animal.

There are other, more formidable enemies against which man does not have the same means of defending himself: natural infirmities, childhood, old age, and illnesses of every kind, sad signs of our weakness, of which the first two are common to all animals, while the last belongs chiefly to men living in society. With regard to childhood, I observe that a human mother, carrying her child with her everywhere, can feed it much more easily than the females of many other species, which are forced to be constantly coming and going, with great fatigue, to seek their own food and to suckle or feed their young. It is true that if a woman perishes, her child is in great danger of perishing with her, but this danger is common to dozens of other species whose young are incapable for a long time of going off to seek their food for themselves; and while childhood is longer among human beings, life is also longer, so that things are more or less equal in this respect, although there are other rules, which are not relevant to my subject, concerning the duration of infancy and the number of young. In old age, when human beings are less active and perspire little, their need for food diminishes with their ability to procure it. Since the savage life protects them from gout and rheumatism, and since old age is, of all ills, the one that human assistance can least alleviate, they finally fade away, without others realizing that they are ceasing to exist, and almost without realizing it themselves.

With regard to illness, I shall not repeat the vain and false statements that most healthy people make against medicine; but I shall ask if there are any reliable observations from which we may conclude that the average length of human life is shorter in those countries where the art of medicine is most neglected than in those where it is most assiduously cultivated. And how could that be the case, if we give ourselves more maladies than medicine can give us remedies? Extreme inequality in ways of living, with excessive idleness for some people and excessive work for others; the ease with which we can arouse and satisfy our appetites and our sensuality; the overrefined foods of the rich, which nourish them with warming juices and plague them with indigestion; the unwholesome food of the poor, who usually do not even have enough of it to satisfy their hunger, and therefore overload their stomachs whenever they have the opportunity; insufficient sleep; excesses of all kinds; immoderate outbursts of all the passions; fatigue; mental exhaustion; the countless sorrows and irritations that afflict people in all walks of life and constantly gnaw at the human soul—these are the pernicious proofs that most of our ills are of our own making, and that we could have avoided nearly all of them by keeping the simple, regular, and solitary way of life prescribed by nature. If nature meant man to be healthy, I might almost venture to say that the state of reflection is an unnatural state, and that a meditating man is a perverted animal. When we think of the healthy constitutions of savages, at least of those whom we have not ruined with our strong liquors; when we know that they have almost no infirmities other than wounds and old age, we are inclined to believe that the history of human maladies could be written by following the history of civil societies. That, at least, was the opinion of Plato, who concluded that since certain remedies, considered inflammatory to various diseases in his own time, were given or approved by Podalirios and Machaon during the siege of Troy, those diseases were then unknown to mankind; and Celsus reports that dieting, so necessary today, was first prescribed by Hippocrates.

With so few sources of sickness, man in the state of nature therefore has little need of remedies, much less of doctors; nor is the human race in worse condition than other species in this respect, and it is easy to learn from hunters whether they find many infirm animals. They do, however, find animals that have had serious wounds which have healed perfectly. Some have broken bones, even limbs, that mend with the help of no other surgeon than time and no other regimen than their usual life, and they recover no less completely than if they had been tormented with incisions, poisoned with drugs, or exhausted by fasting. However useful properly administered medicine may be to us, it is still true that although a sick savage, left to himself, can expect help only from nature, he has nothing to fear but his sickness, and this often makes his situation preferable to ours.

We must therefore avoid the mistake of confusing sav-

age men with the men we have before our eyes. Nature
treats all animals left to her care with a predilection that
seems to show how jealous she is of that right. The horse,
the cat, the bull, and even the donkey are usually larger,
and always more robust, vigorous, strong, and courageous
in the wild than in captivity. They lose half these advantages when they become domesticated; it seems that all our
efforts to feed and treat them well serve only to make
them deteriorate. It is the same with man himself: In becoming social and enslaved, he becomes weak, timorous,
and servile, and his soft, effeminate way of life completes
the enervation of both his strength and his courage. Furthermore, there is an even greater difference between savage and domesticated men than between wild and domesticated animals, for while animals and men are treated
alike by nature, man pampers himself more than the animals he tames, and this makes his degenerate more mar-
kedly.

It is therefore no great misfortune for those primitive
men, and certainly no great obstacle to their survival, that
they go naked; have no houses, and lack all the useless
things that we consider so necessary. If their skin is not
hairy, they have no need of body hair in warm countries,
and in cold countries they soon learn to use the skins of
the animals they have vanquished. If they have only two
feet for running, they have two arms with which to defend
themselves and provide for their needs. Their children
may learn to walk slowly and with difficulty, but their
mothers can easily carry them, an advantage that is lacking in other species, in which the mother, when pursued,
must either abandon her young or match her pace to
theirs. There may be a few exceptions to this, such as the
foxlike animal in the province of Nicaragua which has
feet like a man's hands and, according to Coreal, has a sac
under its belly in which the mother places her young when
she is forced to flee. It is no doubt the same as the animal
called the *tlaquatzin* in Mexico; Laët describes the female as having the same kind of sac, used for the same
purpose. In any case, unless we suppose the combinations
of singular and fortuitous circumstances of which I shall
speak later, and which might very well never have occurred, it is clear that the first man who made clothing or a
dwelling for himself was providing himself with something
for which he had very little need, since he had done with-

out it till then, and since there is no reason to believe that, as a grown man, he could not have continued to endure the same kind of life that he had already endured since childhood.

Alone, idle, and always close to danger, the savage must like to sleep, and his sleep must be light, like that of animals, which think little and can be said to sleep during all the time when they are not thinking. Since self-preservation is almost his only concern, his most highly developed faculties must be those that he uses primarily in attack and defense, either to subjugate a prey or to prevent himself from becoming the prey of another animal. But those organs that are perfected only by softness and sensuality must remain in a state of crudeness which rules out any kind of delicacy in him. His senses are divided in this respect: His touch and taste will be very coarse, while his sight, hearing, and smell will be extremely keen. Such is the state of animals in general, and according to the reports of travelers, it is also the state of most savage peoples. We should therefore not be surprised that the Hottentots of the Cape of Good Hope can, with their unaided eyes, see ships as far out at sea as the Dutch can do with telescopes; or that the savages of America were able to trail the Spaniards by smell as well as the best dogs could have done; or that all these barbarous peoples go naked without discomfort, stimulate their taste with red peppers, and drink European liquors like water.

I have so far considered only the physical aspect of man; let us now try to look at him from a metaphysical and mental point of view.

I see nothing in any animal but an ingenious machine to which nature has given senses to wind itself up and protect itself, up to a certain point, from everything that tends to destroy or disrupt it. I see precisely the same things in the human machine, with this difference: that nature alone does everything in the operations of an animal whereas man, as a free agent, contributes to his own operations. The former chooses or rejects by instinct, the latter by an act of freedom; an animal, therefore, cannot depart from the rules laid down for it, even when it would be advantageous to do so, while man often departs from them to his own disadvantage. Thus a pigeon can die of starvation beside a bowl full of choice meats, and a cat on a pile of fruit or grain, even though either could nourish itself quite well with the foods it disdains, if it would only try them. And thus dissolute men engage in excesses that bring them fever and death, because the mind perverts the senses, and the will still speaks when nature is silent.

Every animal has ideas, since it has senses; it even combines its ideas to some extent; and in this respect, men differ from animals only in degree. Certain philosophers have even maintained that there is more difference between some men and others than between some men and some beasts. What specifically distinguishes man from all other animals is therefore not so much his intelligence as the fact that he is a free agent. Nature commands all animals, and beasts obey. Man feels the same impulses, but he knows that he is free to acquiesce or resist; and it is above all in his awareness of this freedom that the spirituality of his soul is manifested. For physics can, in a way, explain the mechanism of the senses and the formation of ideas; but in our power of willing, or rather of choosing, and in our awareness of that power, we find only purely spiritual acts about which nothing can be explained by the laws of mechanics.

But even if the difficulties surrounding all these questions should leave some room for argument concerning this difference between men and beasts, there is another quite specific quality which distinguishes them and on which there can be no disagreement: the capacity for self-improvement. With the aid of circumstances, this capacity successively develops all others, and it resides in us individually as well as in the species, whereas at the end of a few months a beast is what it will be for the rest of its life, and at the end of a thousand years its species is still what it was at the beginning of that period. Why is man alone subject to becoming imbecilic? Is it not that he thus returns to his original state, and that whereas the beast, which has acquired nothing and so has nothing to lose, always retains its instinct, man loses, through old age or other accidents, everything that his perfectibility has enabled him to acquire, and thereby falls even lower than the beast? It would be sad for us to be forced to admit that this distinctive and almost unlimited faculty is the source of all man's misfortunes; that it is what, with the passing of time, draws him out of his original state, in which his days flowed by in tranquil innocence; that through the centuries it is what gives rise to his knowledge and errors, his vices and virtues, and eventually makes him a tyrant over himself and nature. It would be appalling to be obliged to praise as a benefactor the first man who suggested to the inhabitants of the banks of the Orinoco the use of those boards which they bind to their children's foreheads, and which are responsible for at least part of their imbecility and their primordial happiness.

Savage man, left by nature to his instincts alone, or rather compensated for those that he may lack by faculties capable of first replacing them and then raising him far above them, therefore begins with purely animal functions. Perception and feeling are his first state, which he shares with all animals. Willing and refusing, desiring and fearing: These are the first and almost the only operations of his soul, until new circumstances cause new developments in it.

Whatever moralists may say, human intelligence owes much to the passions, which also owe much to it, as is generally recognized. It is by their activity that our reason is improved; we seek knowledge because we desire enjoyment, and it is impossible to imagine why anyone with neither desires nor fears should take the trouble to reason. The passions in turn have their origin in our needs, and their progress depends on our knowledge, for we can desire or fear things only from the ideas we have of them, or from the simple impulse of nature. Savage man, deprived of all knowledge and understanding, has passions only of the latter kind. His desires do not go beyond his physical needs, and the only needs he experiences are for food, a female, and rest. The only evils he fears are pain and hunger. I say pain and not death, for no animal will ever know what it means to die; knowledge of death and its terrors was one of the first things that man acquired by departing from the animal condition.

It would be easy for me, if it were necessary, to support this view with facts, to show that among all peoples of the world the progress of the mind has been exactly proportionate to the needs given to them by nature or imposed on them by circumstances, and consequently to the passions that impelled them to satisfy those needs. I could show, in Egypt, the arts coming into being and spreading with the overflow of the Nile; I could follow their progress in Greece, where they germinated, grew, and rose to the skies amid the sands and rocks of Attica, without ever being able to take root on the fertile banks of the Eurotas; I could point out that, in general, northern peoples are more inventive than southern ones, because they cannot get along as well without being so, as though nature wanted to equalize things by giving their minds the fertility she refuses to their soil.

But without resorting to the uncertain testimony of history, can anyone fail to see that everything seems to ensure that savage man will have neither the means nor the inclination to change his state? His imagination depicts nothing to him; his heart asks nothing of him. His few needs are so easily satisfied, and he is so far from having enough knowledge to make him want to acquire more, that he has neither foresight nor curiosity. He is indifferent to the spectacle of nature because it is so familiar to him: It is always the same order, the same recurring changes. He does not have enough understanding to be astonished by even the greatest wonders, and he cannot be expected to have the philosophy that a man needs in order to observe once what he has seen every day. His placid soul is wholly absorbed in the feeling of his present existence, with no idea of the future, however near it may be; and his plans, as limited as his intentions, scarcely extend to the end of the day. That is still the extent of the Carib's foresight today: He sells his cotton bed in the morning, then returns in the evening to buy it back, not having foreseen that he would need it that night.

The more we reflect on this subject, the more the distance between pure sensations and the simplest knowledge grows before our eyes, and it is impossible to imagine how a man could have crossed such a wide gap by his own powers, without the aid of communication and the goad of necessity. How many centuries must have passed before men had an opportunity to see any fire other than that of the sky! How many chance events must have been needed to teach them the most common uses of that element! How often they must have let it go out before acquiring the art of reproducing it! And how often each of those secrets must have died with the man who discovered it! What shall we say of agriculture, an art which requires so much work and foresight, depends on so many other arts, can obviously be practiced only in at least an early form of society, and serves not so much to make the earth produce food, for it would do that without our efforts, as to force it to produce those foods that are most to our taste? But let us suppose that men had multiplied to the point where the natural products of the earth were no longer sufficient to sustain them—a supposition which, let me say in passing, would show that such a way of life was quite favorable to the human race. Let us further suppose that at a time when those savages had no forges or workshops, farming implements had fallen into their hands from the sky; that they had overcome the mortal hatred which all savages have for continual work; that they had learned to foresee their needs sufficiently far into the future; that they had guessed how to till the soil, sow grain, and plant trees; that they had acquired the arts of grinding grain and making grapes ferment. They would have had to learn al these things from the gods, for we cannot conceive how they could have discovered them for themselves. But then who would have been so foolish as to exhaust himself in tilling a field that would have been stripped of its crop by the first man or beast that wanted it? And how could each man have accepted the idea of spending his life in arduous toil, knowing that the more he needed the fruits of his labor, the surer he would be to lose them? In short, how could that situation have induced men to practice agriculture unless the land was divided among them, that is, unless the state of nature had been abolished.

If we were to assume that savage man is as skilled in the art of thinking as our philosophers would have us believe; if, following their example, we were to assume that he himself is a philosopher who discovers the most sublime truths of his own accord, and by chains of highly abstract reasoning, arrives at principles of justice and reason drawn from love of order in general, or from the known will of his Creator; in short, if we were to attribute to him a degree of intelligence and enlightenment equal to the degree of stupidity and obtuseness that he must really have, and actually is found to have, what good would the human race derive from all that metaphysics, which could not be communicated, and would perish with the individual who invented it? What progress would mankind make, living in the woods among other animals? And how much would men be able to improve and enlighten each other when they were all without fixed abodes, when none of them had any need of the others, and when it was likely that any two of them would meet only once or twice in their lives, without knowing or speaking to each other?

Let us consider how many ideas we owe to the use of speech, how much grammar exercises the mind and facilitates its operations, and what inconceivable efforts and vast amounts of time must have been required for the invention of language. Then, when we join these considerations to those that I have previously set forth, we can judge how many thousands of centuries were needed for successively developing in the human mind the operations of which it was potentially capable.

At this point I shall briefly discuss the problem of the origin of language. I might content myself with citing or repeating the Abbé de Condillac's conclusions on the subject. They all confirm my own view, and may originally have suggested it to me. But since it is evident, from the way in which this philosopher resolves the difficulties he raises concerning the origin of conventional signs, that he assumes what I question, namely, the existence of a kind of society already established among the inventors of language, I feel that in referring to his reflections I must also add my own, in order to present the same difficulties from a viewpoint relevant to my subject. The first one is to imagine how the problem ever arose. Since men had no dealings with one another, and no need to have any, we cannot understand what induced them to invent language or how it was possible for them to do so, if it was not necessary. I might say, with many others, that language was born of the domestic intercourse among fathers, mothers, and children. But aside from the fact that this would not resolve the difficulties, it would involve the mistake made by those who, when they reason about the state of nature, inject into it ideas that they have taken from society; they always see the family gathered in one dwelling, with its members bound together by ties as close and permanent as those that exist in our own families, where the members are united by so many common interests. The fact is, however, that in that primitive state man had no houses, huts, or property of any kind, so that everyone slept wherever he happened to be and seldom stayed in the same place more than one night. Males and females came together fortuitously, according to chance encounters, opportunities, and desire, with no need of words to express what they had to communicate to each other; and they left each other with the same casual ease. The mother first suckled her children for her own need, and later, when habit had made her fond of them, she fed them for theirs. They left her when they were strong enough to provide for themselves, and since there was almost no way of maintaining contact without keeping each other constantly in sight, they soon became unable even to recognize each other. It should be noted that since the child had to communicate all his needs to his mother, and therefore had more to say to her than she to him, it must have been he who contributed most to the invention of speech, and the language he used must have been largely of his own devising, so that there were as many languages as individuals who spoke them. This diversity was also maintained by men's wandering, vagabond life, which gave no language time to solidify. A description of a mother telling her child the words he must use to ask her for various things is a good illustration of the way in which existing languages are taught, but it does not explain how languages were originally formed.

Let us suppose that this first difficulty has been overcome; let us cross for a moment the immense space that must have separated the pure state of nature from the need for languages; and assuming that they were necessary, let us try to determine how they might have begun to arise. Here we encounter a new difficulty, worse than the first one. for if men needed speech in order to learn to think, they had a still greater need to be able to think in order to acquire the ability to speak; and even if we understood how vocal sounds came to be taken as conventional expressions of some ideas, we would still have to determine what the conventional expressions may have been for ideas which. having no perceptible objects. could not be indicated by either gestures or the voice. We are therefore scarcely able to form tolerable conjectures concerning the art of communicating thoughts and establishing intercourse between minds, a sublime art which is already very far from its origin, but which the philosopher sees as still being at such a prodigious distance from perfection that there is no man rash enough to state that it will ever reach it, even if the disruptions that time necessarily brings were suspended in its favor, even if prejudice were excluded from academies or silenced within them, and their members were able to devote themselves to that thorny problem for whole centuries without interruption.

The first language of mankind, the most universal and forceful language, and the only one that was needed before it became necessary to persuade assembled men, is the cry of nature. Since that cry was brought forth only by a kind of instinct in urgent circumstances, to plead for help in great danger, or for relief from violent pain, it was not often used in the ordinary course of life, in which more moderate feelings prevail. When men began to expand and multiply their ideas, and closer communication was established among them, they sought more numerous signs and a more extensive language. They multiplied the inflections of the voice and combined them with gestures, which by their nature are more expressive, and whose meaning depends less on a prior decision. They indicated visible and mobile objects by gestures, and audible ones by imitative sounds. But since gestures can indicate little more than present or easily described objects and visible actions; since they cannot be used at all times, for darkness or the interposition of an object makes them useless; and since they request attention rather than compelling it, men eventually thought of replacing them with articulate vocal sounds, which, though lacking the same relation to certain ideas, are better able to express all ideas as conventional signs. This substitution could be made only by common consent and in a manner rather difficult to practice for men whose coarse organs were unaccustomed to such a function, and still more difficult to conceive in itself, because that unanimous agreement had to be motivated, and speech seems to have been necessary to establish the use of speech.

We must assume that the first words that were used had a much broader meaning in men's minds than those employed in languages already formed, and that, since men did not know the division of discourse into its constituent parts, they first gave each word the meaning of an entire sentence. When they began to distinguish subjects from attributes, and verbs from nouns, which was no mean effort of genius, substantives were at first only so many proper nouns, the present infinitive was the only tense of verbs, and as for adjectives, the idea of them must have developed only with great difficulty, because every adjective is an abstract word, and abstractions are laborious and un-natural operations.

Each object was at first given a particular name, with-out regard to genus and species, which those originators were unable to distinguish. All individuals presented them-selves to their minds in isolation, as they are in the specta-cle of nature. If one oak was called A, another oak was called B, for the first idea drawn from two things is that they are not the same, and it often takes a long time to observe what they have in common. Therefore, the more limited men's knowledge was, the larger their vocabulary became. The difficulties of having to use all those different names could not easily be overcome, for in order to clas-sify things under common and generic designations, their properties and differences had to be known; men needed far more observations and definitions, that is, natural his-tory and metaphysics, than they could have had at that time.

Moreover, general ideas can be introduced into the mind only with the aid of words, and the understanding can grasp them only by means of propositions. That is one reason why animals cannot form such ideas or ever ac-quire the perfectibility that depends on them. When a monkey goes from one nut to another, are we to believe that he has the general idea of that kind of fruit and com-pares its archetype with those two individuals? Of course not; but the sight of one of those nuts recalls to his mem-ory the sensations he received from the other, and his eyes, altered in a certain way, announce to his palate the alteration it is about to undergo. Every general idea is purely intellectual; if the imagination is involved to the slightest extent, the idea immediately becomes particular. Try to trace in your mind the image of a tree in general; you will never succeed in doing so: In spite of yourself, you will have to see it as small or large, bare or leafy, light or dark, and if you were able to see in it only what is common to all trees, the image would no longer resemble a tree. Purely abstract entities are perceived in the same way, or are conceived only through discourse. The defini-tion of a triangle alone gives you a true idea of it: As soon as you visualize one in your mind, it is that particular triangle and not another, and you cannot avoid giving it visible lines or a colored area. To have general ideas, then, we must enunciate propositions, we must speak; for as soon as the imagination stops, the mind can proceed only with the aid of discourse. Therefore, if the inventors of language were able to give names only to ideas that they already had, it follows that the first substantives could only have been proper nouns.

But when, by means that I cannot conceive, the new grammarians began extending their ideas and generalizing their words, their ignorance must have confined this method to very narrow limits; and as they had at first used too many individual names because they did not know genera and species, they later made too few genera and species because they had not considered entities in all their differences. Carrying this process of division far enough would have required more experience and knowledge than they could have had, and more research and work than they were willing to do. Since even today we are continually discovering new species that we had previously failed to observe, it is easy to imagine how many must have escaped the notice of men who judged things only by their first appearance. As for primary classes and the most general notions, it is superfluous to add that they must also have escaped them. How, for example, could they have imagined or understood the words "matter," "mind," "substance," "mode," "figure," and "motion," when even our philosophers, who have been using them for a long time, have great difficulty in understanding them, and when, since the ideas attached to these words are purely metaphysical, there are no models of them in nature?

I shall now stop after having described those first steps, and ask my judges to interrupt their reading at this point to consider how far language still had to go, after the invention of physical substantives, which are the easiest part of it to invent, before it could express all the thoughts of men, take on a stable form, become capable of being spoken in public, and influence society. I ask them to reflect on how much time and knowledge was needed to discover numbers, abstract words, aorists and all the other tenses of verbs, particles, syntax, connections among propositions, reasoning, and the whole logic of discourse. For my part, I am so appalled by the endless difficulties, and so convinced of the almost demonstrable impossibility of language having been created and established by purely human means, that I leave this difficult question to anyone who may undertake to discuss it: "Which is the more necessary assumption: that language could not have been invented if society had not already been established, or that society could not have been established if language had not already been invented?"

Whatever the origins of society and language may have been, we can at least see, from the little care that nature has taken to bring men closer by mutual needs and facilitate the use of speech for them, how little she has done to prepare them for sociability, and how little she has contributed to what they themselves have done to establish the bonds of society. It is impossible to imagine why, in that primitive state, one man should need another any more than a monkey or a wolf needs another of its kind; or, assuming such a need, what might induce the other man to satisfy it; or, if he was willing to do so, how the two of them could agree on the conditions. I know that it is constantly repeated that nothing could have been more miserable than man in that state; and if it is true, as I believe I have proved, that untold centuries had to pass before he could have the desire and the opportunity to emerge from it, that is an accusation which could be made against nature, but not against the being she thus constituted. But if I understand the word "miserable" correctly, either it has no meaning, or else it denotes only painful privation and suffering of the body or the soul. I would like someone to explain to me what kind of misery could afflict a free man whose heart is at peace and whose body is in good health. I ask whether it is social life or natural life that is more likely to become unbearable to those who live it. We see around us hardly anyone who does not complain about his life; some even put an end to it, insofar as they are able to do so, and divine and human laws combined are scarcely adequate to curb that disorder. I ask whether anyone has heard of a savage living in freedom who ever even thought of complaining about life and killing himself. Let us therefore judge with less pride on which side real misery is to be found. On the contrary, nothing could have been more miserable than savage man dazzled by knowledge, tormented by passions, and reasoning about a state different from his own. Providence was very wise in ordaining that the latent faculties he possessed were to develop only as occasions to exercise them arose, so that they would be neither superfluous and burdensome in the time before they were needed, nor insufficiently developed when they became necessary. In instinct alone, man had all that he required for living in the state of nature; in cultivated reason, he has only what he requires for living in society.

On first consideration it would seem that men in the state of nature, having no kind of moral relations or recognized duties among themselves, could not have been either good or evil, and had neither virtues nor vices, unless we take these words in a physical sense and say that vices are qualities that may be detrimental to the individual's self-preservation, and virtues are qualities that may be favorable to it; in that case, the man who least resisted the simple impulses of nature would have to be called the most virtuous. But if we take the words in their usual sense, we shall do well to mistrust our prejudices and suspend any judgment we might make concerning such a situation until we have carefully considered these questions: whether there are more virtues than vices among civilized men; whether their virtues are more beneficial than their vices are injurious; whether the progress of their knowledge is sufficient compensation for the increasing harm they do to each other as they learn of the good they ought to do; and whether, on the whole, they would not be in a happier situation if they had neither good nor evil to hope or fear from anyone, rather than being subjected to universal dependence and obliged to receive everything from people who accept no obligation to give them anything.

Above all, let us not conclude, with Hobbes, that because man has no natural idea of goodness, he is naturally evil; that he is vicious because he does not know virtue; that he always refuses to do anything for his fellow men which he does not feel he owes to them; or that by virtue of the right, which he justly attributes to himself, to have whatever is necessary to him, he foolishly imagines himself to be the owner of the whole world. Hobbes clearly sees the defect of all modern definitions of natural law, but the conclusions he draws from his own definition show that he takes it in a sense that is equally false. If he had reasoned on the basis of the principles he had established, he would have had to say that since the state of nature is the state in which the efforts we make for our own preservation are least prejudicial to that of others, it is the one that best assures peace, and the most advantageous to mankind. He says exactly the opposite, because of having wrongly intro-

duced into savage man's concern for self-preservation a
need to satisfy a multitude of passions that are the work
of society and have made laws necessary. A bad man, he
says, is a robust child. It remains to be seen whether savage man is a robust child. If we were to grant that he is,
what conclusions could be drawn? That if he is as dependent on others when he is robust as when he is weak, he
will stop at nothing; that he will beat his mother when she
is too slow in giving him her breast; that he will strangle
one of his younger brothers if he finds him bothersome,
and bite another's leg if he is offended or upset by him.
But it is contradictory to suppose that man in the state of
nature is both robust and dependent. Man is weak when
he is dependent, and he is freed from that dependence
when he becomes robust. Hobbes did not see that the
same cause which prevents savages from using their reason, as our jurists maintain, also prevents them from
misusing their faculties, as he himself maintains. It could
therefore be said that savages are not evil precisely because they do not know what it is to be good; for they are
prevented from doing evil not by the development of understanding or the restraint of law, but by the quiescence
of their passions and their ignorance of vice: "Ignorance
of vice is more effective among them than knowledge of
virtue among others." There is, moreover, another factor
that Hobbes overlooked; it is something which, having
been given to man to moderate in certain circumstances
the ferocity of his egotism, or his desire for self-preservation before his egotism came into being, tempers his
ardent concern for his own welfare by an innate dislike of
seeing his fellow men suffer. I believe I need fear no contradiction in attributing to man the only natural virtue
that the most violent detractor of human virtues* was
forced to recognize. I am referring to compassion, an inclination that befits creatures as weak and subject to as
many ills as we are; it is a virtue that is all the more universal and all the more useful to man because it precedes any
kind of reflection in him, and it is so natural that even
beasts sometimes show clear signs of it. Without speaking
of the affection that females have for their young, or of
the dangers they face to save them, I can mention the fre-

*Rousseau is referring to Bernard Mandeville (1670–1733),
author of *The Fable of the Bees,* mentioned below. (Translator's note.)

quently observed reluctance of horses to step on a living body. No animal ever passes by a dead member of its own species without uneasiness; some even give their dead a kind of burial; and the mournful lowing of cattle entering a slaughterhouse shows the impression made on them by the grisly spectacle that strikes them. It is gratifying to see the author of *The Fable of the Bees* forced to recognize man as a compassionate and sensitive being, and abandoning his cold, subtle style in the example he gives. He offers us the tragic image of an imprisoned man who sees, through his window, a wild beast tearing a child from its mother's arms, breaking its frail limbs with murderous teeth, and clawing its quivering entrails. What horrible agitation seizes him as he watches that scene which does not concern him personally! What anguish he suffers from being powerless to help the fainting mother and the dying child!

Such is the pure emotion of nature, prior to all reflection; such is the force of natural compassion, which even the greatest moral depravity still has difficulty in destroying, for whenever the distress of an unfortunate victim is depicted in our theaters, we see tears of pity shed by men who, if they were in the tyrant's place, would increase their enemy's torments still more; like the bloodthirsty Sulla, who was so sensitive to suffering that he had not caused, or Alexander of Pherae, who did not dare to attend a performance of any tragedy, for fear of being seen weeping with Andromache and Priam, yet listened impassively to the cries of all the citizens who were killed every day at his command. "In giving man tears, nature shows that she has given him a tender heart."

Mandeville was well aware that, with all their morality, men would never have been anything but monsters if nature had not given them compassion to support their reasons; but he did not see that all the social virtues, which he tried to deny to man, stem from this quality alone. What is generosity, clemency, or humaneness, if not compassion applied to the weak, the guilty, or the human race in general? Even benevolence and friendship, properly considered, are produced by compassion constantly fixed on a particular object, for is wishing someone to be free of suffering any different from wishing him to be happy? If it were true that commiseration is only a feeling that puts us in a sufferer's place, a feeling that is obscure but strong in savage man, and developed but weak in civilized man, would that not simply reinforce the truth of what I am saying? For commiseration will be all the more forceful as the witnessing animal identifies itself more closely with the suffering animal. It is obvious that this identification must have been much closer in the state of nature than it is in the state of reasoning. It is reason that engenders egotism, and reflection strengthens it. Reflection turns man inward upon himself and separates him from everything that disturbs or afflicts him. It is philosophy that isolates him, and makes him say in secret, at the sight of another's suffering, "Perish, if you will; I am secure." Only a danger to all of society can trouble the philosopher's tranquil sleep and draw him from his bed. A murder can be committed with impunity under his window; he has only to put his hands over his ears, and argue with himself a little, to prevent nature, which is rebelling within him, from identifying him with the victim of the murder. Savage man does not have that admirable talent; lacking wisdom and reason, he always thoughtlessly obeys his first humane impulse. When there is a riot or a street brawl, the populace gathers while the prudent man walks away; it is the rabble, the marketplace women, who separate the combatants and prevent decent people from killing each other.

It is thus certain that compassion is a natural feeling which, by moderating the activity of each individual's self-love, contributes to the preservation of the whole species. It is compassion that makes us go, without reflection, to the assistance of those we see suffering; in the state of nature, it takes the place of laws, morality, and virtue, with the advantage that no one is tempted to disobey its gentle voice; it prevents the robust savage from robbing weak children and disabled old men of their laboriously acquired sustenance, if he expects to find his own elsewhere; instead of this sublime maxim of reasoned justice: "Do unto others as you would have others do unto you," compassion inspires all men with another maxim, much less perfect, but perhaps more useful: "Do good to yourself with as little harm to others as possible." In short, it is in this natural feeling, rather than in subtle arguments, that we must seek the cause of the reluctance to do evil that all men would feel even without the moral principles that have been taught to them. Although men with minds

like that of Socrates may be able to acquire virtue by reason, the human race would long since have ceased to exist
if its preservation had depended only on the reasoning of
its members.

With such torpid passions and such a salutary restraint,
men were more wild than malicious, more concerned with
avoiding harm to themselves than tempted to harm others,
and not subject to very dangerous conflicts. Since they
maintained no kind of relations among themselves and
therefore knew nothing of vanity, respect, esteem, and
contempt; since they had not the slightest notion of "mine
and thine," and no true idea of justice; since they regarded
any violence that might befall them as a misfortune that
could easily be repaired, rather than as an offense that had
to be punished; and since they had no inclination to take
revenge, except perhaps automatically and on the spot,
like a dog biting a stone that has been thrown at him,
their quarrels would seldom have had bloody consequences
if they had never been caused by anything that aroused
stronger emotions than a dispute over food. But I believe
there was a more dangerous source of conflict, which I
must now discuss.

Among the passions that stir the human heart, there is
an ardent, impetuous one that makes one sex necessary to
the other, a terrible passion that braves all dangers, over-
comes all obstacles, and, in its fury, seems calculated to
destroy the human race that it is destined to preserve.
What will become of men in the grip of that frenzied, brutal urge if they are without shame or restraint, and risk
bloodshed every day in fighting over mates?

We must first acknowledge that the more violent the
passions are, the more necessary it is to have laws to curb
them. But, disregarding the fact that laws are inadequate
to achieve that purpose, as is shown by the disorders and
crimes which these passions cause among us every day, it
would still be good to inquire whether those disorders did
not arise from the laws themselves, for in that case, even
if the laws were capable of repressing them, the least one
could expect of them would be that they put a stop to
evils which would not exist without them.

Let us begin by distinguishing between the mental and
physical elements in the feeling of love. The physical element is the general desire that impels one sex to unite
with the other. The mental element is what directs that

desire and fixes it on one object exclusively, or at least gives it a greater degree of energy for that preferred object. Now it is easy to see that the mental element in love is an artificial feeling born of social usage and extolled by women with great care and cleverness, to establish their power and give dominance to the sex that ought to obey. This feeling, founded on certain notions of merit or beauty that a savage is not in a position to have, and on comparisons that he is not in a position to make, must be almost nonexistent for him. Since his mind is unable to form abstract ideas of regularity and proportion, his heart is not subject to feelings of admiration and love, which, even though we may not be aware of it, are produced by the application of those ideas. He follows only the temperament given to him by nature, not tastes that he is unable to acquire; he therefore looks on all women as adequate for his need.

When they are limited to the physical side of love, and fortunate enough to be ignorant of those preferences which stimulate desire and increase the difficulties of satisfying it, men must feel amorous ardor less often and less intensely, and must consequently have fewer and less violent conflicts among themselves. Imagination, which causes such ravages among us, does not speak to savage hearts; each man peacefully awaits the impulse of nature, obeys it without choice, with more pleasure than furor, and loses all desire as soon as his immediate need has passed.

It is therefore incontestable that only in society has love, like all the other passions, acquired the impetuous ardor that so often makes it harmful to men. It is all the more ridiculous to represent savages as constantly killing each other in fights caused by their brutal lust, because that view is directly contrary to experience. Of all existing peoples, the Caribs have least departed from the state of nature, and it is they who are most peaceful in their sex lives and least subject to jealousy, even though they live in a hot climate, which always seems to make these passions more active.

As for any inferences that might be drawn, in the case of certain animal species, from the combats between males which cause bloodshed in our poultry yards all year round, and in springtime make our forests resound with the cries that accompany battles over females, we must begin by excluding all species that obviously differ from us in the proportion which nature has established between the power of one sex and that of the other; thus no inferences concerning the human race can be drawn from fights between cocks. In species in which a better proportion is observed, such fights can be caused only by a scarcity of females in relation to the number of males, or by the existence of periods during which females consistently reject the advances of all males, which amounts to a scarcity of females, for if each of them is sexually receptive during only two months of the year, it is as if, in this respect, their total number were reduced by five-sixths. Neither of these two cases is applicable to the human species, in which there are generally more females than males, and in which the females, unlike those of other species, have never been observed to have periods of heat and exclusion, even among savages. In some species, moreover, all individuals become inflamed at once, and there is then a terrible time of common ardor, of tumult, disorder, and combat. Such times are unknown to the human species, in which love is never periodical. We therefore cannot conclude, from certain animals' combats for possession of females, that the same thing would happen to man in the state of nature; and even if that conclusion were valid, there would still be no reason to believe that such strife would destroy the human race, since it does not destroy other species. It would obviously do less damage in the state of nature than it does in society, especially in countries that still attach some importance to morality, where the jealousy of lovers and the vengeance of husbands daily cause duels, murders, and even worse; where the duty of eternal fidelity only gives rise to adultery; and where the very laws of continence and honor necessarily increase debauchery and multiply the number of abortions.

Let us conclude that, wandering in the forests, without industry, speech, a fixed dwelling, war, or ties of any kind, with no need of his fellow creatures and no desire to harm them, perhaps not even recognizing any of them individually, self-sufficient and subject to few passions, savage man had only the knowledge and feelings that were appropriate to his state; that he felt only his real needs and took notice only of what he considered important for him to see; and that his intelligence made no more progress than his vanity. If by chance he made a discovery, he was all the less able to communicate it to others because he did not even know his own children. Every art perished with its inventor. There was neither education nor progress; generations succeeded one another fruitlessly: Since each one always started from the same point, centuries went by without any change in the crudeness of the earliest times; the species was already old, and man still remained a child.

I have dwelt at such length on the supposition of that primordial condition because, having ancient errors and inveterate prejudices to destroy, I felt that I ought to dig down to the root and show, by depicting the true state of nature, how far even natural inequality is from having as much reality and influence in that state as our writers maintain.

It is easy to see that many of the differences among men which are regarded as natural are actually the work of habit and the various ways of life that men adopt in society. Whether one has a robust or a delicate constitution, for example, and the strength or weakness that goes with it, is often determined more by whether one was brought up in a harsh or an effeminate manner than by the original attributes of the body. The same is true of mental abilities. Not only does education make the difference between cultivated and uncultivated minds, but it also increases the differences among the former, in proportion to their various degrees of culture, for if a giant and a dwarf are walking on the same road, each step that they both take places the giant farther ahead of the dwarf. Now if we compare the prodigious diversity of educations and ways of life that exists in the civil state with the simplicity and uniformity of animal and savage life, in which all individuals eat the same foods, live in the same way, and do exactly the same things, we can understand how much smaller the differences among men must be in the state of nature than in that of society, and how greatly the natural inequalities of the human race must be augmented by socially created inequalities.

But even if nature were as partial in distributing her gifts as she is claimed to be, what advantages would the most favored men enjoy, to the detriment of others, in a state that would allow almost no kind of relations between them? Where there is no love, what is the advantage of beauty? Of what use is wit to those who do not speak, or guile to those who have no dealings with others? I often hear it said that the strong will oppress the weak, but I would like to know what is meant by the word "oppress." Some will dominate violently, the others will groan in servitude, subjected to all their whims. That is precisely what I observe among us; but I do not see how it could be said of savage man, to whom it would be difficult even to explain the meaning of servitude and domination. One man may be able to seize the fruit that another has gathered, the game he has killed, or the cave in which he has taken shelter; but how can he ever succeed in making him obey him, and what bonds of dependency can there be among men who have no possessions? If I am driven from one tree, I have only to go to another; if I am tormented in one place, what is to prevent me from going elsewhere? If there should be a man so much stronger than I am, and furthermore so depraved, so lazy and cruel, that he forces me to provide for his sustenance while he remains idle, he must resign himself to never taking his eyes off me for a moment, and keeping me carefully bound while he sleeps, for fear that I may escape, or kill him; in short, he must voluntarily submit to a hardship greater than the one he seeks to avoid, and the one he imposes on me. After all that, if he relaxes his vigilance for an instant, if an unexpected noise makes him look away from me, I will run off; as soon as I have gone twenty paces into the forest, my chains will be broken and he will never see me again.

Without my discussing such details at unnecessary length, it should be clear to anyone that since the bonds of servitude are formed only by men's mutual dependence and the reciprocal needs that unite them, it is impossible for one man to enslave another without having first made himself necessary to him. Since this cannot occur in the state of nature, everyone in that state is free of domination by others, and the law of the strongest is inoperative.

Having demonstrated that inequality is scarcely felt in the state of nature, and that its influence is almost nonexistent, I must next show its origin and describe its progress in the successive developments of the human mind. Having shown that perfectibility, the social virtues, and the other faculties that natural man possessed in latent form could never have developed of themselves, that they required the fortuitous concurrence of a number of extraneous causes which might never have arisen and without which man would have remained eternally in his original condition, I must next consider and correlate the various accidents that may have improved human reason while deteriorating the species, made man malicious while making him sociable, and, from that remote beginning, brought him and the world to the point where we see them now.

I admit that there are several different ways in which the events I am going to describe may have happened, and that I can choose among them only on the basis of conjectures; but such conjectures become reasons when they are the most probable that can be derived from the nature of things and the only means we can have of discovering the truth, and the consequences I intend to deduce from mine will not be conjectural, for on the principles I have just established, it would be impossible to construct any other system which would not provide me with the same results, and from which I could not draw the same conclusions.

This will make it unnecessary for me to show in detail that the passing of time compensates for the unlikelihood of events; that very slight causes can be surprisingly powerful when they act unceasingly; that there are hypotheses which cannot be destroyed, even though they cannot be given the certainty of facts; that when two facts given as real are to be connected by a series of intermediate facts that are unknown or regarded as such, it is the task of history to provide the connecting facts when possible; that when historical evidence is lacking, it is the task of philosophy to describe facts which may have formed the connection; and finally, that in the case of events, similarity reduces the facts to a much smaller number of different classes than one might imagine. It is enough for me to have presented these ideas to the consideration of my judges, and to have seen to it that the general reader will have no need to consider them.

PART TWO

The first man who, having enclosed a piece of land, took it into his head to say, "This is mine," and found people simple enough to believe him, was the true founder of civil society. The human race would have been spared endless crimes, wars, murders, and horrors if someone had pulled up the stakes or filled in the ditch and cried out to his fellow men, "Do not listen to this impostor! You are lost if you forget that the fruits of the earth belong to everyone, and the earth to no one!" But it is highly probable that by then things had already reached a point where they could no longer continue as they had been, for this idea of property, depending on many prior ideas which could only have arisen successively, was not formed all at once in the human mind. Men had to make great progress, acquire many kinds of knowledge and skill, and transmit and augment them from one age to another, before they reached that final stage in the state of nature. Let us therefore go farther back and try to consider that slow succession of events and discoveries from a single point of view, in their most natural order.

Man's first feeling was that of his own existence; his first concern was self-preservation. The earth produced everything he needed, and instinct prompted him to make use of it. Hunger and other appetites made him successively experience different ways of existing. There was one which invited him to perpetuate his species, and that blind urge, devoid of any sentiment of the heart, led to a purely animal act. Once their need had been satisfied, the two sexes ceased paying any attention to each other; even the child no longer meant anything to its mother as soon as it could do without her.

Such was the condition of earliest man. It was the life of an animal limited at first to pure sensations. Far from even thinking of forcing anything from nature, he scarcely took advantage of the gifts she offered him. But he soon encountered difficulties and had to learn to overcome them. The height of trees that prevented him from gathering their fruit, the competition of other animals seeking the same food, the ferocity of those intent on killing him—everything obliged him to develop his physical abilities. He had to become vigorous in combat, agile, and swift-footed. He soon found natural weapons: stones and clubs. He learned to surmount the obstacles of nature, to fight other animals when necessary, to compete even with other men for his sustenance, and to make up for what he had to yield to those stronger than himself.

As the human race multiplied, its cares increased. Differences in terrains, climates, and seasons must have forced men to alter their ways of living. Barren years, long, harsh winters, and hot summers that seared everything made new skills necessary. On the seashore and the banks of rivers, they invented the hook and line, and became fishermen and fish-eaters. In cold regions they covered themselves with the skins of the animals they had killed. Lightning, a volcano, or some lucky accident made them acquainted with fire, a new resource against the rigors of winter. They learned to conserve it, then to reproduce it, and finally to use it for cooking meat, which they had previously eaten raw.

As man repeatedly interacted with various living beings and observed their interactions with one another, he must naturally have been led to perceive certain relations. These relations, which we express by the words "large," "small," "strong," "weak," "fast," "slow," "cowardly," "brave," and so on, were compared when necessary, almost unthinkingly, and finally produced in him a kind of reflection, or rather an automatic prudence which indicated to him the precautions that were most important for his security.

The new understanding that resulted from this development increased his superiority to other animals by making him aware of it. He became skilled in setting traps for them and outwitted them in countless ways. Although some surpassed him in speed or strength, in time he became the master of those that could be useful to him, and the scourge of those that could harm him. Thus his first contemplation of himself gave him his first surge of pride. Still scarcely able to grasp the concept of a hierarchical order, he saw that his species ranked above all others, and this was the remote beginning of the idea of rank among individuals.

Although his fellow men were not to him what ours are to us, and although he had little more to do with them than with other animals, they were not forgotten in his observations. The conformities that he eventually perceived among them, and between himself and his female, made him judge those that he did not perceive. Seeing that others all acted as he would have done in similar circumstances, he concluded that their ways of thinking and feeling were the same as his own. When this important truth had been firmly established in his mind, an intuition that was as reliable as dialectical reasoning and more rapid, prompted him to behave toward them in accordance with the rules best suited to furthering his own advantage and security.

Taught by experience that love of well-being is the sole motive of human actions, he was able to distinguish the rare occasions when mutual interest ought to make him rely on the assistance of his fellow men, and the still rarer occasions when competition ought to make him wary of them. In the first case, he joined them in a herd, or at most in some sort of free association that obligated no one and lasted only as long as the temporary need that had formed it. In the second case, everyone sought his own advantage, either by open force, if he believed himself capable of it, or by adroitness and cunning, if he felt that he was too weak to do otherwise.

That is how men may have gradually acquired a crude idea of mutual commitments and the advantage of fulfilling them, but only insofar as their present and obvious interest required it, because they knew nothing of foresight, and far from concerning themselves with the distant future, they did not even think of the next day. If a group of them set out to take a deer, they were fully aware that they would all have to remain faithfully at their posts in order to succeed; but if a hare happened to pass near one of them, there can be no doubt that he pursued it without a qualm, and that once he had caught his prey, he cared very little whether or not he had made his companions miss theirs.

It is easy to understand that such undertakings did not require a language much more refined than that of crows and monkeys, which troop together in almost the same

way. For a long time the universal language must have
been composed of inarticulate cries, many gestures, and a
few imitative noises. When these were augmented in each
country by a few conventional articulate sounds, whose establishment, as I have already said, is not very easy to explain, there were individual languages, crude and imperfect, similar to those still spoken by various savage peoples
today.

Urged on by the passing of time, the great number of
things I have to say, and the almost imperceptible rate of
the progress that took place at the beginning, I am swiftly
passing over multitudes of centuries; for the more slowly
events succeeded one another, the more rapidly they can
be described.

These first advances finally enabled men to make others
more quickly. The more their minds were enlightened, the
more their skills were improved. They ceased sleeping under trees or in caves and found various tools of hard,
sharp stone which they used for cutting wood, digging,
and making huts of branches, which they later learned to
cover with clay and mud. This was the period of a first
revolutionary change that established and distinguished
families, and introduced a kind of property, already a
source of much quarreling and fighting. However, since
the strongest were no doubt the first to make dwellings
that they felt capable of defending, we may assume that
the weak found it quicker and safer to imitate them,
rather than trying to dislodge them; and as for those who
already had huts, none of them must have had any great
inclination to take possession of his neighbor's, less because it did not belong to him than because he did not
need it, and because he could not have seized it without
the danger of a fierce fight with the family that occupied
it.

The first developments of the heart were the result of a
new situation in which husbands and wives, fathers and
children, were united in a common dwelling. The habit of
living together gave rise to the sweetest feeling known to
man: conjugal love and paternal love. Each family became a small society, all the better united because mutual
attachment and freedom were its only ties. This was the
time when the first differences appeared in the two sexes'
ways of living, which had previously been the same. The
women grew more sedentary and became accustomed to

keeping the hut and the children while the men went off in search of food for all. With their somewhat softer life, both sexes began to lose some of their ferocity and vigor; but while individuals became less capable of fighting wild beasts separately, it was easier for them to assemble to resist them in common.

In this new state, with a simple and solitary life, very few needs, and implements that they had invented to provide for those needs, men had abundant leisure and used it to procure various kinds of conveniences that had been unknown to their forefathers. This was the first yoke that they had unwittingly imposed on themselves, and the first source of evils that they prepared for their descendants. For besides continuing to soften their bodies and minds, through habit these conveniences lost all their charm and degenerated into real needs, so that the pain of being deprived of them was much greater than the pleasure of having them, and men were unhappy to lose them without being happy to possess them.

We can see a little better at this point how the use of speech gradually arose, or became improved, within each family; and we can also conjecture how various particular causes may have extended language and accelerated its progress by making it more necessary. Great floods or earthquakes caused inhabited areas to be surrounded by water or precipices; upheavals of the earth broke off parts of the mainland and made them islands. It is clear that a common language must first have been formed among men thus brought together and forced to live with one another, rather than among those who wandered freely in the forests of the mainland. It is therefore quite possible that after their first attempts at seafaring, islanders brought the use of speech to other men; and it is at least highly probable that society and languages came into existence on islands and were well developed there before they became known on the mainland.

Everything now began to take on a new aspect. After having previously roamed the forests, men became more settled, slowly began coming together in different bands, and finally formed in each region a separate nation, with shared customs and a distinctive character, unified not by regulations and laws, but by a single way of life, the same kinds of food, and the common influence of climate. With time, permanent proximity could not fail to bring about certain connections among different families. Young people of both sexes lived in neighboring huts; the fleeting relations demanded by nature soon led them, by way of regular contact with each other, to form equally pleasant and more lasting relations. They became accustomed to considering different men or women and making comparisons; they gradually acquired ideas of merit and beauty that produced feelings of preference. Seeing each other often gave them a need to continue seeing each other. A sweet, tender feeling permeated their souls, and was turned into an impetuous fury by the slightest opposition. Jealousy was thus born with love; discord triumphed, and the gentlest of passions received sacrifices of human blood.

As ideas and feelings succeeded one another, as the mind and the heart grew more active, the human race continued to become more sociable. Connections were extended, ties became closer. People acquired the habit of gathering in front of their huts or around a large tree; singing and dancing, true children of love and leisure, became the amusement, or rather the occupation, of idle men and women who had formed themselves into groups. Each began looking at the others and wanting them to look at him; public esteem came to be valued, and it went to those who were the best singers or dancers, the most beautiful or handsome, the strongest, the most dexterous, or the most eloquent. This was the first step toward inequality, and also toward vice. From these first preferences arose vanity and contempt, on the one hand, and shame and envy, on the other; and the fermentation caused by these new leavens finally produced compounds that were deadly to happiness and innocence.

As soon as men had begun evaluating each other and the idea of esteem had been formed in their minds, everyone claimed a right to it and it was no longer possible to withhold it from anyone with impunity. Hence came the first duties of civility, even among savages; and hence any deliberate wrong that was done to someone became an outrage, for besides being harmed by it, he also saw it as evidence of contempt for him, which was often more intolerable than the harm itself. Each man punished contempt that had been shown for him in a manner proportionate to the esteem in which he held himself; it was thus that vengeance became terrible, and men bloodthirsty and cruel. This is precisely the stage that has been reached by

most of the savage peoples known to us. Because some
writers have not made adequate distinctions among their
ideas, and have not discerned how far these peoples already are from the first state of nature, they have hastily
concluded that man is naturally cruel and needs political
rule to keep his cruelty under control. The fact is that
nothing is gentler than man in his original state; placed by
nature at an equal distance from the stupidity of brutes
and the pernicious understanding of man in the civil state,
and limited by both instinct and reason to warding off
dangers that threaten him, he is restrained by natural
compassion from harming others needlessly, even if he has
been harmed by them. For, according to the axiom of the
wise Locke, "Where there is no property there is no injustice."

But it must be noted that early society, and the relations already established among men, required qualities
different from those given to them by their original constitution. When morality had begun to be introduced into human acts and, before the existence of laws, each man was
the sole judge and avenger of offenses committed against
him, the goodness that had suited the state of nature was
not the kind that was called for by the newborn society.
Punishments had to become more severe as opportunities
for offenses became more frequent, and fear of vengeance
had to perform the restraining function of law. Thus, although men had become more irascible and natural compassion had already deteriorated to some extent, this
period of development of human faculties, midway between the indolence of the original state and the irrepres-
sible activity of our egotism, must have been mankind's
happiest and most stable epoch. The more we reflect on it,
the more clearly we see that this state was the least subject to upheavals and the best for man, and that he must
have left it as the result of some unfortunate accident
which, for the common good, should never have happened. The example of savages, most of whom have been
found in this state, seems to confirm the view that the human race was meant to remain in it forever, that it is the
true youth of the world, and that while all later advances
have appeared to be so many steps toward the perfection
of the individual, they have actually been leading toward
the decay of the species.

As long as men were content with their rustic huts, as

long as they limited themselves to making clothes of animal skins sewn together with thorns or fish bones, to adorning themselves with feathers and shells, painting their bodies in various colors, improving or embellishing their bows and arrows, using sharp-edged stones as tools for making fishing boats and crude musical instruments; in short, as long as they limited themselves to artifacts that could be made by one man, and to arts that did not need the concurrence of several hands, they were as free, healthy, good, and happy as their nature permitted them to be, and they continued to enjoy the pleasures of independent intercourse with one another. But as soon as one man needed another's help, as soon as one man realized that it was useful to have enough provisions for two, equality disappeared, property came into being, work became necessary, and vast forests were changed into smiling fields which man had to water with his sweat, and in which slavery and poverty soon germinated and grew with the crops.

Metallurgy and agriculture were the two arts whose invention produced this great revolution. To the poet it is gold and silver, but to the philosopher it is iron and grain that made men civilized and brought on the downfall of the human race. They were both unknown to the savages of America, who for that reason are still savages. Other peoples seem to have remained barbarians as long as they practiced one of those arts without the other. And perhaps one of the best reasons why Europe has been, if not longer, at least more constantly and better civilized than any other part of the world, is that it is both the most abundant in iron and the most fertile in grain.

It is very difficult to conjecture how men first came to know and use iron, for it is impossible to believe that, of themselves, they thought of mining ore and preparing it for smelting, before knowing what the result would be. On the other hand, it is all the more implausible to attribute the discovery to an accidental fire, because mines are formed only in arid regions that are bare of trees and plants; it almost seems as if nature had taken precautions to withhold that fateful secret from us. There remains only the extraordinary possibility that a volcano ejecting molten metal may have been observed by men who conceived the idea of imitating that operation of nature. We must further assume that they were industrious enough to undertake such a laborious task, and had the great foresight that they would have needed in order to realize the advantages they could gain from it, which almost necessarily presupposes minds more highly developed than theirs must have been.

As for agriculture, its principle was known long before its practice was established; it is scarcely possible that men, constantly occupied in obtaining food from trees and plants, should not have soon gained some understanding of the ways in which nature assures the propagation of plant life. But they probably did not begin to turn their industry in that direction until very late, either because trees, which along with hunting and fishing supplied their food, had no need of their care; or because they did not know how to use grain, or had no implements with which to cultivate it; or, finally, because they had no means of preventing others from appropriating the fruits of their labor. We may assume that when they became more industrious, they began by cultivating a few vegetables or roots around their huts, using sharp stones and pointed sticks, long before they knew how to prepare grain and had the implements necessary for cultivation on a large scale. Moreover, to sow a field for such cultivation, one must resolve to lose something in the present in order to gain much more in the future, and this attitude is alien to the mind of savage man, who, as I have said, finds it very difficult even to think in the morning of what he will need at night.

The invention of other arts was therefore necessary to make the human race apply itself to the art of agriculture. When men were needed for smelting and forging iron, others had to feed them. The more the number of artisans increased, the fewer hands there were to obtain food for the community, with no decrease in the number of mouths to feed; and since the artisans required food in exchange for their iron, the others finally found means of using iron to increase the amount of food available. Thus plowing and agriculture arose, on the one hand, and the art of working metals and multiplying their uses, on the other.

The division of land necessarily followed from its cultivation, and once property had been recognized it gave rise to the first rules of justice, for if each man is to be assured of what is rightfully his, all must be able to have something. Furthermore, when men began to look forward into the future and realize that they had something to lose, they all had reason to fear reprisals for any wrongs they might do to others. This origin is all the more natural because it is impossible to imagine property arising from anything but labor, since the only way in which a man can take possession of something he has not made is to put his own work into it. It is work alone that gives a farmer title to the produce of the land he has tilled, and consequently to the land itself, at least until he has harvested his crop. If this possession is continued uninterruptedly from year to year, it is easily transformed into ownership. When the ancients, says Grotius, called Ceres "the lawgiver" and gave the name of Thesmaphoria to a festival celebrated in her honor, they implied that the division of land had produced a new kind of right: the right of property, different from that which derives from natural law.

Things in this state might have remained equal if abilities had been equal and if, for example, the use of iron and the consumption of food had always remained in the same proportion. But this proportion, which nothing worked to preserve, was soon broken. The strongest did more work; the most skillful turned their efforts to better advantage; the most ingenious found ways to shorten their labor; the farmer needed more iron, or the blacksmith more grain; and doing equal amounts of work, some prospered while others were barely able to stay alive. It is thus that natural inequality gradually becomes accentuated by inequalities of exchange, and differences among men, developed by differences in circumstances, become more noticeable and more permanent in their efforts, and begin to influence the fate of individuals in the same proportion.

Things having reached this point, it is easy to imagine the rest. I shall not take time to describe the successive inventions of the other arts, the progress of language, the testing and employment of talents, the inequailty of fortunes, the use or abuse of wealth, and all the details connected with them, which the reader can easily supply for himself. I shall limit myself to taking a glance at the human race in that new state of affairs.

Let us assume, then, that all human faculties had developed, memory and imagination were functioing, egotism had come into play, reason had become active, and the mind had almost reached the greatest perfection of which it was capable. Let us assume that all natural qualities were in action, and that each man's rank and condition had been established, on the basis not only of his property and his power to help or harm others, but also of his wit, beauty, strength, skill, merit, and talent. Since these were the only qualities that could win respect, it soon became necessary for him either to have them or seem to have them; for his own advantage, he had to show himself as different from what he actually was. Being and appearing became two quite different things, and from that distinction came ostentation, deceptive guile, and all the vices that follow in their wake. On the other hand, whereas man had previously been free and independent, his multitude of new needs now placed him in subjection to all of nature, so to speak, and especially to his fellow men. He became their slave, in a sense, even when he became their master: If he was rich, he needed their services; if he was poor, he needed their help; and no condition anywhere between those two extremes enabled him to do without them. He therefore had to be constantly seeking to make them take an interest in his fate and see their advantage, real or apparent, in working to further his. This made him crafty and devious with some, harsh and imperious with others, and forced him to deceive all those whom he needed, when he could not make them fear him and did not feel that it was to his interest to be useful to them. Finally, consuming ambition, a drive to raise the relative level of their fortunes, less from real need than from a desire to place themselves above others, aroused in all men a vile inclination to harm one another, a secret jealousy that was all the more dangerous because it often wore the mask of benevolence in order to strike its blow more safely; in short, there was competition and rivalry on the one hand, opposition of interests on the other, and always the hidden desire to profit at the expense of others. All these evils were the first effect of property, and the inseparable accompaniments of incipient inequality.

Before the invention of signs to represent wealth, it could scarcely have consisted of anything but land and livestock, the only real property that men can have. When inheritances had grown in number and size to the point where they covered all the land and bordered on one another, a man could increase his property only at the expense of others. Those who were excluded from ownership, who because of weakness or indolence had acquired nothing, became poor without having lost anything, because while everything around them was changing, they themselves had not changed. They were forced to receive or steal their sustenance from the rich, and this gave rise, according to differences of character, to domination and servitude, or violence and theft. As soon as the rich had discovered the pleasure of dominating, they disdained all others; using their present slaves to acquire new ones, they thought only of subjugating their neighbors, like those ravenous wolves which, once they have tasted human flesh, reject all other food and seek only to devour men.

Thus, when both the poorest and the most powerful men had come to regard their poverty or their power as a kind of right to take the belongings of others which was equivalent, in their view, to the right of property, the destruction of equality was followed by terrible disorders; and it was thus that the usurpations of the rich, the banditry of the poor, and the unbridled passions of both, stifling natural compassion and the still weak voices of justice, made men grasping, ambitious, and malicious. Between the right of the strongest and the right of first occupancy, there arose constant conflicts which inevitably led to fighting and murder. Nascent society gave way to the most horrible state of war; the human race, degraded and devastated, unable to retrace its steps or give up the unfortunate acquisitions it had made, and working only for its shame by misusing the faculties that honor it, brought itself to the brink of ruin. "Terrified by this new evil, rich and miserable, he wants to flee from wealth, and now hates what he once desired."

It is impossible that men should not eventually have begun to reflect on this wretched situation and on the calamities that overwhelmed them. The rich, especially, must soon have become aware of how disadvantageous it was for them to be in a state of incessant warfare whose cost was borne by them alone, and in which the risk of death was common to all, while the risk of losing property was individual. Moreover, no matter how they might try to place their usurpations in a favorable light, they knew that they rested on a precarious and spurious title, and that since they had acquired them only by force, they would have no right to complain if they were taken away from them by force. Even those who had become rich only through their own industry could scarcely base their ownership on a better title. It was useless for them to say, "I built this wall myself; I earned this land by my own work," because others could reply to them, "Who marked off the boundaries for you, and by what right do you expect to be paid at our expense for work that we never forced you to do? Do you not see that many of your brothers are dying or suffering for lack of what you have too much of? Only the express and unanimous consent of the whole human race could have entitled you to take more from the common resources than what you require for your own needs." Lacking valid arguments to justify himself and sufficient forces to defend himself; easily able to crush an individual, but crushed himself by troops of bandits; alone against everyone, and unable, because of mutual jealousy, to unite with his equals against enemies who were united by the common hope of pillage, the rich man, pressed by necessity, finally devised the most shrewdly conceived plan that ever entered the human mind: to employ in his favor the very strength of those who attacked him, to turn his adversaries into his defenders, to instill different principles into them, and to give them different institutions that would be as favorable to him as natural right was unfavorable.

With this in mind, after having depicted to his neighbors the horrors of a situation which armed them all against each other and made their possessions as burdensome as their needs, and in which no one could find security in either wealth or poverty, he easily invented specious arguments to make them accept his plan. "Let us unite," he said to them, "to protect the weak from oppression, restrain the ambitious, and assure everyone of possessing what belongs to him; let us institute rules of justice and peace that will be binding on everyone and give preference to no one, and will to some extent make up for the whims of fortune by subjecting both the weak and the strong to mutual obligations. In short, rather than turning our forces against each other, let us assemble them in a supreme power that will govern us in accordance with wise laws, protect and defend all members of the association, repulse our common enemies, and keep us always in harmony."

Much less than an equivalent of this speech was needed to convince men who were so unsophisticated and easy to lead astray, and who, moreover, had too many disputes to settle among themselves to do without arbitrators, and too much greed and ambition to do without masters for very long. They all hastened to enchain themselves, believing that they were assuring their freedom; for although they had enough intelligence to realize the advantages of a political establishment, they did not have enough experience to foresee its dangers. Those most capable of anticipating abuses were precisely those who expected to profit from them; and even the wisest saw that they had to resign themselves to sacrificing part of their freedom to save the rest, as a wounded man allows his arm to be cut off to save the rest of his body.

Such was, or probably was, the origin of society and laws, which gave new fetters to the weak and new strength to the rich, permanently destroyed natural freesom, established the law of property and inequality forever, turned adroit usurpation into an irrevocable right, and for the advantage of a few ambitious men, subjected all others to unending work, servitude, and poverty. It is easy to see how the establishment of one society made others necessary, for if men were to hold their own against united forces, they had no choice but to unite theirs also. Societies rapidly multiplied and expanded until they covered the whole surface of the earth; it was no longer possible for a man to find any place in the world where he could escape servitude and withdraw his head from beneath the sword that everyone always saw suspended above him, often precariously. When civil laws had thus become the common rule of all citizens, the law of nature subsisted only among the different societies, where, under the name of the law of nations, it was tempered by a few tacit agreements to make commerce possible and serve as a substitute for natural compassion, which, between one society and another, lost nearly all the strength it had between one man and another, and no longer exists in that form except in a few great cosmopolitan souls who cross the imaginary barriers that separate peoples, and following the example of the Sovereign Being who created them, include the whole human race in their benevolence.

Remaining thus in the state of nature among themselves, societies soon began to feel the effects of the disadvantages that had forced individuals to leave that state, and it became even more harmful among those great bodies than it had been among the individuals who composed them. Hence came the national wars, battles, murders, and reprisals which offend reason and make nature shudder, and all those horrible prejudices which cause the shedding of human blood to be regarded as an honor and a virtue. Even the most decent citizens learned to consider killing their fellow men as one of their duties. Finally men began slaughtering one another by the thousands, without knowing why, and more murders were committed in one day of combat, and more atrocities in the capture of a single town, than had been committed in the state of nature during many centuries, all over the world. Such were the first perceptible results of the division of the human race into different societies. Let us return to the founding of those societies.

I know that a number of writers have attributed other origins to political societies, such as conquests by the strongest men, or the union of the weak. So far as what I wish to establish is concerned, it makes no difference which of these origins is chosen. It seems to me, however, that the one I have just described is the most natural, for the following reasons. (1) In the first case, since the right of conquest is not a true right, it could not have been the basis of any other; the conqueror and the conquered people remained in a state of war, unless the people, restored to full freedom, voluntarily chose its conqueror as its leader. At that point, since whatever agreements had been made were founded on violence and were *ipso facto* invalid, there could have been no real society or body politic, and no other law than the law of the strongest. (2) The words "strong" and "weak" are ambiguous in the second case. In the interval between the establishment of the right of property or of first occupancy and that of political governments, the meanings of these words are better expressed by "rich" and "poor," for before the existence of laws a man could subjugate his equals only by attacking their possessions or giving them a share of his own. (3) Since the poor had nothing to lose but their freedom, it would have been sheer madness on their part to give up their only possession voluntarily, without gaining anything in exchange. But since the rich were, so to speak, sensitive in all parts of their possessions, it was much easier to hurt them and consequently they had to take more precautions to protect themselves. And finally, it is reasonable to assume that something was invented by those to whom it was beneficial, rather than by those to whom it was harmful.

At its inception, government had no fixed, stable form. Lacking philosophy and experience, men could see only present evils, and thought of remedying others only as they arose. Despite all the efforts of the wisest lawgivers, the political state remained imperfect because it was almost the work of chance. Since it had been badly begun, time could only reveal defects in it and suggest remedies, without ever being able to correct its basic flaws. Men were constantly patching it up, whereas they should first have cleared the ground and discarded all the old materials, then built a good edifice, as Lycurgus did in Sparta. At first, society consisted only of a few general agreements that everyone obligated himself to keep, with the whole community guaranteeing them with regard to each individual. Experience had to show how weak such a constitution was, and how easily violaters could avoid conviction or punishment when the public alone had to be the witness and judge of their misdeeds; the law had to be evaded in countless ways; and finally, drawbacks and disorders had to multiply continually, before anyone thought of giving the dangerous trust of public authority to individuals and empowering magistrates to enforce obedience to the decisions of the people. The idea that leaders were chosen before the confederation was formed, and that ministers of the law existed before the law itself, is a supposition that requires no serious rebuttal.

It would be equally absurd to believe that peoples began by throwing themselves into the arms of an absolute master, unconditionally and irrevocably, and that when proud and indomitable men decided to guarantee their common security, the first means of doing so that occurred to them was to plunge themselves into slavery. Why should they have voluntarily submitted to superiors, if not in order to be defended against oppression, and for protection of their possessions, their freedom, and their lives, which were, so to speak, the constituent elements of their being? Since, in relations between man and man, the worst that can happen is for one to find himself at the mercy of the other, would it not have been contrary to common sense for them to begin by surrendering to a leader the only things for whose preservation they needed his help? What equivalent could he have offered them in exchange for granting him such a right? And if he had dared to demand it on the pretext of defending them, would he not have immediately received the reply given in the fable: "What more will the enemy do to us?" It is therefore incontestable, and the fundamental axiom of all political right, that peoples gave themselves leaders because they expected them to defend their freedom, not to enslave them. "If we have a monarch," Pliny said to Trajan, "it is so that he will save us from having a master."

Our political theorists write the same kind of sophistries about love of freedom as our philosophers do about the state of nature. On the basis of things they see, they judge very different things which they do not see. They attribute a natural propensity for servitude to man because the men they observe endure their servitude so patiently. They do not realize that freedom is like innocence and virtue, in that only those who have it are aware of its value, and when they lose it they also lose their taste for it. "I know the delights of your country," Brasidas said to a satrap who was comparing life in Sparta to life in Persepolis, "but you cannot know the pleasures of mine."

As an unbroken horse bristles, paws the ground, and struggles violently against any attempt to put a bit in his mouth, while a trained horse remains docile under the whip and the spur, the barbarian will not bow his head to the yoke that civilized man bears without a murmur, and he prefers the stormiest freedom to peaceful slavery. It is therefore not from the degradation of subjugated peoples that we must judge man's natural disposition for or against servitude, but from the prodigious efforts that all free peoples have made to save themselves from oppression. I know that subjugated peoples are always boasting of the tranquillity they enjoy in their chains, and that "they give the name of peace to the most wretched slavery." But when I see free peoples sacrificing pleasures, peace, wealth, power, and life itself to the preservation of that good which is regarded so disdainfully by those who have lost it; when I see freeborn animals with such an abhorrence of captivity that they break their heads against the bars of their cages; and when I see multitudes of naked savages despising European pleasures and defying hunger, fire, the sword, and death solely to keep their independence, I feel that slaves are not entitled to argue about freedom.

As for paternal authority, which some writers see as the origin of absolute government and all society, it is enough to point out, without recapitulating the contrary demonstrations of Locke and Sidney, that nothing is farther removed from the ferocious spirit of despotism than the gentleness of that authority. It is more concerned with the advantage of him who obeys than with that of him who commands. By the law of nature, the father is master of the child only so long as his help is necessary; they then become equals, and the son, completely independent of the father, owes him only respect, not obedience, for gratitude is a duty that should be fulfilled, but not a right that can be demanded. Rather than saying that civil society derives from paternal authority, we ought to say that the latter draws its greatest strength from the former. No man was ever recognized as the father of several children until children began remaining with their fathers. The father's property, which is truly his to dispose of as he chooses, is the tie that keeps his children under his domination; he can make their share of it depend on the extent to which they please him by always deferring to his wishes. But far from being able to expect any such favor from a despot, his subjects are reduced to regarding it as a boon when he allows them to keep some of their own possessions, for they and everything they have are his property, or so he maintains. He is just when he despoils them, and merciful when he permits them to live.

If we were to continue thus examining fact from the standpoint of right, we would find no more solidity than truth in the view that tyranny was established voluntarily, and it would be difficult to demonstrate the validity of a supposed contract that binds only one of the parties, with all commitments on one side and none on the other, and can be prejudicial only to the party that assumes an obligation. This odious system is far from being, even today, that of wise and good monarchs, especially the Kings of France, as can be seen in various portions of their edicts, and particularly in the following passage from a famous document published in 1667 by order of Louis XIV and in his name:

Let it therefore not be said that the sovereign is not subject to the laws of his state, since the contrary is a truth of the law of nations. It has sometimes been attacked by flatterers, but good monarchs have always defended it as a tutelary divinity of their states. How much more legitimate it is to say, with the wise Plato, that the perfect felicity of a kingdom is achieved when the subjects obey the monarch, the monarch obeys the law, and the law is just and always directed to the public good!

I shall not pause here to examine whether, since freedom is the noblest human faculty, men do not degrade their nature, lower themselves to the level of beasts enslaved by instinct, and even offend their Creator when they unconditionally renounce the most precious of all his gifts, and consent to commit all the crimes that he has forbidden, to please a ferocious or mad master; or whether seeing his finest work destroyed must anger that sublime Artisan more than seeing it dishonored. I shall not appeal to the authority of Barbeyrac, who states emphatically, following Locke, that no man can sell his freedom to the point of making himself subject to an arbitrary power that can treat him according to its whims, "for," he adds, "that would be selling his own life, which he has no right to do." I shall ask only by what right a man who did not shrink from debasing himself to that point was able to subject his descendants to the same ignominy, depriving them, without their consent, of goods which they would not have owed to his generosity, and without which life itself is a burden to those who are worthy of it.

Pufendorf says that just as we may transfer our property to others by agreements and contracts, we may also surrender our freedom to someone. This, it seems to me, is very bad reasoning. For in the first place, any property that I transfer becomes completely foreign to me and I do not care whether or not it is abused, but it is important to me that my freedom shall not be abused, and I cannot expose myself to the possibility of becoming an instrument of crime without making myself guilty of any evil that I may be compelled to do. Furthermore, since the right of property is based only on human agreements, anyone may dispose of his possessions as he sees fit, but it is not the same with the essential gifts of nature, such as life and freedom: Although it is permissible to enjoy them, it is at least doubtful that anyone has a right to divest himself of them. If a man gives up his freedom, he degrades his being; if he gives up his life, he annihilates that being insofar as it is within his power to do so. Since no temporal good can make up for the loss of either, it would be an offense against both nature and reason to relinquish them at any price. But even if a man could alienate his freedom as he does his property, there would still be a great difference as far as his children were concerned. Children assume ownership of their father's property only by transfer of his right to it; freedom, however, is a gift that they receive from nature simply by virtue of being human, and their parents consequently have no right to deprive them of it. Therefore, as violence had to be done to nature in order to establish slavery, nature had to be changed in order to perpetuate it; the jurists who have gravely decided that the child of a slave woman is born a slave have stated, in effect, that a human being is not born human.

Thus it seems certain to me not only that governments did not begin with arbitrary power, whch is actually a perversion of them, an extreme limit that finally brings them back to the law of the strongest which they were originally intended to remedy, but that even if they had begun with such power, since it is by nature illegitimate it could not have served as the basis of social rights or, consequently, of artificial inequality.

I shall not at present enter into the inquiries that remain to be made concerning the nature of the fundamental agreement that underlies all government; I shall here limit myself, following the common opinion, to considering the establishment of the body politic as a real contract between the people and the leaders it chooses for itself, a contract by which both parties obligate themselves to observe the laws that are stipulated in it and form the bonds of their union. Since, with regard to social relations, the people has combined all its wills into one, all articles in which this will is explained become so many fundamental laws that obligate all members of the state without exception. One of these laws regulates the selection and power of magistrates who are charged with assuring execution of the rest. They are empowered to do whatever is necessary to maintain the constitution, but they are not authorized to change it. They are given honors designed to enhance respect for the law and its ministers, as well as personal prerogatives to compensate them for the arduous work required by good administration. Each magistrate, for his part, obligates himself to use the power entrusted to him only in accordance with the intentions of his constituents, to uphold their right to peaceful enjoyment of what belongs to them, and always to let the public good take precedence over his private interest.

Before the inevitable abuses of such a constitution had been shown by experience, or before knowledge of the human heart had caused them to be foreseen, it must have seemed all the better because those who were charged with its preservation were also those who had the greatest interest in it; for magistracy and the rights pertaining to it were based only on the fundamental laws, so that if those laws had been destroyed, the magistrates would immediately have ceased to be legitimate and the people would no longer have been obligated to obey them; and since the essence of a state is constituted not by the magistrates but by the laws, everyone would then have rightfully reverted to his natural freedom.

A little attentive reflection on all this will confirm it with new reasons, and consideration of the nature of the contract will show that it cannot be irrevocable; for if there were no superior power capable of ensuring the fidelity of the contracting parties and forcing them to fulfill their mutual commitments, they would be the sole judges of their own case, and each would always have the right to renounce the contract as soon as he felt that the other had violated its terms, or as soon as he ceased to find those terms to his liking. It seems that the right to abdicate may be founded on this principle. Considering only the human aspect of the institution, as we are doing here, it can be seen that if the magistrate, who holds all power and appropriates all the advantages of the contract, had the right to relinquish his authority, the people, which pays for all its leaders' mistakes and misconduct, should be all the more entitled to renounce its dependence. But the terrible dissensions and endless disorders that would necessarily arise from that dangerous power show, more than anything else, how greatly human governments needed a base more solid than reason alone, and how necessary it was for public peace that the divine will should intervene to give the sovereign authority a sacred and inviolable character that would deprive the subjects of the pernicious right to dispose of it. If religion had given only that benefit to men, it would be enough to make them all obliged to cherish and adopt it, even with its abuses, since it avoids even more bloodshed than fanaticism causes. But let us follow the thread of our hypothesis.

The various forms of government owe their origin to the greater or lesser differences that existed among individuals at the time when a state was founded. If one man was preeminent for his power, virtue, wealth, or prestige, he was elected the sole magistrate, and the state became monarchical. If several men, more or less equal among themselves, stood out above all the rest, they were elected jointly, and an aristocracy was created. Those whose wealth or abilities were less disproportionate, and who had remained closer to the state of nature, held the supreme administration in common and formed a democracy. Time showed which of these forms was most advantageous to men. Some peoples remained entirely under the rule of law, others soon came to obey masters. Citizens were intent on keeping their freedom; subjects thought only of taking away that of their neighbors, for they could not tolerate seeing others enjoy a good that they themselves had lost. In short, wealth and conquest arose on one side, happiness and virtue on the other.

In these different governments, all offices were at first elective. When wealth did not prevail, preference went to merit, which gives natural ascendancy, and to age, which gives experience in conducting affairs and cool-headedness in deliberations. The elders of the Hebrews, the gerontes of the Spartans, the senators of the Romans, and even the etymology of our word *seigneur,** show how greatly age was respected in the past. The more old men were chosen, the more often elections had to be repeated, and the more their drawbacks became a problem. Corruption appeared, factions came into being and developed bitter enmities, civil wars broke out; the blood of citizens was sacrificed to the supposed good of the state, and men were on the verge of falling back into the anarchy of earlier times. Ambitious leaders took advantage of these circumstances to perpetuate their offices within their own families; the citizens, already used to dependence, peace, and the conveniences of life, and already incapable of breaking their chains, consented to let their servitude be increased in order to make their tranquillity more secure. It was thus

---

*"Lord"; the word has the same etymology as the English "senior." (Translator's note.)

that leaders, having made their offices hereditary, became accustomed to regarding them as family possessions and themselves as the owners of the state, of which they had originally been only agents; to calling their fellow citizens their slaves; to counting them among their belongings, like cattle; and to calling themselves the equals of the gods, and kings of kings.

If we follow the progression of inequality through these various changes, we find that the establishment of law and the right of property was its first phase, the institution of magistracy its second, and the transformation of legitimate power into arbitrary power its third and last. The first gave rise to the distinction of rich and poor, the second to that of weak and powerful, and the third to that of master and slave, which is the ultimate degree of inequality and the one to which the others all lead, until new changes dissolve the government completely, or bring it back to legitimacy.

To understand why this progression is inevitable, we must consider not so much the reasons for the establishment of the body politic as the form it takes in operation and the disadvantages that follow from it, for the vices that make social institutions necessary are the same that make their abuses unavoidable. Except in the single case of Sparta, where the education of children was the main concern of the law, and where Lycurgus established a kind of morality that almost made laws superfluous, laws are less strong than passions and restrain men without changing them; it would therefore be easy to demonstrate that any government which unfailingly fulfilled the purpose for which it was created, without corruption or deterioration, would have been instituted unnecessarily, and that a country where no one evaded the law or misused public office would have no need of either magistrates or laws.

Political distinctions necessarily produce civil distinctions. The growing inequality between the people and its leaders is soon felt by individuals, and is modified among them in countless ways, according to passions, abilities, and circumstances. A magistrate cannot seize illegitimate power without being forced to share some of it with accomplices. Moreover, the citizens allow themselves to be oppressed only insofar as they are driven by blind ambition; looking more below themselves than above, they come to cherish domination more than independence, and they consent to bear chains in order to impose them on others. A man who does not seek to command is very difficult to reduce to obedience; the most adroit politician would never succeed in enslaving men who wanted only to be free. But inequality can easily be implanted among ambitious and cowardly souls who are always ready to run the risks of fortune and are almost as willing to serve as to dominate, depending on the vagaries of chance. Thus there must have come a time when the people was so beguiled that its leaders had only to say to the lowliest of men, "Be great, you and all your descendants," to make him appear great to everyone, including himself. And his descendants gained stature in proportion to the number of generations that separated them from him. The effect continued to increase as the cause grew more remote and obscure; the more worthless idlers a family could count among its ancestors, the more illustrious it became.

If this were the place to go into details, I could easily explain how, even with no intervention by the government, inequality in influence and authority is inevitable as soon as the union of individuals in a single society forces them to make comparisons among themselves and take into account the differences they discover in the course of their dealings with one another. These differences are of several kinds, but since wealth, nobility or rank, power, and personal merit are generally the main distinctions by which men are measured in society, I could show that the harmony or conflict of these various forces is the surest indication that a state is well or badly constituted. I could show that among these four kinds of inequality, personal qualities are the origin of all the others and wealth is the one to which they are all eventually reduced, for, being the most immediately useful and the easiest to transfer, it can readily be used to buy all the rest. This observation enables us to judge rather precisely the extent to which a people has departed from its original constitution, and how far it has moved toward the ultimate stage of corruption. I could point out how this universal desire for reputation, honors, and preferments, which consumes us all, exercises our abilities and powers and causes comparisons to be made among them; how it stimulates and multiplies the passions; and how, making all men competitors, rivals, or rather enemies, it daily causes setbacks, triumphs, and catastrophes of all kinds, by making so many aspirants run the same course. I could show that it is to this ardent desire to be talked about, this eagerness to distinguish ourselves which nearly always holds us in its grip, that we owe what is best and worst among men: our virtues and our vices, our knowledge and our errors, our conquerors and our philosophers; that is, a multitude of bad things and a few good ones. I could demonstrate, finally, that if we see a handful of rich and powerful men at the peak of eminence and fortune, while the great majority languish in obscurity and poverty, it is because the former value things only insofar as others are deprived of them; without changing their condition, they would cease to be happy if the people ceased to be wretched.

But these details alone could form the subject matter of a long book that would weigh the advantages and disadvantages of all governments with respect to the rights of the state of nature, and examine all the aspects under which inequality has appeared thus far and may appear in the future, according to the nature of governments and the changes in them that time will necessarily bring. We would see the multitude oppressed from within as the result of the very precautions it had taken against the dangers that threatened it from without; we would see oppression growing steadily, while the oppressed never knew where it would end or what legitimate means were left to them for stopping it; we would see national freedoms and the rights of citizens gradually dying out, and the protests of the weak treated as sedition; we would see politics restricting the honor of defending the common cause to a mercenary segment of the people; we would see this giving rise to the need for taxes, and the disheartened farmer leaving his fields, even in time of peace, abandoning his plow to gird on a sword; we would see the birth of the strange and baneful rules of the code of honor; we would see the defenders of the fatherland sooner or later becoming its enemies, constantly holding a dagger above their fellow citizens; and the time would come when they would be heard saying to the oppressor of their country, "If you order me to plunge my sword into my brother's chest or my father's throat, or even into the entrails of my pregnant wife, my arm will be reluctant to obey, but I will do it."

We would see a multitude of prejudices, equally contrary to reason, happiness, and virtue, arising from the extreme inequality of conditions and fortunes, the diversity of passions and abilities, useless or pernicious arts, and shallow knowledge. We would see leaders fomenting everything that might weaken united men by turning them against each other; everything that might give society apparent harmony while sowing seeds of real division; everything that might make the different social classes mistrust and hate each other by placing their rights and interests in opposition, thereby strengthening the power that restrained them all.

It is in the midst of these disorders and upheavals that despotism, gradually raising its hideous head and devouring everything good and healthy that it sees in any part of the state, finally succeeds in trampling the laws and the people underfoot and establishes itself on the ruins of the republic. The time that precedes this last change is a time of agitation and calamities, but in the end everything is swallowed up by the monster, and the people no longer has leaders or laws, but only a tyrant. From then on, also, there is no longer any question of morality and virtue, for despotism "can expect nothing from honor," and wherever it reigns it tolerates no other master; as soon as it speaks, integrity and duty lose all meaning, and its slaves can have no other virtue than blind obedience.

This is the final phase of inequality, and the extreme point that closes the circle and touches the point from which we started; it is here that individuals become equal again, because they are nothing, and since the subjects now have no other law than the will of their master and he has no other rule than his passions, all ideas of right and all principles of justice vanish again; it is here that everything reverts entirely to the law of the strongest, and consequently to a new state of nature that differs from the one with which we began, in that the first was the state of nature in its purity, while the second is the result of excessive corruption. Otherwise, however, there is so little difference between these two states, and the contract of government is so thoroughly dissolved by despotism, that the despot remains in power only so long as he is the strongest. If he is ousted, he has no right to complain of violence. An uprising that kills or dethrones a sultan is as legitimate as the acts by which he disposed of the lives and possessions of his subjects the day before. He maintained himself by force alone, and force alone has overthrown him. Everything thus happens in accordance with the natural order, and no matter what the outcome of these brief and frequent revolutions may be, no one can complain of the injustice of others, but only of his own imprudence or misfortune.

In thus discovering and following the lost and forgotten paths that must have led man from the natural state to the civil state, and in restoring, along with the intermediate positions that I have just marked, those which lack of time has made me omit, or which my imagination has not suggested to me, an attentive reader cannot fail to be struck by the vast distance that separates those two states. In that slow succession of events he will see the solution to a host of moral and political problems that philosophers cannot solve. He will realize that since the human race of one era is not the human race of another era, the reason why Diogenes did not find his man is that he was searching among his contemporaries for a man of a time that had passed. Cato, he will say, perished with Rome and freedom because he did not fit his time; that greatest of men only astonished a world that he would have ruled five centuries earlier. In short, he will show men's souls and passions gradually deteriorate until they can almost be said to have changed their nature; why our needs and pleasures eventually take new objects; and why, original man having vanished by degrees, society no longer offers to the eyes of the sage anything but an aggregation of artificial men and factitious passions that are the work of all those new relations and have no real foundation in nature. What reflection teaches us on this subject is fully confirmed by observation: Savage man and civilized man differ so greatly in the depths of their hearts and in their inclinations that what constitutes the supreme happiness of one would reduce the other to despair. Savage man is steeped in peace and freedom; he wants only to live and remain idle; not even the ataraxia of the Stoic can approach his profound indifference to every other object. Civilized man, on the other hand, is always active and restless, always sweating and tormenting himself to find still more laborious occupations. He continues working to the end, and even hastens his death to place himself in a situation that will permit him to live, or renounces life to acquire immortality. He pays court to men in high positions, whom he hates, and to the rich, whom he despises; he stops at nothing to obtain the honor of serving them; he haughtily boasts of his baseness and their patronage; and, proud of his slavery, he speaks scornfully of those who do not have the honor of sharing it. What a spectacle the arduous and envied labors of a European government minister would be to a Carib Indian! That indolent savage would prefer the cruelest death to the horror of such a life, which is often not even alleviated by the pleasure of doing good. But in order for him to see the object of all that concern, the words "power" and "repute" would have to have some meaning in his mind; he would need to learn that there is a kind of man who attaches importance to the attention of others and is able to draw happiness and self-satisfaction from what they say about him, rather than what he thinks of himself. Here is the real cause of all these differences: Savage man lives within himself, while social man, always outside himself, can live only in the opinion of others, and it is only from their judgment that he draws, so to speak, the feeling of his own existence. It is beyond my present subject to show how this frame of mind produces such indifference to good and evil, along with such lofty discourses on morality; how, since everything is reduced to appearances, everything becomes artificial and affected: honor, friendship, virtue, and often even our vices, which we eventually succeed in turning into reasons for boasting; how, in short, always asking others what we are and never daring to ask ourselves, in the midst of all our philosophy, benevolence, politeness, and sublime principles we have nothing but frivolous and deceptive appearances: honor without virtue, reason without wisdom, and pleasure without happiness. It is enough for me to have shown that this is not the original state of man, and that it is only the spirit of society, and the inequality that society engenders, which thus change and debase our natural inclinations.

I have tried to describe the origin and development of inequality, and the establishment and abuse of political societies, to the extent that they can be deduced from the nature of man solely by the light of reason, independently of sacred dogmas that give sovereign authority the sanction of divine right. It follows from this description that inequality, being almost negligible in the state of nature, owes its strength and growth to the development of our faculties and the progress of the human mind, and finally becomes stable and legitimate by the establishment of property and laws. It also follows that moral inequality, authorized only by socially prescribed right, is contrary to natural right whenever it is not accompanied by a proportionate degree of physical inequality. This is enough to determine what we ought to think, in this respect, of the kind of inequality that prevails in all civilized nations, because it is obviously contrary to the law of nature, however it may be defined, for a child to command an old man, for an imbecile to lead a wise man, and for a handful of people to wallow in luxury while the starving multitude lacks the necessities of life.

DISCOURSE

Which won the Prize of the Academy of Dijon in the year 1750, on this question Proposed by the Academy:

Has the restoration of the arts and sciences been conducive to the purification of morals?

———◆———

By a Citizen of Geneva

Here I am a barbarian because I am not understood.

—OVID

PREFACE

Here is one of the greatest and noblest questions that have ever been discussed. This discourse will not deal with those metaphysical subtleties that have spread into nearly all branches of literature and are not always absent from academic curricula; it will deal, rather, with one of those truths that are closely bound up with the happiness of the human race.

I foresee that I shall not readily be forgiven for the position I have dared to take. Directly opposing everything that is now most admired, I can expect only universal condemnation; I cannot count on the approval of the public because a few wise men have honored me with theirs. I have therefore resolved not to concern myself with pleasing superficial intellectuals or men of the world. There will always be men of the kind who remain in subjection to the opinions of their time, their country, and their social group. There are those who pass for freethinkers and philosophers today, but would have been regarded only as fanatics in the days of the Catholic League. No one should write for such readers if he wants to live beyond his own time.

One more remark and I shall finish. Not expecting the honor that was bestowed on me, after sending in this discourse I revised and expanded it to the point where it had almost become a new work. I now feel obliged to present it as it was when it received the prize. I have merely inserted a few footnotes and left two easily recognizable additions, of which the Academy might not have approved. I believe that fairness, respect, and gratitude require me to point this out.

DISCOURSE

> "We are deceived by the outward
> appearance of right."

Has the restoration of the arts and sciences been conducive to the purification or the corruption of morals? That is the question I am about to examine. What position shall I take on it? The position, gentlemen, of an honest man who knows nothing and esteems himself none the less for it.

I am aware that it will be difficult to adapt what I have to say to the tribunal before which I am appearing. How shall I dare to condemn the sciences before one of the most erudite assemblies in Europe, praise ignorance in a famous Academy, and reconcile contempt for study with respect for true scholars? I saw these incongruities from the start, and they did not dishearten me. "I shall not be mistreating science," I told myself, "I shall be defending virtue before virtuous men." Integrity is even dearer to upright men than erudition to the learned. What, then, do I have to fear? The sagacity of the assembly that will be listening to me? I do fear it, I confess, but because of the composition of the discourse, not the views of the speaker. Equitable sovereigns have never hesitated to pronounce judgment against themselves in dubious discussions, and a just claim has the greatest chance of being upheld when it is defended against a righteous and enlightened adversary who is the judge of his own case.

In addition to this consideration, which encourages me, there is another that is decisive to me: I know that when I have pleaded the cause of truth to the best of my natural ability, there is one prize which I cannot fail to receive, no matter how my efforts may be judged: I shall find it within my heart.

PART ONE

It is a great and noble spectacle to see man emerging from nothingness, so to speak, by his own efforts, dissipating by the light of his reason the thick darkness in which nature had enveloped him, rising above himself, soaring into the heavens by means of his mind, striding with giant steps, like the sun, across the vast reaches of the universe, and, what is still greater and more difficult, returning into himself to study man and know his nature, his duties, and his end. All these wonders have been renewed within the past few generations.

Europe had relapsed into the barbarism of the earliest ages. A few centuries ago, the peoples of this now enlightened part of the world were living in a state worse than ignorance. A kind of scientific jargon even more despicable than ignorance had usurped the name of knowledge and erected an almost insurmountable obstacle to its return. A revolution was needed to bring men back to common sense. When it finally came, it was from the least expected direction. It was the obtuse Mussulman, the eternal scourge of letters, who caused them to be reborn among us. The fall of the throne of Constantine brought the remaining fragments of ancient Greece to Italy, and France was in turn enriched by those precious relics. The sciences soon followed literature; the art of writing preceded the art of thinking, an order which may seem strange, but may be all too natural. The main advantage of communion with the Muses now became apparent: that of making men more sociable by giving them a desire to please one another with works worthy of their mutual approval.

The mind has its needs, as well as the body. Those of the body are the foundation of society; those of the mind create its amenities. Government and its laws provide for the security and well-being of men united in society, while literature, the sciences, and the arts, less despotic and more powerful, perhaps, strew garlands of flowers on the iron chains that bind them, make them forget the original freedom for which they seem to have been born, cause them to love their slavery, and turn them into what is known as a civilized people. Thrones were erected by need; the arts and sciences strengthen them. Powers of the earth, cherish talents and those who cultivate them.[1] Civilized peoples, cultivate them; to them, happy slaves, you owe the delicate, refined taste on which you pride yourselves, the gentleness of character and urbanity of manner which make your personal relations so easy and amiable; in short, you owe to them the appearance of all virtues, none of which you actually have.

It was by this kind of refinement, all the more gracious as it least affects to show itself, that Athens and Rome distinguished themselves in the vaunted days of their magnificence and glory, and it is no doubt in that respect that our time and our nation will rise above all others. A tone of philosophy without pedantry, a manner that is natural yet engaging, as far removed from German awkwardness as from Italian effusiveness—such are the fruits acquired by good education and improved by social intercourse.

How pleasant it would be to live among us if our outer appearances always mirrored what was in our hearts, if decorum were virtue, if our maxims were our rules of conduct, and if true philosophy were inseparable from the title of philosopher! But all those qualities are too seldom found together, and virtue almost never appears amid such great pomp. Luxurious clothes may indicate an opulent man, and elegant ones a man of taste, but a healthy and robust man is recognized by other signs: It is beneath the rustic attire of a plowman, not the gold braid of a courtier, that bodily strength and vigor are to be found. Finery is equally alien to virtue, which is the strength and vigor of the soul. The upright man is like a wrestler who prefers to fight naked: He scorns all those vile trappings which would hinder the use of his strength and were invented, in most cases, only to hide some deformity.

Before art had fashioned our manners and taught our passions to speak an artificial language, our habits were rustic but natural, and differences in behavior were obvious signs of differences in character. Human nature was basically no better than it is now, but men found security in being easily able to discern each other's feelings and intentions, and this advantage, whose values we no longer appreciate, spared them many vices.

Now that more subtle refinements and more delicate taste have reduced the art of pleasing to a set of rules, there is a base and deceptive uniformity in our behavior, and minds seem to have been cast in the same mold. Politeness and propriety make incessant demands on us; we always follow social usage, never our personal inclinations. We no longer dare to appear to be what we are. Under that constant constraint, the men who make up the herd known as society will always do the same things in the same circumstances, unless some more powerful cause drives them to do otherwise. Thus we can never be sure of whom we are dealing with, and to know our friends we must wait until some serious situation arises; that is, we must wait until it is too late, for it is precisely when such a situation arises that it is essential to know one's friends already.

What a train of vices accompanies this uncertainty! There can be no sincere friendship, no genuine esteem, no justified confidence. Suspicion, resentment, fear, coldness, reserve, hatred, and betrayal are always hidden behind that uniform and treacherous veil of politeness, behind that vaunted urbanity which we owe to the intellectual advances of our time. The name of the Master of the Universe is no longer profaned by oaths, but he is insulted by blasphemies that do offend our delicate ears. We do not boast of our merits, but we denigrate those of others. We do not hurl crude vituperation at our enemies, but we slander them adroitly. Hatred of other nations is dying out, but so is love of our own. Ignorance is despised, but it has been replaced by dangerous skepticism. Some excesses are banished and some vices are dishonored, but others are adorned with the name of virtues, and one must either have them or pretend to have them. Anyone who may wish to extol the moderation of our modern sages is free to do so, but for my part I see it only as a refinement of intemperance that is as unworthy of my praise as their artful simplicity.[2]

Such is the purity that our morals have acquired. It is thus that we have become virtuous men. Let literature, the arts, and the sciences claim the share they have had in that salutary achievement. I will add only one observation: Let us imagine an inhabitant of some remote country who judges European morals on the basis of the state of the sciences among us, the perfection of our arts, the propriety of our public entertainments, the refinement of our manners, the amiability of our conversations, our endless professions of good will, and those animated gatherings of people of all ages and conditions who seem eager to oblige each other from morning to night; such a foreigner would form an idea of our morals which would be directly contrary to what they actually are.

Where there is no effect, there is no cause to be sought; but here the effect is certain, the depravity is real, and our souls have been corrupted in proportion as our sciences and arts have advanced toward perfection. Will it be said that this is a misfortune peculiar to our time? No, gentlemen, the evils caused by our vain curiosity are as old as the world. The state of morals is as closely controlled by the progress of the arts and sciences as the daily ebb and flow of the tides by the moon. We have seen virtue flee as the light of the arts and sciences rose above our horizon, and the same phenomenon has been observed in all times and places.

Consider Egypt, that first school of mankind, that fertile land under a cloudless sky, that illustrious country from which Sesostris set forth to conquer the world. Egypt became the mother of philosophy and the fine arts, and soon afterward she was conquered by Cambyses, then the Greeks, the Romans, the Arabs, and finally the Turks.

Consider Greece, once peopled by heroes who twice vanquished Asia: first at Troy, then on their own soil. Her nascent literature had not yet corrupted her people's hearts; but the progress of the arts, the dissolution of morals, and the yoke of the Macedonian came in close succession, and Greece, always learned, pleasure-loving, and enslaved, gained nothing from any of her revolutions but a change of master. All the eloquence of Demosthenes was unable to revive a body that had been enervated by luxury and the arts.

It was in the time of men like Ennius and Terence that Rome, founded by a shepherd and made illustrious by tillers of the soil, began to degenerate. But after Ovid, Catullus, Martial, and that host of obscene writers whose very names are an offense to modesty, Rome, once the shrine of virtue, became a center of crime, an object of opprobrium to other nations, and the plaything of barbarians. That capital of the world finally fell under the yoke that she had imposed on so many peoples, and shortly before her fall she gave one of her citizens the title of Arbiter of Good Taste.

What shall I say of that metropolis of the Eastern Empire which, by its position, seemed destined to be the metropolis of the entire world; that refuge of the arts and sciences which had been banished from the rest of Europe, perhaps more by wisdom than by barbarism? The most shameless debauchery and corruption, the foulest betrayals, assassinations, and poisonings, an aggregation of all the most atrocious crimes—this is what makes up the history of Constantinople; this is the pure source of the enlightenment on which our age prides itself.

But why go back to remote times for proofs of a truth that is clearly demonstrated to us in the present? There is in Asia an immense country where learning is so honored that it takes men to the highest positions in the state. If the sciences purified morals, taught men to shed their blood for their country, and animated their courage, then the peoples of China ought to be virtuous, free, and invincible. But there is no vice that does not dominate them, no crime that is not common among them. If that vast empire could not be saved from the yoke of the crude and ignorant Tartars by the sagacity of its ministers, the supposed wisdom of its laws, and the great number of its inhabitants, of what use to it were all its scholars? What has it gained from all the honors heaped upon them, other than the distinction of being peopled by slaves and scoundrels?

Let us, by contrast, consider the morals of that small number of nations which, preserved from the contagion of vain knowledge, have by their virtues made themselves happy and set an example for other nations. Such were the early Persians, who formed a singular nation in which virtue was taught as science is now taught in Europe; they easily subjugated Asia and earned the glory of having the history of their institutions regarded as a philosophical novel. Such were the Scythians, of whom such magnificent praise has come down to us. Such were the ancient Germans, whose simplicity, innocence, and virtues were described with relief by a man who had grown weary of

writing about the crimes and infamies of an educated, opulent, and pleasure-seeking people. Such was even Rome,
in the time of her poverty and ignorance. And such is still
that rustic nation so renowned for its courage, which adversity has never overcome, and for its fidelity, which no
example has ever corrupted.[3]

It was not from stupidity that these peoples preferred
other activities to those of the mind. They knew that in
some countries there were idle men who spent their time
arguing about the supreme good, or vice and virtue, and
that those proud reasoners, lavishing the highest praise on
themselves, lumped other peoples together under the con-
temptuous name of barbarians. But they considered the
morals of those men and learned to despise their doctrines.[4]

Let us not forget that in the heart of Greece itself arose
that city as famous for its happy ignorance as for the wisdom of its laws, that republic of demigods rather than
men, so far superior did their virtues seem to anything human. O Sparta, you are an eternal rebuke to vain doctrines! While vices were being introduced into Athens under the guidance of the fine arts, and while her tyrant was
carefully gathering the works of the prince of poets, you
were expelling the arts and artists, the sciences and scholars, from your walls.

This difference was accentuated by later events. Athens
became the seat of refinement and good taste, the city of
orators and philosophers. The elegance of her buildings
was matched by that of her language. On all sides, one
could see canvas and marble animated by the hands of the
most accomplished masters. From Athens came those astonishing works that will always serve as models in corrupt ages. The picture of Sparta is less sumptuous.
"There," said other peoples, "men are born virtuous; the
very air of the city seems to inspire virtue." Her inhabitants have left us only the memory of their heroic acts.
Are such monuments worth less to us than the curious
marble relics that have come down to us from Athens?

It is true that a few Athenian wise men withstood the
general torrent and preserved themselves from vice in the
company of the Muses. But let us listen to the judgment
that the greatest and most unfortunate of them pronounced
on the artists and learned men of his time.

"I have examined poets," he said,*

and I consider them to be men whose talent deceives them and others; they present themselves as wise men, and are regarded as such, while in reality they are anything but wise.

From poets I turned to artists. No one was more ignorant of the arts than I; no one was more convinced that artists possessed sublime secrets. But I saw that their condition is no better than that of poets, and that both share the same misconception: Because the most skillful of them excel in their domain, they consider themselves the wisest of men. This presumption tarnishes their knowledge, so far as I am concerned. Putting myself in the place of the oracle, I asked myself which I would rather be: what they are, knowing what they have learned, or what I am, knowing that I know nothing. I answered, to myself and to the oracle, that I would rather remain what I am.

None of us—sophists, poets, orators, artists, and myself—knows what truth is, or goodness, or beauty. But there is one difference between us: The others all know nothing but believe they know something, and while I, too, know nothing, I at least have no doubt of my ignorance. Therefore all the superior wisdom attributed to me by the oracle consists only in being convinced that I am ignorant of what I do not know.

Thus we have praise of ignorance spoken by Socrates, the wisest of men in the judgment of the gods, and the most learned of the Athenians in the opinion of all of Greece. If he were to return to life now, would our scholars and artists make him change his mind? No, gentlemen, that just man would continue to despise our vain sciences; he would not help to swell the flood of books that overwhelms us on all sides, and the only precept he would give us would be the one he left to his disciples and our descendants: the example and memory of his virtue. That is the noblest way of educating mankind.

Cato the Elder continued in Rome what Socrates had

---

*Rousseau is here paraphrasing, rather than quoting, a passage from Plato's *Apology* in which Socrates is speaking. (Translator's note.)

begun in Athens: He inveighed against those subtle and cunning Greeks who perverted the virtue of his fellow citizens and undermined their courage. But the sciences, the arts, and dialectics prevailed again: Rome became filled with philosophers and orators; military discipline was neglected, agriculture was despised, sects were formed, and the fatherland was forgotten. The sacred names of freedom, unselfishness, and obedience were succeeded by the names of Epicurus, Zeno, and Arcesilaus. "Since learned men began appearing among us," said their own philosophers, "upright men have disappeared." Till then, the Romans had been content to practice virtue; all was lost when they began to study it.

O Fabricius, what would your great soul have thought if, having the misfortune of being called back to life, you had seen the pomp and luxury of the city which you had saved, and which had been made more illustrious by your revered name than by all its conquests? You would have cried out to the gods and said, "What has become of those thatched roofs and rustic hearths that were once the home of moderation and virtue? What noxious splendor has replaced Roman simplicity? What is this foreign language? What are these effeminate ways? What is the meaning of these statues, these paintings, these edifices? Fools! What have you done? You, the masters of nations, have made yourselves the slaves of the frivolous men you conquered! You are now ruled by glib orators! Was it to enrich architects, painters, sculptors, and actors that you shed your blood in Greece and Asia? Are the spoils of Carthage to be the prize of a flute-player? Romans, hasten to demolish these amphitheaters, break these statues, and burn these paintings; cast out these slaves who hold you in subjection, and whose pernicious arts corrupt you. Let other hands win fame by vain talents; the only talent worthy of Rome is that of conquering the world and making virtue rule it. When Cinneas looked on our Senate as an assembly of kings, he was not dazzled by empty pomp or affected elegance. He heard none of that meaningless eloquence which is the study and delight of fatuous men. What, then, did Cinneas see that was so majestic? Citizens, he saw a spectacle that all your wealth and arts will never produce, the noblest spectacle that has ever appeared beneath the heavens: an assembly of two hundred virtuous men, worthy of commanding Rome and governing the world."

But let us return through time and space and see what is happening here and now; or rather, let us avoid odious descriptions that would offend our delicacy, and spare ourselves the effort of repeating the same things under different names. It was not in vain that I evoked the spirit of Fabricius: I attributed no sentiments to that great man which I could not equally well have atttributed to Louis XII or Henry IV. Among us, it is true, Socrates would not have drunk the hemlock; but he would have drunk something even more bitter: contempt and insulting mockery that would have been a hundred times worse than death.

Thus we see how luxury, dissolution, and slavery have always been the punishment of our proud efforts to emerge from the happy ignorance in which eternal wisdom placed us. The thick veil with which that wisdom has covered all its operations should have been sufficient warning to us that we were not meant to embark on that vain quest. But have we been able to profit from any of the lessons taught to us by Providence, and are there any that we have neglected with impunity? Peoples of the earth, know that nature intended to preserve you from knowledge, as a mother snatches a dangerous weapon from the hands of her child; that all the secrets which nature hides from you are so many evils from which she protects you; and that the difficulty you encounter in extending your knowledge is not the least of her blessings. Men are perverse; they would be even worse if they had the misfortune of being born learned.

How humiliating these observations are to mankind! How mortifying they should be to our pride! What! Integrity is the child of ignorance? Learning and virtue are incompatible? What conclusions might be drawn from these suppositions? But to reconcile these apparent contradictions, we have only to examine closely the vanity and emptiness of the proud titles which we give so gratuitously to human knowledge, and which serve only to blind us. Let us therefore consider the arts and sciences in themselves. Let us see what must result from their progress; and let us not hesitate to accept all conclusions in which our reasoning is confirmed by historical inductions.

PART TWO

There was an ancient tradition that passed from Egypt to Greece, according to which the sciences were invented by a god who wanted to destroy the peace of mankind.[5] What, then, must have been thought of them by the Egyptians themselves, among whom they had been born and who had a close view of the sources that produced them? Whether we study the history of the world or use philosophical investigation to make up for the uncertainty of chronicles, we shall not find an origin of any field of human knowledge that corresponds to the idea we like to form of it. Astronomy arose from superstition; rhetoric from ambition, hatred, flattery, and falsehood; geometry from avarice; physics from idle curiosity; and all, even moral philosophy, from human pride. The arts and sciences therefore owe their birth to our vices; we would be less doubtful of their advantages if they owed it to our virtues.

The flaw of their origin is all too plainly reflected in their objects. What would become of the arts without the luxury that sustains them? Without human injustice, what would be the use of jurisprudence? What would history be without tyrants, wars, and conspirators? In short, who would want to devote his life to barren study and meditation if everyone acted only in accordance with the duty of man and the requirements of nature, and had time only for his country, the unfortunate, and his friends? Were we meant to die at the edge of the pit into which truth was withdrawn? This reflection alone should be enough to discourage at the outset anyone who seriously seeks to enlighten himself by the study of philosophy.

Countless dangers and wrong paths await us in the investigations of the sciences. To reach truth, we must pass through errors a thousand times more dangerous than truth is useful. Our handicap is obvious, for falsity can appear in an infinite number of combinations, while truth has only one mode of existence. Even with the best of intentions, by what signs can we be sure of recognizing it? Amid all our divergent opinions, what criterion shall we agree upon for judging it?[6] And there is still this most difficult question of all: If we are eventually fortunate enough to find truth, who among us will know how to make good use of it?

The effects produced by our sciences are even more dangerous than their objects are vain. Born in idleness, they in turn foster it, and an irreparable loss of time is the first detrimental effect that they inevitably have on society. In politics as in morality, it is a great evil not to do good; every useless citizen must be regarded as a pernicious man. Tell me, illustrious philosophers—you from whom we have learned the ratios in which bodies are attracted to one another in a vacuum; the relations among the spaces traversed in a given time by the revolutions of the planets; which curves have acnodes, flexes, or cusps; how man sees everything in God; how the soul and the body act together without connection, like two clocks; which planets may be inhabited; which insects reproduce themselves in an extraordinary manner—tell me, you from whom we have received all that sublime knowledge: If you had never taught us any of those things, would we be less numerous, less well governed, less formidable, or more perverse? Reconsider the importance of your achievements; and since the labors of our most enlightened scholars and our best citizens are of so little use to us, tell us what we are to think of that multitude of obscure writers and idle men of letters who consume the substance of the state without giving anything in return.

Idle, did I say? Would to God that they were! Morals would be healthier and society more peaceful. But those vain and frivolous phrasemongers go everywhere, armed with their baneful paradoxes, undermining the foundations of faith and annihilating virtue. They smile disdainfully at such old words as "fatherland" and "religion," and devote all their talents and philosophy to destroying or degrading everything that is most sacred to men. Not that they have any deep-seated hatred of virtue or our dogmas: Public opinion is the real object of their attacks; to turn them into ardent supporters of religion, one would have only to banish them to a land of atheists. Such is the power of a compelling urge to make oneself different from others.

Misuse of time is a great evil. Even worse evils flow from literature and the arts. One is luxury, which, like them, is born of the idleness and vanity of men. Luxury is seldom found without the arts and sciences, and they are never found without it. I know that our philosophy, always fertile in singular maxims, maintains, against the experience of all ages, that luxury is what makes the splendor of a state; but even if that philosophy overlooks the need for sumptuary laws, will it deny that good morals are essential to the duration of empires, and that luxury is diametrically opposed to good morals? Let luxury be regarded as a sure sign of wealth; let it even be credited with increasing wealth—what are we to conclude from this paradox, so worthy of having arisen in our time? And what will become of virtue if wealth must be acquired at any cost? Ancient political philosophers were always speaking of morals and virtue; ours speak only of commerce and money. One of them will tell you that in a certain country a man is worth the amount for which he could be sold in Algiers; another, following the same rule, will find countries where a man is worth nothing, and others where he is worth less than nothing. They evaluate men like herds of cattle. According to them, a man's worth to the state is only that of what he consumes; thus one Sybarite would have been worth thirty Spartans. But I would like them to tell me which of those two republics, Sparta and Sybaris, was subjugated by a handful of peasants, and which made Asia tremble.

The monarchy of Cyrus was conquered with thirty thousand men by a king poorer than the lowliest of Persian satraps; and the Scythians, the poorest of all peoples, withstood the world's most powerful monarchs. Two famous republics once vied with each other for control of the world; one was very rich, the other had nothing, and it was the latter that destroyed the former. The Roman Empire in its turn, after having swallowed up all the world's wealth, fell prey to peoples that did not even know what wealth was. The Franks conquered Gaul, and the Saxons England, with no other treasures than their courage and their poverty. A band of poor mountaineers, whose greed was limited to a few sheepskins, first humbled the pride of Austria, then crushed the opulent House of Burgundy, which had made the potentates of Europe tremble. And finally, all the power and wisdom of the heir of Charles V of Germany, supported by all the treasures of the Indies, was unable to overcome a handful of herring-fishers. Let our political philosophers lay aside their calculations to reflect on these examples; let them learn once and for all that money can buy anything but morals and citizens.

What, then, is the essential question in this discussion of luxury? The following: Is it better for an empire to be brilliant and short-lived, or virtuous and lasting? I say "brilliant," but what kind of brilliance is possible for such an empire? A taste for ostentation almost necessarily excludes a taste for honesty. No, souls that have been degraded by a multitude of trivial concerns can never rise to anything great; and even if they had the strength, they would lack the courage to do so.

Every artist wants to be applauded. The praise of his contemporaries is the most precious part of his reward. What will he do to obtain it if he has had the misfortune of being born in a nation and a time in which the learned men who have become fashionable have placed frivolous youth in the position of setting the tone of society; in which men have sacrificed their taste to the tyrants of their freedom;[7] in which, since one of the sexes dares to approve only of what is proportionate to the faintheartedness of the other, masterpieces of dramatic poetry are ignored and wonders of harmony are rejected? What will he do, gentlemen? He will lower his genius to the level of his age, and he will prefer to produce commonplace works that will be admired during his lifetime, rather than marvels that would not be admired until long after his death. Tell us, famous Arouet,* how many strong and manly beauties you have sacrificed to our false delicacy, and how many great things the spirit of gallantry, so fertile in small ones, has cost you.

It is thus that the dissolution of morals, the necessary result of luxury, in turn brings about the corruption of taste. If, among men of extraordinary talent, there should happen to be one with enough firmness of soul to refuse to comply with the spirit of his time and degrade himself by producing puerile works, woe to him! He will die in indi-

---

*Voltaire, whose name was originally François-Marie Arouet. (Translator's note.)

gence and oblivion. Carle and Pierre,† the time has come when your brushes, destined to augment the majesty of our temples with sublime and holy images, will either fall from your hands or be prostituted to decorating the panels of a carriage with lascivious paintings. And you, inimitable Pigalle, rival of Praxiteles and Phidias, you whom the ancients would have commissioned to create statues of gods that would have excused their idolatry in our eyes—your hand will either resign itself to polishing the belly of a grotesque figurine, or be forced to remain idle.

We cannot reflect on morals without taking pleasure in recalling the image of the simplicity of the earliest times. It is like a beautiful shore, adorned only by the hand of nature, to which we continually look back as we regretfully feel ourselves moving away from it. When men were innocent and virtuous, they liked to have the gods as witnesses of their acts, and lived with them in the same huts; but when they became wicked, they grew tired of those bothersome onlookers and banished them to magnificent temples. Finally they expelled them from the temples so that they themselves could live in them, or at least the temples of the gods became indistinguishable from the houses of citizens. This was the height of depravity; vice was never carried farther than when it was seen at the entrances of powerful men's palaces, supported, so to speak, by marble pillars, and engraved on Corinthian capitals.

As the conveniences of life are multiplied, as the arts are perfected and luxury spreads, true courage fades, the military virtues vanish, and this is the work of the sciences and all those arts, which secretly exert their influence in governmental chambers. When the Goths ravaged Greece, they refrained from burning all the libraries because one of them said that they ought to leave their enemies in possession of something that was so effective in turning them away from military exercises and diverting them with idle and sedentary occupations. Charles VIII became master of Tuscany and the Kingdom of Naples almost without having drawn his sword, and his whole court attributed the unexpected ease of his success to the fact that the monarchs and noblemen of Italy were more concerned with cultivating wit and learning than with training themselves to

---

†Carle Van Loo and Jean-Baptiste-Marie Pierre, French painters who were contemporaries of Rousseau. (Translator's note.)

be vigorous warriors. In fact, says the sensible man* who cites these two examples, experience has always shown that in military matters and everything similar to them, study of the sciences tends much more to make men soft and effeminate than to stir and strengthen their courage.

The Romans admitted that military virtue had declined among them in proportion as they became connoisseurs in painting, sculpture, and the art of the goldsmith, and began cultivating the fine arts; and, as though that famous country were destined always to serve as an example to other nations, the rise of the Medici and the restoration of literature obliterated again, and perhaps forever, the martial reputation that Italy seemed to have recovered a few centuries ago.

With the wisdom that shone in most of their institutions, the ancient Greek republic forbade their citizens to engage in any of those tranquil and sedentary occupations which debilitate and corrupt the body and at the same time weaken the vigor of the soul. If men are overwhelmed by the slightest lack, and repelled by the slightest effort, how can they be expected to face hunger, thirst, fatigue, danger, and death? How tenaciously will soldiers endure strenuous exertion if they are entirely unaccustomed to it? How resolutely will they make forced marches under officers who do not even have the strength to travel by horseback? It would not be a valid objection to cite the renowned valor of all those modern warriors who are so skillfully disciplined. Their courage in a one-day battle may be admirable, but how well do they endure excessive fatigue, and how well do they withstand the rigors of the seasons and inclement weather? It takes only a little sunshine or snow, or lack of a few unnecessary supplies, to make the best of our armies weaken and collapse in a few days. Intrepid warriors, listen for once to the truth which you hear so seldom: You are brave, I have no doubt of it; you would have triumphed with Hannibal at Cannae and at Trasimenus; with you, Caesar would have crossed the Rubicon and subjugated his country; but you would not have crossed the Alps with the former, or vanquished your ancestors with the latter.

The outcome of a war does not always depend on combat, and for a general there is an art superior to that of

---

*Montaigne. (Translator's note.)

winning battles. A man may be fearless under fire, but still be a very bad officer; and even with common soldiers, a little more strength and vigor might be more useful than great courage, which does not protect them from death. What does it matter to the state whether its troops perish by fever and cold or by the sword of the enemy?

If cultivation of the sciences is prejudicial to martial qualities, it is still more so to moral qualities. Beginning in our earliest years, our absurd education embellishes our minds and corrupts our judgment. I see everywhere immense establishments in which our youth are educated at great expense, and taught everything but their duty. Your children will be ignorant of their own language, but will speak others that are not in use anywhere; they will be able to write poetry which they themselves can scarcely understand; although they will not know how to distinguish between truth and error, they will be skilled in the art of making both unrecognizable to others by specious arguments. But magnanimity, equity, temperance, humanity, and courage will be only meaningless words to them; the cherished name of the fatherland will never fall upon their ears; and if they are ever told anything about God, it will be more to arouse fear of him than reverent awe.[8] "I would as soon that my schoolboy had spent his time on a tennis court," said a wise man; "at least his body would have been in better condition." I know that children should be kept occupied, and that idleness is the danger most to be feared for them. But what should they learn? That is assuredly a great question! Let them learn what they ought to do when they become men,[9] not what they ought to forget.

Our gardens are adorned with statues and our galleries with paintings. What would you expect to be shown by those masterpieces of art, exposed to the admiration of the public? Great men who have defended their country, or those still greater ones who have enriched it with their virtue? No. They are images of all the aberrations of the heart and the mind, carefully drawn from ancient mythology and presented to the budding curiosity of our children, no doubt in order that they may have models of misconduct before their eyes even before they are able to read.

What is the source of all these abuses, if not the pernicious inequality created among men by the distinction of talents and the debasement of virtues? That is the most obvious effect of all our studies, and the most dangerous of all their consequences. We no longer ask if a man has integrity, but if he has talent; we ask not if a book is useful, but if it is well written. Rewards are lavished on cleverness, and virtue is left unhonored. There are countless prizes for fine discourses, and none for noble acts. But is the glory attached to the best of all the discourses that will ever win the prize of this Academy comparable to the merit of having established that prize?

The wise man does not run after fortune, but he is not insensitive to glory. When he sees it so badly distributed, his virtue, which a little emulation would have animated and turned to the advantage of society, becomes languid and fades away in poverty and oblivion. That is what must eventually happen wherever agreeable talents are preferred to useful ones, as has been demonstrated all too clearly by experience since the renewal of the arts and sciences. We have physicists, geometers, chemists, astronomers, poets, musicians, and painters, but we no longer have citizens; or if there are still a few left, scattered over our forsaken countrysides, they die there, indigent and despised. Such are our feelings for those who give us food for ourselves and milk for our children, and such is the state to which they have been reduced.

I admit, however, that the evil is not as great as it might have become. By placing health-giving herbs alongside poisonous plants and making the substance of a number of noxious animals provide a remedy for the wounds they inflict, eternal Providence has taught sovereigns, who are its ministers, to imitate its wisdom. It was by following this example that a great monarch, whose glory will continue to gain new luster in every age, drew from within the arts and sciences, which are such an abundant source of dissolution, those famous learned societies which, along with the dangerous trust of human knowledge, also hold the sacred trust of morality, for each of them is devoted to maintaining moral purity within itself, and requires the same purity of those whom it admits to membership.

These wise institutions, strengthened by their founder's successor and imitated by all the kings of Europe, will at least serve to restrain men of letters, who, all aspiring to membership in the academies, will keep watch over themselves and try to make themselves worthy of it by useful works and irreproachable morals. For the prizes with which they honor literary merit, these academies will choose subjects capable of animating love of virtue in the hearts of citizens, and by their own morality, will show that the same love also reigns among them. They will give nations the rare pleasure of seeing learned societies imparting to mankind not only agreeable enlightenment, but also salutary instructions.

At this point an objection might be raised which would actually be another proof of what I am saying. The fact that so many efforts are being made shows all too clearly how necessary they are; one does not seek remedies for ills that do not exist. Why must these remedies share the nature of ordinary ones by being inadequate? Because so many institutions have been created to favor erudition, they are all the more capable of inspiring respect for the objects of the sciences and making men turn their attention to cultivating them. From the precautions that have been taken, it would seem that we had too many farmers and were afraid of running short of philosophers. I will not venture to make a comparison between agriculture and philosophy, because I know it would not be tolerated. I will ask only these questions: What is philosophy? What is contained in the writings of the most famous philosophers? What are the lessons taught by those friends of wisdom? Listening to them, we have the impression that they are mountebanks in a public square, each one shouting, "Come to me! Only I will tell you the truth!" One claims that there is no body and that everything is only an appearance, another that nothing exists but matter and that there is no God but the world. One maintains that there are no virtues or vices and that moral good and evil are illusions, another that men are wolves and may devour each other with a clear conscience. O great philosophers, if only you would limit those profitable lessons to your friends and children! You would soon reap the benefit of them, and then we would have no need to fear finding one of your disciples among our own friends and children.

Such are the wonderful men who enjoy the esteem lavished on them by their contemporaries while they are alive, and then attain immortality after their demise. Such are the wise maxims that we receive from them and continue to pass on from one generation to the next. Did paganism, rich in all the aberrations of human reason, leave to posterity anything comparable to the shameful monuments that have been erected by printing during the reign of the Gospel? The impious writings of men like Leucippus and Diagoras perished with them. The art of eternizing the extravagances of the human mind had not yet been invented. But thanks to typographical characters[10] and the use we make of them, the dangerous musings of Hobbes and Spinoza will endure forever. Such famous writings, which our ignorant, rustic forefathers would have been incapable of producing, will survive among our descendants, along with those even more dangerous works which reek of the moral corruption of our time, and together they will provide future centuries with a faithful history of the progress and advantages of our arts and sciences. If our descendants read them, they will have no doubt about the question we are now discussing, and unless they are even more foolish than we, they will raise their hands toward heaven and say in the bitterness of their hearts, "Almighty God, you who hold the minds of men in your hand, deliver us from the knowledge and the baneful arts of our forefathers, and give us ignorance, innocence, and poverty, the only goods that can make us happy and are precious in your sight."

But if the progress of the arts and sciences has added nothing to our real happiness, if it has corrupted our morals, and if moral corruption has adulterated the purity of our taste, what are we to think of that host of elementary writers who have removed the difficulties which guarded the approach to the Temple of the Muses, and which nature had placed before it to try the strength of those who were tempted to seek knowledge? What are we to think of those compilers of works that have rashly broken open the door of the sciences and brought into their sanctuary a populace unworthy of approaching it, whereas it would have been better if all those who were incapable of making great advances in the career of learning had been disheartened at the outset, and had then turned to arts that are useful to society? A man who will now spend his whole life being a bad versifier or an inferior geometer might have become an outstanding cloth manufacturer. Those destined by nature to have disciples do not need masters. Men like Bacon, Descartes, and Newton, the teachers of mankind, have themselves had no teachers. What guide could have led them to where their vast genius has taken them? An ordinary master would only have lessened their understanding by confining it within the narrow limits of his own. It was from the first obstacles that they learned to exert themselves and develop the abilities that enabled them to cover such immense distances. If a few men must be permitted to apply themselves to the study of the arts and sciences, it should be only those who feel strong enough to follow their predecessors' footsteps alone, and go beyond them. Only a few are capable of raising monuments to the glory of the human mind. But if nothing is to be above their genius, nothing must be above their hopes. That is the only encouragement they need. The soul is gradually proportioned to the objects with which it concerns itself, and it is great occasions that produce great men. The prince of eloquence was a Roman consul, and the greatest of all philosophers, perhaps, was Lord Chancellor of England. If one had been only a professor at some university and the other had obtained only a modest stipend from an academy, can there by any doubt that their work would have been affected by their situation? Let kings not disdain to admit into their councils those men most capable of giving them good advice; let them renounce the old prejudice, invented by the pride of those in high positions, that the art of ruling nations is more difficult than that of enlightening them, as if it were easier to induce men to do good voluntarily than to compel them to do it by force. Let them give honorable refuge in their courts to learned men of the first order. Let those men obtain there the only reward worthy of them: that of contributing by their influence to the happiness of the peoples to whom they have taught wisdom. Only then shall we see what can be done by virtue, knowledge, and authority, animated by noble emulation and working together toward the felicity of the human race. But as long as power is alone on one side, and knowledge and wisdom are alone on another, learned men will seldom turn their thoughts to great things, monarchs will do noble things even more seldom, and peoples will continue to be abject, corrupt, and unhappy.

As for us ordinary men, whom heaven has not endowed with such great talents and destined to such great glory, let us remain in our obscurity. Let us not pursue a reputation which would escape us and which, in the present state of things, would never repay us for what it had cost us, even if we were all qualified to obtain it. Why should we seek our happiness in the opinion of our fellow men if we can find it in ourselves? Let us leave to others the task of instructing peoples in their duties, and limit ourselves to fulfilling our own; if we can do that, we have all the knowledge we need.

O virtue, sublime science of simple souls, are such efforts and complications required in order to know you? Are your principles not engraved in all hearts? To learn your laws, is it not enough for us to withdraw into ourselves and listen to the voice of our conscience while our passions are silent? That is true philosophy; let us learn to be content with it. And without envying those famous men who make themselves immortal in the Republic of Letters, let us place between them and us that glorious distinction which was observed between two ancient peoples: that one knew how to speak well, the other how to act rightly.

1. Monarchs are always glad to see a taste for superfluities and the agreeable arts, which do not result in the exportation of money, increase among their subjects, for they know that such things foster the smallness of soul that goes so well with servitude, and that all the needs which a people gives itself are so many more chains that bind it. When Alexander wanted to keep a fish-eating people under his domination, he made them give up fishing and eat foods common to other peoples; and the savages of America, who go barefoot and live entirely on what they obtain by hunting, have always been impossible to subdue. What yoke can be imposed on men who need nothing?

2. "I like discussion and argument," says Montaigne, "but only with a few people, and for my own enjoyment. Serving as an entertainment for the rich and powerful, and vying with others in displaying one's wit and glib chatter, is a trade that I consider unbecoming to a man of honor." It is the trade of all our intellectuals, except one.

3. I dare not speak of those happy peoples that do not even know the names of the vices we have such difficulty in curbing: the savages of America, who govern themselves in a simple, natural way which Montaigne prefers, without hesitation, not only to Plato's laws, but also to the most perfect ideas of government that philosophy will ever be able to imagine. He cites many examples of their conduct that are striking to anyone capable of admiring them. "But never mind," he says, "they wear no breeches!"

4. Let me ask in good faith what opinion the Athenians themselves must have had of eloquence, when they were so careful to exclude it from that upright tribunal whose judgments could not be appealed even by the gods. What did the Romans think of medicine, when they banished it from their republic? And when a vestige of humane feeling prompted the Spaniards to forbid their lawyers to go to America, what idea must they have had of jurisprudence? Perhaps they felt that by that one act they could make up for all the evil they had done to the unfortunate Indians.

5. It is easy to see the allegory in the fable of Prometheus; and it does not appear that the Greeks, who chained him to Mount Caucasus, thought much better of

him than the Egyptians did of their god Theuth. The satyr, says an ancient fable, wanted to kiss and embrace fire the first time he saw it, but Prometheus cried out to him, "Satyr, you will mourn the loss of the beard on your chin, because fire burns when it is touched."

6. The less we know, the more we think we know. Did the Peripatetics have any doubts about anything? Did not Descartes construct the universe with cubes and vortices? And even today, in Europe, are there any physicists who do not boldly explain the profound mystery of electricity, which will perhaps be forever the despair of real philosophers?

7. I am far from thinking that this ascendancy of women is bad in itself. It is a gift that nature has given them for the happiness of the human race: Better directed, it might do as much good as it now does evil. We are not sufficiently aware of the advantages to society that would result if a better education were given to that half of the human race which rules the other. Men will always be what it pleases women for them to be; therefore, if you want men to be great and virtuous, teach women the meaning of greatness of soul and virtue. The reflections which are suggested by this subject, and which Plato made in the past, deserve to be better developed by a writer worthy of following such a great master and defending such a great cause.

8. *Pensées philosophiques* [by Diderot].

9. Such was the education of the Spartans, according to the greatest of their kings. It is noteworthy, says Montaigne, that in the excellent government of Lycurgus, which was almost monstrous in its perfection, yet devoted such great care to the upbringing of children, regarding it as its main responsibility, there are so little mention of doctrine, even at the very seat of the Muses. It was as if those noble-hearted youths scorned any other yoke, and had to be given, instead of our teachers of science, only teachers of valor, prudence, and justice.

Let us see how that same author speaks of the ancient Persians. Plato, he says, reports that the heir to their throne was thus brought up: At birth he was given into the care not of women, but of eunuchs who were in high standing with the king because of their virtue. They undertook to make his body beautiful and healthy. When he was seven, they taught him to ride and hunt. At fourteen, he was placed in the hands of four men: the wisest, the most just, the most temperate, and the bravest in the kingdom. The first taught him religion; the second, to be always truthful; the third, to conquer his covetousness; the fourth, to fear nothing. All of them, let me point out, tried to make him good; none tried to make him learned.

Astyages, in Xenophon, asks Cyrus to tell him about his last lesson, and Cyrus replies, "It was this: In our school a big boy who had a small cloak gave it to a little boy and took away his cloak, which was larger. Our teacher asked me to judge the dispute. I decided that the matter should be allowed to stand as it was, since each boy now had a better-fitting cloak than before. The teacher then told me that I had made a bad judgment, for I had considered only what was appropriate, whereas my first concern should have been justice, which requires that no one shall be forcibly deprived of what belongs to him." And he says that he was punished, just as pupils in our villages are punished if they forget the first aorist of τύπτω. A modern teacher will have to give me a fine speech, in *genere demonstrativo*, before he can convince me that his school is as good as that one.

10. If we consider the frightful disorders that printing has already caused in Europe, and if we judge the future by the progress that its evils continue to make from day to day, it is easy to foresee that sovereigns will soon make as many efforts to banish that terrible art from their states as they made to establish it in them. Sultan Ahmed, yielding to the insistence of a few self-styled men of good taste, consented to allow a printing press to be installed in Constantinople; no sooner was it in operation than he had to have it demolished, and the pieces thrown into a well. It is said that when Caliph Omar was asked what was to be done with an Alexandrian library, he replied, "If the books in that library contain things contrary to the Koran, they are evil and must be burned. If they contain only the doctrine of the Koran, burn them anyway, for they are superfluous." Our learned men have cited that reasoning as the height of absurdity. But imagine Gregory the Great in the place of Omar, and the Gospel in the place of the Koran: The library would still have been burned, and that might have been the finest act of the illustrious pontiff's life.

The Creed
*of a Savoyard Priest**

❖━━━◆━━━❖

**The Creed of a Savoyard Priest* is a section of Rousseau's
Emile. In it, the priest is speaking to a young man whom he is
in the process of saving from cynicism and despair. (Translator's note.)

My son, do not expect learned discourse or profound reasoning from me. I am not a great philosopher, and I have little desire to be one. But I sometimes have common sense, and I always love truth. I do not wish to argue with you, or even to try to convince you; it will be enough for me to tell you what I think in the simplicity of my heart. Consult your own while I speak; that is all I ask of you. If I am mistaken, it is in good faith, and my error therefore cannot be charged to me as a crime. If you are mistaken in the same way, you can be accused of no great wrong. I believe I am right in assuming that you and I are both endowed with reason, and have the same interest in listening to it. Why should you not think as I do?

I was born poor and a peasant, destined by my condition to till the soil, but my parents felt that it would be better for me to make my living as a priest, and they succeeded in enabling me to have the necessary education. Neither they nor I had any concern for my learning what was good, true, or useful, but only what was needed for me to be ordained. I learned what I was expected to learn, I said what I was expected to say, I assumed the required obligations, and I was made a priest. But I soon became aware that in committing myself to not being a man, I had promised more than I could fulfill.

We are told that conscience is the work of prejudice; I know from my own experience, however, that conscience persists in following the order of nature despite all the laws of men. We may be forbidden to do this or that, but remorse is always weak if what we do is permitted by well-ordered nature, and weaker still if we are obeying one of her commands. My good young man, she has not yet spoken to your senses; may you long remain in the happy state in which her voice is that of innocence. Remember that we offend her even more by anticipating her than by opposing her. To know when we may yield without doing wrong, we must begin by learning to resist.

From my youth onward, I have respected marriage as the first and holiest institution of nature. Having renounced the right to it for myself, I resolved not to profane it, for the simple and regular life that I had always led had allowed my mind to keep all the clarity of its natural discernment, in spite of my schooling and my studies. It had not been dimmed by worldly maxims, and my poverty kept me away from the temptations put forward by the sophistry of vice.

That very resolution was what led me into disaster: My respect for the bed of marriage made my misconduct easy to discover. The scandal had to be expiated. I was arrested, suspended by the Church, and forced to leave. I was much more the victim of my scruples than of my incontinence, and I had reason to conclude, from the reproaches that accompanied my disgrace, that one can often escape punishment by making one's crime still worse.

Such experiences have a profound effect on a thoughtful mind. My melancholy reflections overturned my former concepts of justice, honesty, and all the duties of man. Each day I lost another of the opinions I had accepted. Those that remained were not enough to form a body of ideas that could stand alone. I felt the self-evidence of my principles being gradually obscured in my mind, and finally, when I had been reduced to no longer knowing what to think, I reached the point where you are now, with this difference: that since my unbelief had developed with greater difficulty and at a later age, it would be all the harder to destroy.

I was in the state of uncertainty and doubt that Descartes considers essential to the search for truth. It is not likely to be lasting, because it is disquieting and painful. Only a lazy mind or the interest of vice can keep us in it. My heart had not been corrupted enough to make me willing to remain in it, and nothing maintains the habit of reflection better than being more satisfied with oneself than with one's situation.

I meditated on the sad fate of mortals adrift on that sea of human opinions, without rudder or compass, at the mercy of their stormy passions, with no other guide than an inexperienced pilot who knows neither from where he has come nor where he is going. I said to myself, "I love truth, I seek it, and cannot find it. Show me where it is and I will hold fast to it. Why must it hide from a heart that is eager to worship it?"

Although I have often experienced greater suffering, I have never led such a constantly unpleasant life as during that time of confusion and anxiety when I was incessantly wandering from one doubt to another, and gaining nothing from my long meditations but uncertainty, obscurity, and contradictions with regard to the cause of my being and the rule of my duties.

How can anyone be a systematic and sincere skeptic? I do not understand it. Either there really are no such philosophers, or they are the unhappiest of men. Doubt concerning the things most important for us to know is a stress too great for the human mind to endure very long. We cannot help putting an end to our doubt in one way or another, because we would rather be mistaken than believe nothing.

My perplexity was made still worse by the fact that since I had been born into a Church that decides everything and permits no doubt, rejecting one of its tenets made me reject all the rest, and my inability to accept its many absurd decisions turned me against those that were not absurd. Having been told to believe everything prevented me from believing anything, and I did not know where to stop.

I turned to the philosophers: I studied their books and examined their various opinions. I found them all to be proud, assertive, and dogmatic, even in their supposed skepticism. They know everything, prove nothing, and ridicule each other; only on this last point do I feel that all of them are right. They are triumphant when they attack, and feeble when they defend themselves. If you weigh their arguments, they all prove to be destructive; if you examine their doctrines, you find that each man is limited to his own; they agree only in wrangling with each other. Listening to them was not the way for me to cast off my uncertainty.

It became clear to me that the inadequacy of the human mind is the first cause of that prodigious diversity of views, and that pride is the second. The vast mechanism of the world is beyond our grasp. We cannot calculate its ratios; we know neither its first laws nor its final cause. We do not know ourselves; we know neither our nature nor the primary force that moves us; we scarcely know whether man is a simple or a composite being. We are surrounded by impenetrable mysteries that lie beyond the realm of perception. We believe that we have the intelligence needed to fathom them, but we can use only our imagination. Through this imaginary world, each man clears a path which he believes to be the right one, but he cannot determine whether or not it leads toward the goal. Yet we want to know and understand everything. We are unable to accept our ignorance of what we cannot know. We prefer to choose our certainties at random and believe in illusions, rather than admit that none of us can perceive reality. We are small parts of a great whole whose limits we cannot see and whose Maker leaves us to our foolish disputes, yet we are vain enough to want to decide what that whole is in itself, and what we are in relation to it.

Even if philosophers were able to discover the truth, which of them would take any interest in it? Each knows quite well that his system has no better foundation than the others, but he upholds it because it is his own. There is not one of them who, if he succeeded in distinguishing the true from the false, would not prefer a falsehood that he had invented to a truth discovered by someone else. Where is the philosopher who would not deceive the whole human race, without hesitation, for the sake of his own glory? Is there a single one of them who, in the secret depths of his heart, has any other goal than making himself famous? If he can rise above the crowd and outshine his rivals, what more does he ask? The first thing he must do is to think differently from others. Among believers, he is an atheist; among atheists, he would be a believer.

The first benefit I derived from these reflections was learning to limit my inquiries to what concerned me directly, to be willing to remain in profound ignorance of everything else, and to trouble myself to the point of doubt only with regard to things that were important for me to know.

I also realized that, far from ridding me of my useless doubts, the philosophers would only multiply those that tormented me, without resolving any of them. I therefore took another guide. "I must follow the inner light," I told myself. "It will mislead me less than they do, or at least my error will be my own, and I shall be less perverted if I follow my illusions than if I believe their lies."

Then, turning over in my mind the various opinions that had successively swayed me since my birth, I saw that although none was self-evident enough to produce immediate conviction, some were more plausible than others, and that my inner assent was given to them or withheld from them in varying degrees. Having made this observation, I compared all those different ideas without prejudice and found that the first and most common was also the simplest and most sensible, and that the only reason why it was not accepted by everyone was that it was not the latest to be proposed. Imagine all our philosophers, ancient and modern, having first exhausted their strange systems of forces, chance, fate, necessity, atoms, an animate world, living matter, and materialism of every kind, and then, after all of them, the illustrious Clarke enlightening the world, proclaiming at last the Being of Beings and the Giver of all things. What universal admiration and unanimous applause would have greeted that new system! It is so great, so comforting, so sublime, so well suited to uplifting the soul and giving virtue a foundation, and at the same time so striking, so illuminating, so simple; and it seems to me that while it contains some things that are incomprehensible to the human mind, their number is smaller than that of the utter absurdities in any other system. I said to myself, "Every system has its insoluble problems, because man's mind is too limited to solve them. Such problems therefore cannot be used as justification for rejecting one system in favor of another. But what differences there are in the direct evidence for all those systems! Should we not prefer the one that explains everything, yet presents no more difficulties than the others?"

Thus, with love of truth as my only philosophy, and as my only method a simple and easy rule that enabled me to dispense with vain and subtle arguments, I resumed my examination, with the help of that rule, of the knowledge that concerned me. I resolved to accept as self-evident all propositions that I could not sincerely refuse to believe, to regard as true all those that seemed to follow necessarily from them, and to leave all others in uncertainty, neither rejecting nor accepting them, without bothering to clarify them if they had no bearing on practical reality.

But who am I? What right do I have to judge things, and what determines my judgments? If they are forced upon me by the impressions I receive, it is futile for me to expend any energy in such inquiry, because they will either occur or not occur, without any effort on my part to direct them. First, therefore, I must examine myself, to become acquainted with the instrument I intend to use and learn the extent to which I can rely on it.

I exist, and I have senses by which I am affected. That is the first truth which strikes me and forces me to accept it. Do I have an independent feeling of my existence, or do I feel it only by means of my sensations? That is my first doubt. For the present, I cannot resolve it: Since I am continually affected by sensations, either immediately or in memory, how can I know if the feeling of my *self* is something outside those sensations and if it can be independent of them?

My sensations take place within me, since they make me aware of my existence; but their cause is external to me, since they affect me whether I am willing or not, and I can neither produce nor abolish them of my own volition. I therefore clearly understand that a sensation, which is inside me, and its cause or object, which is outside of me, are not the same thing.

Thus, not only do I exist, but other entities exist also, namely, the objects of my sensations; and even if those objects are only ideas, it is still truth that they are distinct from me.

Everything which I feel to be outside of me, and which acts on my senses, I call matter; and all particles of matter which I perceive as being combined into separate entities, I call bodies. Thus all the disputes between idealists and materialists mean nothing to me: Their distinctions between the appearance and the reality of bodies are idle fancies.

I am now already as sure of the existence of the universe as I am of my own. Next I consider the objects of my sensations, and finding in myself the ability to compare them, I discover that I am endowed with an active force which I previously did not know I possessed.

To perceive is to feel; to compare is to judge; judging and feeling are not the same. By sensation, objects are presented to me as separate, isolated, as they are in nature; in comparing them, I move and rearrange them, so to speak, I place one over another to see whether they are alike or different and to ascertain, in general, all their relations. In my opinion, the distinctive faculty of an ac-

tive or intelligent being is the ability to give meaning to
the word "is." In purely sentient beings I fail to find that
intelligent force which superposes and then judges; I cannot see it in nature. Such a passive being will feel each object separately, or will even feel a total object formed by
two together, but having no power to place one upon the
other, it will never compare them, it will not judge them.

Seeing two objects at once is not seeing their relations
or judging their differences; perceiving several objects distinct from one another is not counting them. I may simul-
taneously have the idea of a large stick and a small stick
without comparing them, without judging that one is smaller than the other, just as I may see my whole hand without counting my fingers.[1] Such comparative ideas as
"larger" and "smaller," and the numerical ideas of "one,"
"two," etc., certainly not sensations, even though they
are always accompanied by sensations when my mind produces them.

We are told that a sentient being distinguishes sensations
by the differences between them. This calls for explanation. When the sensations are different, the sentient being
distinguishes them by their differences; when they are
alike, it distinguishes them because it feels them to be separate from each other. Otherwise, how could it distinguish
two equal objects in a simultaneous sensation? It would
necessarily have to confuse the two objects and take them
for one, especially in a system which maintains that ideas
representing extension have no extension.

When the two sensations to be compared are perceived,
their impression is made, each object is felt, both are felt,
but their relation is nevertheless not felt. If the judgment
of that relation were only a sensation, and came to me
solely from the object, my judgments would never deceive
me, because it is never false that I feel what I feel.

Why, then, am I mistaken about the relation between
these two sticks, especially when they are not parallel?
Why do I say, for example, that the large stick is three
times as long as the small one, when it is actually four
times as long? Why is the image, which is the sensation
unlike its model, which is the object? Because I am active
when I judge, and the operation of comparison is faulty;
in judging relations, my understanding mingles its errors
with the truth of sensations, which show only objects.

Let me add to this a consideration that will strike you, I

am sure, when you have reflected on it: If we were purely passive in the use of our senses, there would be no communication among them; it would be impossible for us to know that the object we touch and the object we see are the same. Either we would never be aware of anything outside ourselves, or there would be for us five perceptible substances whose identity we would have no means of perceiving.

Let any name be given to the power of my mind which brings together my sensations and compares them, let it be called attention, meditation, reflection, or whatever you like; it is still true that it is in me and not in things, that it is I alone who produce it, even though I produce it only when I receive impressions from objects. Though I have no control over whether I feel or not, I do control the extent to which I examine what I feel.

I am therefore not merely a passive sentient being, but an active and intelligent being, and no matter what philosophy may say, I dare to claim the honor of thinking. I know only that truth is in things, not in the mind that judges them, and that the less of myself I put into my judgments of them, the surer I am to approach truth; thus my rule of relying more on feeling than on reason is confirmed by reason itself.

Having made sure of myself, so to speak, I begin looking outside myself, and I consider myself with a kind of shudder, cast into this vast universe, lost in the immense number of entities without knowing what they are, either among themselves or in relation to me. I study them, I observe them; and the first object that presents itself to me as a basis for comparison is myself.

Everything that I perceive through my senses is matter, and I deduce all the essential properties of matter from the sensory qualities that make me perceive it and are inseparable from it. I see it sometimes in motion and sometimes at rest,[2] from which I infer that neither rest nor motion is essential to it; but motion, being an action, is the effect of a cause of which rest is only the absence. Therefore, when nothing acts on matter it does not move, and for the very reason that it can be either in motion or at rest, indifferently, its natural state is the state of rest.

I perceive in bodies two kinds of motion: imparted motion and spontaneous or voluntary motion. In the first, the cause of motion is external to the body that moves, and in the second it is in the body itself. I do not conclude from this that the motion of a watch, for example, is spontaneous; for if nothing external to the spring acted on it, it would not tend to straighten itself and would not pull the chain. For the same reason, I do not attribute spontaneity to fluids, or even to the fire that causes their fluidity.[3]

If you ask me if the movements of animals are spontaneous, I will answer that I do not know, but that analogy would seem to indicate that they are. If you ask me how I know that there are spontaneous movements, I will answer that I know it because I feel it. If I will to move my arm, I move it, and its movement has no other immediate cause than my will. It would be futile for anyone to try to destroy that feeling in me by reasoning, because it is stronger than any logic he could use; he might as well try to prove to me that I do not exist.

If there were no spontaneity in men's actions, or in anything that happens on earth, it would be all the more difficult to imagine the first cause of all motion. For my part, I am so thoroughly convinced that matter is at rest in its natural state, and has no power to move of itself, that whenever I see a body in motion I immediately judge that either it is a living body or its motion was imparted to it. My mind rejects the idea of inorganic matter moving of itself, or producing any action.

Yet this visible universe consists of matter, scattered and dead matter,[4] which as a whole has none of the cohesion, organization, or common feeling of the parts of a living body, for it is certain that we, who are parts, have no feeling of ourselves in the whole. This same universe is in motion, and in its movements, which are ordered, uniform, and subject to fixed laws, it has none of the freedom that appears in the movements of men and animals. The world is therefore not a great animal that moves of itself; its movements have a cause external to it, which I do not perceive. But inner conviction makes that cause so real to me that I cannot see the sun moving across the sky without imagining a force that drives it, and when I think of the earth turning I seem to feel a hand that makes it turn.

If I am forced to accept general laws whose essential relations to matter I do not perceive, am I any better off than before? Since those laws are not real entities, substances, they must have some other foundation that is unknown to me. From experiment and observation we have learned the laws of motion. These laws determine effects without showing causes; they are inadequate to explain the structure and workings of the universe. With dice, Descartes formed heaven and earth; but he was unable to set his dice in motion, or start his centrifugal force, without the aid of a rotary movement. Newton discovered the law of gravity, but gravity alone would soon reduce the universe to a motionless mass; a propelling force had to be added to that law to make the heavenly bodies describe their curves. Let Descartes tell us what physical law made his vortices whirl; let Newton show us the hand that launched the planets in the tangents of their orbits.

The first causes of motion are not in matter; it receives motion and transmits it, but does not produce it. The more I observe the action and reaction of natural forces acting on one another, the more I see that, going from effect to effect, we must always arrive at some will as a first cause, for to suppose an infinite regression of causes is to suppose none at all. In short, any movement that is not caused by another movement can come only from a spontaneous, voluntary act; inanimate bodies act only by motion, and there is no real action without will. This is my first principle. I believe that a will moves the universe and animates nature. This is my first dogma, or my first article of faith.

How does a will produce a physical and corporeal act? I do not know, but I perceive in myself that it does so. I will to act, and I act; I will to move my body, and my body moves. But it is incomprehensible and unprecedented that an inanimate body, at rest, should move of itself and produce motion. Will is known to me by its acts, not by its nature. I know it as a cause of motion; but to conceive matter producing motion is clearly to conceive an effect without a cause: it is to conceive absolutely nothing.

It is no more possible for me to conceive how my will moves my body than how my sensations affect my soul. I do not even know why one of those mysteries has seemed more explainable than the other. As for me, either when I am passive or when I am active, the means of uniting the two substances seems completely incomprehensible to me. It is strange that others take that very incomprehensibility as their point of departure for combining the two substances, as though operations so different in nature could be better explained in one subject than in two.

It is true that the dogma I have just established is obscure, but it does have some meaning and there is nothing in it that is contrary to reason or observation. Can the same be said of materialism? It is clear that if motion were essential to matter, it would be inseparable from it, always in it to the same degree, always the same in each particle of matter; it would be incommunicable, and could neither increase nor diminish; and we could not even conceive of matter at rest. When someone tells me that motion is not essential to matter but is necessary to it, he is trying to mislead me with words that would be easier to refute if they had a little more meaning. For either the motion of matter comes from matter itself and is therefore essential to it, or else it comes from an external cause, in which case it is necessary to matter only insofar as the cause acts on it, and we return to the original difficulty.

General and abstract ideas are the soul of men's greatest errors; the jargon of metaphysics has never led to the discovery of a single truth, and it has filled philosophy with absurdities that we are ashamed of as soon as we have stripped them of their grandiose words. Tell me, my friend, if when someone speaks to you of a blind force spread throughout nature, he presents any real idea to your mind. Those who think they say something by such vague words as "universal force" and "necessary motion" do not say anything at all. The idea of motion is nothing other than the idea of transference from one place to another; there is no motion without a specific direction, for no entity can move in all directions at once. In what direction, then, does matter necessarily move? Does all the matter in a body have uniform motion, or does each atom have its own? According to the first idea, the whole universe must form a solid and indivisible mass; according to the second, it must form only a diffuse and incohesive fluid in which no two atoms can ever unite. What would be the direction of that motion common to all matter? Would it be in a straight line, upward, downward, left, or right? If each molecule of matter had its own particular direction, what would be the causes of all those directions and all those differences? If each atom or molecule of matter only revolved on its own axis, nothing would ever leave its place and no motion could be imparted; and even then, that circular motion would have to have a direction. To attribute motion to matter by abstraction is to speak words that mean nothing; and to attribute a specified motion to it is to presuppose a determining cause. The more I multiply particular forces, the more new causes I have to explain, and I can never find any common agent that controls them. Far from being able to imagine any order in the fortuitous concurrence of the elements, I cannot even imagine them as being in conflict, and a chaotic universe is less conceivable to me than a harmonious one. I realize that the mechanism of the world may not be intelligible to the human mind; but if a man sets out to explain it, he must say things that men can understand.

If moving matter shows me a will, matter moving in accordance with certain laws shows me an intelligence: that is my second article of faith. Acting, comparing, and choosing are operations of an active and thinking being; therefore that being exists. You may ask me where I see him existing. I see him not only in the revolving heavens and in the sun that gives us light, not only in myself, but also in a grazing sheep, a flying bird, a falling stone, a windblown leaf.

I judge the order of the world even though I do not know its purpose, because to judge it I have only to compare its parts with one another, to study their connections and relations, and to observe how they work together. I do not know why the universe exists, but that does not prevent me from seeing how it is modified, or from perceiving the close interconnections by which the entities that compose it aid one another. I am like a man who, seeing an open watch for the first time, admires its mechanism even though he does not know its function and has not seen its dial. "I do not know what the whole machine is designed to do," he might say, "but I see that each part of it is made for the others, I admire its maker in the details of his work, and I am sure that its parts all move together in this way for some common purpose which I cannot perceive."

Let us compare the particular ends, the means, the ordered relations of every kind, and then listen to our inner feeling. What healthy mind can reject its testimony? What unprejudiced eye can fail to see the obvious order of the universe as evidence of a supreme intelligence? How many sophistries must a man amass before he becomes blind to the harmony of all parts of that universe and the admirable way in which each works to preserve the others? Anyone may speak to me of combinations and chances as much as he likes, but what good will it do him to reduce me to silence if he cannot convince me? And how can he deprive me of the involuntary feeling that continues to deny what he says? If organized bodies came together in countless fortuitous ways before taking on stable forms, if there were first stomachs without mouths, feet without heads, hands without arms, and imperfect organs of all kinds which perished because they were unable to preserve themselves, why are none of those imperfect attempts still to be seen in the world? Why did nature finally lay down laws for herself to which she was not subject before? I grant that I ought not to be surprised if something that is possible actually happens, and if the number of attempts compensates for the improbability of the event. But if I were told that printer's type had been thrown at random and the letters had fallen in such a way as to spell out the entire *Aeneid*, I would not deign to take one step to investigate that falsehood. "You are overlooking the number of throws," I might be told. But how many throws must I assume in order to make the combination plausible? Since I see the result of only one, to me the odds are infinity to one that it was not the effect of chance. Furthermore, since combinations and chances never yield anything but products of the same nature as the elements combined, the organization of life cannot result from a random aggregation of atoms, and a chemist making compounds will never cause them to feel and think in his crucible.[5]

I have read Nieuwentyt with surprise, and almost with shock. How could he set out to write a book of the wonders of nature which show the wisdom of the Creator of nature? If his book had been as big as the world, it would still not have exhausted its subject; and as soon as we try to enter into detail, the greatest wonder of all escapes us: the harmony and concord of the whole. The generation of living organic bodies is in itself an unfathomable mystery to the human mind. The insurmountable barriers that nature has placed among the various species, so that they will not become mingled, make her intentions abundantly clear. She has not simply established order: She has also taken effective measures to prevent it from being disturbed.

There is no entity in the universe that cannot be regarded in some respect as the common center of all the others, around which they are all ordered, so that they are all reciprocally ends and means in relation to one another. The mind is confused and lost in that infinity of relations, not one of which is confused or lost in the multitude of the others. What absurd assumptions are needed to deduce all that harmony from the blind mechanism of matter moving at random! Those who deny the unity of intention manifested in the relations of all parts of that great whole vainly cover their gibberish with abstractions, coordinations, general principles, and symbolic terms; no matter what they do, it is impossible for me to conceive such an immutably ordered system of entities without also conceiving an intelligence that orders it. It is not in my power to believe that passive, lifeless matter could have produced living, feeling beings, that blind chance could have produced intelligent beings, that anything which does not think could have produced thinking beings.

I therefore believe that the world is governed by a wise and powerful will; I see that, or rather I feel it, and it is important for me to know it. But is the world eternal or created? Is there a single source of all things? Are there two, or more? And what is their nature? I do not know, and what does it matter to me? When knowledge of those things becomes important to me, I will try to acquire it; until then, I will refrain from speculating on idle questions, which, though they may trouble my vanity, are irrelevant to my conduct and beyond my reason.

Always remember that I am not urging you to accept my views: I am simply presenting them to you. Whether matter is eternal or created, whether there is a passive source or not, it is still certain that the whole is one, and proclaims a single intelligence, for I see nothing that is not ordered within the same system and does not work toward the same end, namely, maintaining the whole in the established order. The being who has both will and power, who is active of himself, who moves the universe and orders all things—that being, whatever he may be, I call God. I add to that name the ideas of intelligence, power, and will, which I have assembled, and that of goodness, which necessarily follows from them; but in attributing that idea to him, I have no better knowledge of him. He remains beyond the reach of both my senses and my understanding. The more I think about him, the more perplexed I am; I know with certainty that he exists, and that he exists of himself; I know that my existence is subordinate to his, and that the same is true of all things known to me. I perceive God everywhere in his works, I feel him within myself, I see him all around me; but as soon as I try to contemplate him in himself, as soon as I try to discover where he is, what he is, what his substance is, he eludes me, and my troubled mind no longer perceives anything.

Deeply aware of my inadequacy, I will never reason about the nature of God unless I am forced to do so by the feeling of his relation to me. Such reasoning is always rash; a wise man should engage in it only with trepidation and the conviction that he is incapable of attaining ultimate truth, for what is most insulting to God is not refraining from thinking about him at all, but thinking about him wrongly.

After having discovered those of his attributes by which I conceive his existence, I return to myself and try to ascertain the rank I occupy in the order of things which he governs and which I can examine. I find that I an incontestably in the foremost rank because of the species to which I belong, for by my will and the means of executing it that I have at my disposal, I have more power to act on all things around me, or to accept or avoid their action as I choose, than any of them has to act on me against my will by mere physical impulsion; and by my intelligence, I am the only one able to examine the whole. What earthly entity except man can observe all others, measure, calculate, and foresee their movements and effects, and join, so to speak, the feeling of common existence to that of his individual existence? What is so ridiculous in thinking that all things were made for me, if I alone am able to relate them to myself?

It is therefore true that man is lord of the earth on which he lives, for not only does he subdue all animals, not only does he control the elements by his skills and industry, but he alone on earth is able to control them, and in contemplation he even takes possession of the heavenly bodies that are beyond his physical grasp. Show me another animal on earth that can make use of fire and admire the sun. What! I can observe and know the parts of the world and their relations; I can comprehend the meaning of order, beauty, and virtue; I can contemplate the universe and raise myself toward the hand that governs it; I can love good and do it—and yet I should compare myself to an animal? Abject soul, it is your wretched philosophy that makes you resemble an animal; or rather, you try in vain to degrade yourself, but your spirit testifies against your principles, your charitable heart belies your doctrine, and the very misuse of your faculties proves their excellence in spite of you.

I have no system to uphold; I am a simple and honest man, unaffected by the jealous spirit of any faction and with no aspiration to the honor of being the head of a sect. I am content with the place assigned to me by God. After God, I see nothing better than my species. If I had to choose my place in the order of existence, what more could I choose than to be a man?

I am deeply moved by this thought, rather than being made proud by it, for my state did not result from my own choice; it could not have been determined by the merit of a being who did not yet exist. Can I see myself thus distinguished without being thankful that I hold this honorable position, and without blessing the hand that placed me in it? My first return to self-contemplation gives rise in my heart to a feeling of gratitude and exaltation toward the Creator of my species, and from this feeling comes my first homage to the benevolent Divinity. I worship his supreme power and I am touched by his kindness. This worship is not something that must be taught to me: it is dictated to me by nature herself. Is it not a natural consequence of our self-love to honor what protects us and to love what is benevolently inclined toward us?

But when, seeking to learn my individual place in my species, I consider the various ranks in it and the men who occupy them, what am I to think? What a spectacle! Where is the order I had observed? The panorama of nature showed me only harmony and proportion; that of the human race now shows me only confusion and disorder! Concord reigns among the elements, and men are in chaos! The animals are happy, and their lord is miserable! O Wisdom, where are your laws? O Providence, is this how you order the world? O Benevolent Being, what has become of your power? I see evil on earth.

Would you believe, my dear friend, that it was from these sad thoughts and apparent contradictions that my mind conceived the sublime idea of the soul, to which my reflections had not yet led me? As I meditated on the nature of man, I seemed to discover two distinct principles in him. The first elevated him to the study of eternal truths, to love of justice and moral beauty, to those realms of the intellectual world that the wise delight in contemplating. The second drew him downward into himself, subjected him to the power of his senses and the passions that are their ministers, and counteracted, through them, everything inspired in him by the first principle. Feeling myself swayed and torn by those two conflicting tendencies, I said to myself, "No, man is not one: I both exert my will and fail to exert it; I feel both enslaved and free; I see what is good, I love it, and I do evil; I am active when I listen to my reason and passive when I am carried away by my passions; and when I give in to them, my worst torment is the feeling that I could have resisted them."

Young man, listen to me with confidence, because I will always speak to you in good faith. If conscience is the work of prejudice, I am undoubtedly wrong, and there is no demonstrably true morality; but if giving oneself preference over all others is a natural inclination of man, and if the first feeling of justice is nevertheless inborn in the human heart, let those who maintain that man is not a compound being resolve that contradiction, and I will acknowledge that there is only a single substance.

Let me point out that by the word "substance" I mean, in general, a being endowed with some primary quality, apart from all particular or secondary modifications. If, then, all the primary qualities that are known to us can be combined in a single being, we must grant that there is only one substance; but if some primary qualities exclude each other, there are as many different substances as there are such exclusions. Reflect on that; as for me, whatever Locke may say, I need only know matter as extended and divisible in order to be assured that it cannot think. If a philosopher tells me that trees feel and rocks think,[6] it will be useless for him to perplex me with his subtle arguments; I can see him only as an insincere sophist who would rather attribute feeling to stones than a soul to man.

Let us suppose that a deaf man denies the existence of sound because he has never heard it. I show him a stringed instrument and make it sound in unison with another instrument which is hidden from him. He sees the string vibrating and I say to him, "That is caused by sound."

"Not at all," he replies. "The cause of the string's vibration is in the string itself; such vibration is a quality common to all bodies."

"Then show it to me in other bodies," I say, "or at least show me its cause in this string."

"I cannot do that," answers the deaf man. "I do not understand how the string vibrates, but why should I explain it by your sound, of which I know nothing? That would be explaining an obscure fact by a cause that is even more obscure. Either make your sound perceptible to me, or I will say that it does not exist."

The more I reflect on thought and the nature of the human mind, the more similarity I find between the reasoning of materialists and that of the deaf man. They are deaf to the inner voice that cries out to them in a tone that is difficult to ignore, "A machine does not think. Neither motion nor form can produce reflection. Something within you tries to break the bonds that restrain it. Space is not your measure, the whole universe is not large enough for you. Your feelings, your desires, your anxiety, and even your pride have another origin than the limited body in which you feel yourself imprisoned."

No material entity is active of itself, and I am active in that way. It is futile to present me with arguments against this: I feel it, and that feeling which speaks to me is stronger than the reason that opposes it. I have a body on which other bodies act, and which acts on them. There can be no doubt of that reciprocal action; but my will is independent of my senses; I succumb or I resist, and it is always perfectly clear to me whether I have done what I willed to do or whether I have only given in to my passions. When I yield to temptation, I act according to the impulsion of external objects. When I reproach myself with that weakness, I listen only to my will; I am a slave in my vices and a free man in my remorse. The feeling of freedom within me is effaced only when I degrade myself, when I finally prevent the voice of the soul from speaking out against the power of the body.

I know will only through the feeling of my own will, and intelligence is no better known to me. If I am asked what cause determines my will, I ask in turn what cause determines my judgment, for it is clear that those two causes are one. If we realize that man is active in his judgments and that his intelligence is only the power of comparing and judging, we see that his freedom is only a similar power, or one derived from it: He chooses good as he chooses truth; if his judgment is false, his choice is wrong. What, then, is the cause that determines his will? It is his judgment. And what is the cause that determines his judgment? It is his faculty of intelligence, his power to judge; the determining cause is within him. Beyond that, I understand nothing.

No doubt I am not free not to will my own good, I am not free to will harm to myself; but my freedom lies in the very fact that I can will only what is good for me, or what I regard as such, without being determined by anything external to me. Does it follow that I am not my own master because I am unable to be anything other than myself?

The source of every act is the will of a free being; we cannot go beyond that. It is not the word "freedom" that is meaningless, but the word "necessity." To suppose an act, an effect, that does not derive from an active origin is truly to suppose an effect without a cause: it is to fall into a vicious circle. Either there is no first impulsion or no first impulsion has an antecedent cause, and there is no true will without freedom. Man is therefore free in his acts, and as such, animated by an immaterial substance. That is my third article of faith. From these first three articles you can easily deduce all the others, without my continuing to state them.

If men are active and free, they act of themselves. What they do freely is not part of the system ordained by God, and cannot be imputed to him. He does not will the evil they do when they misuse the freedom he has given them, but neither does he prevent them from doing it, whether because the evil done by such weak beings is as nothing in his eyes, or because he cannot prevent it without restricting their freedom and doing a greater evil by degrading their nature. He has made them free not in order that they may do evil, but that they may do good by choice. He has given them the ability to make that choice by rightly using the faculties with which he has endowed them, but he has so limited their powers that misuse of their freedom cannot disrupt the general order. The evil that they do falls back upon them without changing anything in the system of the world, without preventing the human race from being preserved in spite of itself. To complain that he does not prevent them from doing evil is to complain that he has given them an excellent nature, that he has endowed their acts with the morality that ennobles them, that he has given them a right to virtue. Supreme happiness lies in being content with oneself; it is in order to deserve that contentment that we are placed on earth and endowed with freedom, that we are tempted by the passions and restrained by conscience. What more could divine power itself have done for us? Could it have placed contradiction in our nature and given the reward for having done good to a man who was incapable of doing evil? What! To prevent man from being wicked, should he have been limited to instinct and made an animal? No, God of my soul, I will never reproach you for having made me in your image, so that I may be free, good, and happy, like you.

It is misuse of our faculties that makes us unhappy and wicked. Our sorrows, cares, and sufferings come from ourselves. Moral evil is undeniably our own work, and physical ills would be nothing without our vices, which have made us sensitive to them. Is it not to preserve us that nature makes us feel our needs? Is not bodily pain a sign that the machine is out of order, and a warning that we must attend to it? Death. . . . The wicked poison their lives and ours. Who would want to live forever? Death is the remedy for the ills we bring upon ourselves; nature does not wish to make us suffer forever. Man living in primitive simplicity is subject to so few ills! He lives almost without sickness, as well as without passions. He neither foresees nor feels death; when he does feel it, his miseries make it desirable to him, and then it is no longer an evil for him. If we were content to be what we are, we would have no reason to complain of our fate; but in seeking an imaginary good, we cause ourselves a thousand real evils. He who cannot endure a little suffering must expect to suffer greatly. When a man has ruined his constitution by a dissolute life, he tries to restore it with remedies; to the ills that he feels, he adds those that he fears. Anticipation of death makes it horrible and hastens its approach; the more we try to flee from it, the more we feel it, and we die of fear throughout a whole lifetime, protesting against nature for the ills that we have inflicted on ourselves by offending her.

Man, look no farther for the author of evil: that author

is yourself. There is no evil but the evil you do and the evil you suffer, and both come from yourself. Evil in general can arise only from disorder, and in the system of the world I see only unfailing order. Particular evil is only in the feeling of the suffering being; man did not receive that feeling from nature: he gave it to himself. Pain has little power over someone who, having thought little, has neither memory nor foresight. Take away our baneful progress, take away our errors and vices, take away the work of man, and all is well.

Where all is well, nothing is unjust. Justice is inseparable from goodness, and goodness is the necessary effect of boundless power and the self-love that is an essential attribute of all sentient beings. The all-powerful Being extends his existence, so to speak, with that of others. Producing and preserving are the everlasting work of power; it does not act on what does not exist. God is not the God of the dead; he could not be destructive and wicked without harming himself. The all-powerful Being can will only what is good.[7] Therefore the Being who is supremely good because he is supremely powerful must also be supremely just; otherwise he would contradict himself, for the love of order that produces order is called goodness, and the love of order that preserves order is called justice.

It is sometimes said that God owes nothing to his creatures. I believe that he owes them everything he promised them when he brought them into being; and in giving them the idea of good and making them feel the need of it, he promised it to them. The more I turn inward and reflect on myself, the more clearly I read these words written in my soul: "Be just and you will be happy." Yet, considering the present state of things, this is not true: The wicked prosper and the just are oppressed. And what indignation flares up in us when that expectation is disappointed! Conscience rebels and protests against its Author; it groans and cries out to him, "You have deceived me!"

"I have deceived you, rash creature? Who told you that? Has your soul been destroyed? Have you ceased to exist? O Brutus, O my son, do not sully your noble life in ending it; do not leave your hope and glory with your body in the fields of Philippi. Why do you say, 'Virtue is nothing,' when you are about to enjoy the reward of your own? You are about to die, you think; no, you will live, and then I will keep all my promises to you."

From the complaints of impatient mortals, one might think that God owed them a reward before they earned it, that he was obliged to pay them for their virtue in advance. No! Let us first be good, and then we shall be happy. Let us not demand our prize before our victory, or our wages before our work. "It is not while they are on the racetrack that the winners in our sacred games are crowned," says Plutarch, "but after they have run their course."

If the soul is immaterial, it may survive the body; and if it does so, Providence is justified. If I had no other proof of the immateriality of the soul than the triumph of the wicked and the oppression of the just in this world, that alone would prevent me from doubting it. Such a flagrant discord in the universal harmony would make me seek to resolve it. I would say to myself, "Everything does not end for us when life ends; death puts everything back in order." I would have to ask myself, it is true, what becomes of a man when all his perceptible aspects have been destroyed, but that question ceases to be a difficulty for me as soon as I recognize the existence of two substances. It is quite simple that during my bodily life, when I perceive only through my senses, everything that lies beyond them escapes me. I can understand that when the union of the body and the soul has been broken, one may be dissolved and the other preserved. Why should the destruction of one cause the destruction of the other? Being so different in nature, they are in an unstable condition during their union; when that union ceases, each returns to its natural state: The active, living substance regains all the force it used in moving the passive, dead substance. Alas, my vices make it all too clear to me that man is only half alive during his life: The life of the soul begins only with the death of the body.

But what is that life? Is the soul immortal by nature? My limited mind cannot grasp anything limitless: everything that is called infinite escapes me. What can I deny or affirm? How can I reason with regard to what I cannot conceive? I believe that the soul survives the body long enough to assure the maintenance of order; who knows if that is enough to make it endure forever? But although I understand how the body is worn out and destroyed by the division of its parts, I cannot conceive such a destruction of a thinking being; and unable to imagine how it could die, I assume that it does not die. Since that assumption is comforting and not unreasonable, why should I fear to accept it?

I feel my soul, I know it by feeling and thought, I know that it exists even though I do not know its essence; I cannot reason concerning ideas that I do not have. What I do know is that the identity of the self is prolonged only through memory, and that in order to continue being the same, I must remember having existed in the past. After death I cannot remember what I was during my life without also remembering what I felt and consequently what I did; and I have no doubt that such memories will some day bring happiness to the good and torments to the wicked. In this world, a host of ardent passions absorb our inner feeling and distract our remorse. The humiliations and disfavor that result from the practice of virtue prevent us from feeling all its charms. But when, freed of the illusions imposed on us by the body and the senses, we enjoy contemplation of the Supreme Being and the eternal truths that flow from him, when all the powers of our soul respond to the beauty of order, and when we are wholly absorbed in comparing what we have done with what we should have done, then the voice of conscience will regain its strength and authority, and the pure happiness of being content with oneself, or the bitter regret of having degraded oneself, will determine, by inexhaustible feelings, the fate that each of us has prepared for himself. Do not ask me, my good friend, if there will be other sources of happiness and torment; I do not know. Those that I have imagined are enough to console me for this life and make me hope for another. I do not say that the virtuous will be rewarded, for what other good can an excellent being expect than to exist according to his nature? But I do say that they will be happy, because their Maker, the Author of all justice, having made them sensitive, did not make them to suffer. Since they have not misused their freedom on earth, they have not deviated from their destiny by their own fault, and yet they have suffered in this life; they will therefore be compensated for it in another life. This idea is based not so much on man's merit as on the idea of goodness that seems to me inseparable from the divine essence. I am only assuming that the laws of order are observed, and that God remains true to himself.[8]

Do not ask me if the torments of the wicked will be everlasting, if the goodness of the Author of their being can condemn them to suffer forever; I do not know that, either, and I have no vain curiosity about such useless questions. Is it important for me to know what will become of the wicked? I have little interest in their fate. It is difficult for me to believe, however, that they are condemned to endless torments. If supreme justice takes vengeance, it does so in this life. O nations, you and your errors are its ministers! It uses the evils you inflict on yourselves to punish the crimes that cause them. It is in your insatiable hearts, consumed with envy, greed, and ambition, that the avenging passions punish your iniquities in the midst of your false prosperity. What need is there to look for hell in another life? It is here, in this life, in the hearts of the wicked.

When our fleeting needs and mad desires come to an end, our passions and our crimes must also end. What kind of perversity can pure spirits have? Needing nothing, why should they be wicked? If, lacking our gross senses, they find their whole happiness in the contemplation of other beings, they can only will the good; and when someone has ceased to be wicked, can he be miserable forever? I am inclined to believe that he cannot, though I have not troubled myself to settle the question in my mind. O good and merciful Being, whatever your decrees may be, I worship them! If you punish the wicked eternally, I abandon my feeble reason before your justice; but if the remorse of those wretched souls is extinguished with time, if their suffering eventually ceases, if the same peace awaits all of us some day, I praise you for it. Is not the wicked man my brother? How often have I been tempted to be like him! If, delivered from his misery, he also loses the malignancy that accompanies it, and if he is as happy as I, then, far from arousing my jealousy, his happiness will only add to mine.

It is thus that, contemplating God in his works and studying him in those of his attributes that it concerns me to know, I have gradually come to expand and augment the idea, imperfect and limited at first, which I have formed of that immense Being. But if that idea has become nobler and greater, it is also less proportionate to human reason. As I approach in spirit the eternal light, its brightness dazzles and confuses me, and I am forced to abandon all the earthly notions that helped me to conceive it. God is no longer corporeal and perceptible; the supreme intelligence that governs the world is no longer the world itself; I try to grasp its essence, but all the efforts of my mind are in vain. When I think that it is that intelligence that gives life and activity to the living, active substance that controls animate bodies, and when I hear it said that my soul is spiritual and that God is a spirit, I rebel against that debasement of the divine essence. As if God and my soul were of the same nature! As if God were not the only absolute Being, the only one who truly acts, feels, thinks, and wills of himself, the only one from whom we receive thought, feeling, activity, will, freedom, and existence! We are free only because he wills our freedom, and his inexplicable substance is to our souls as our souls are to our bodies. I cannot say whether he created matter, bodies, minds, and the whole world. The idea of creation baffles me and surpasses my understanding; I accept it to the extent that I can conceive it. But I know that God formed the universe and everything that exists, that he made and ordered everything. He is undoubtedly eternal, but can my mind grasp the idea of eternity? Why should I be content with words that convey no idea to me? What I understand is that God existed before all things, that he will exist as long as they do, and that he will continue to exist even if they cease to be. The idea that a Being beyond my understanding gives existence to other beings is merely obscure and incomprehensible, but the idea that being and nothingness can convert themselves into each other of their own accord is an obvious contradiction, a flagrant absurdity.

God is intelligent; but how? Man is intelligent when he reasons, but the supreme intelligence has no need to reason. For God, there are neither premises nor conclusions, there are not even propositions: He is purely intuitive, he sees both what is and what may be. All truths are to him a single idea, as all places are a single point and all times a single moment. Human power acts through means; the divine power acts of itself. God is able to act because he wills to do so; his will is his power. God is good, nothing could be more certain than that; but man's goodness is love of his fellow man, and God's goodness is love of order, for it is by order that he maintains what exists, and binds each part to the whole. God is just, I am convinced of it: it is a consequence of his goodness. The injustice of men is their own work, not his. Moral disorder, which to philosophers is evidence against the existence of Providence, is to me proof of it. But men's injustice consists in giving everyone his due, while God's justice consists in calling everyone to account for what he has given him.

If I have succeeded in discovering, one after another, those attributes of which I have no absolute idea, I have done so by drawing necessary conclusions, by correctly using my reason; but I affirm them without understanding them, and that is actually the same as affirming nothing. I may say to myself, "God is thus; I feel it, I have proved it to myself," but it changes nothing: I am still unable to understand how he can be thus.

In short, the more I try to contemplate his infinite essence, the less I comprehend it; but it is, and that is enough for me; the less I conceive it, the more I worship it. I humbly say to God, "Being of Beings, I am because you are; in constantly meditating on you, I am rising to my source. The worthiest use that I can make of my reason is to renounce it before you. The delight of my mind, and the charm of my weakness, is to feel myself overwhelmed by your greatness."

Having thus deduced the main truths that it concerns me to know, from the impressions of perceptible objects and the inner awareness that leads me to judge causes in accordance with my natural understanding, it remains for me to determine the principles of conduct I must derive from them, and what rules I must lay down for myself in order to fulfill my destiny on earth, according to the intention of the Being who placed me here. Still following my method, I do not draw those rules from the principles of a lofty philosophy: I find them in the depths of my heart, indelibly written there by nature. I have only to consult myself about what I want to do: What I feel to be right is right, what I feel to be wrong is wrong. Conscience is the best of all casuists; only when we bargain with it do we resort to the subtleties of reasoning. Our first concern is for ourselves, yet how often the inner voice tells us that in seeking our own good at the expense of others we are doing wrong! We believe that we are following the impulsion of nature when we are actually resisting her; listening to what she says to our senses, we despise what she says to our hearts; the active being obeys, the passive being commands. Conscience is the voice of the soul, the passions are the voice of the body. Is it surprising that these two voices often contradict each other? To which must we listen? Reason deceives us all too often, and we have acquired all too good a right to disregard it, but conscience never deceives us. It is man's true guide; it is to the soul what instinct is to the body;[9] whoever follows it obeys nature, and has no fear of going astray. This is an important point; let me dwell on it awhile, to make it clearer.

All the morality of our acts is in the judgment that we ourselves pass on them. If it is true that good is good, then it must be good within our hearts as well as in what we do; the first reward of justice is to feel that we are practicing it. If moral goodness is in conformity with our nature, man can have a sound mind and a healthy constitution only insofar as he is good. If it is not, if man is naturally wicked, he cannot cease to be wicked without corrupting himself, and goodness in him is an unnatural vice. If we are made to harm our fellow man as a wolf is made to kill its prey, a humane man is so contrary to nature as a merciful wolf, and only virtue can make us feel remorse.

Let us look into ourselves, my young friend, and setting aside all personal interest, let us try to see the direction of our inclinations. Which sight pleases us more: the sufferings of others, or their happiness? Which is more enjoyable for us to do, and leaves us with a more pleasant feeling afterward: a kind act, or a malicious one? When you see a play, which characters win your sympathy? Do you take pleasure in seeing crimes? Do you weep when the criminals are punished? It is said that nothing matters to us except self-interest; but the fact is that the sweetness of friendship and compassion consoles us in our sorrows, and even in our pleasures we would be lonely and miserable if we had no one with whom to share them. If there is nothing moral in man's heart, what is the source of his transports of admiration for heroic deeds and his enraptured love of great souls? What connection is there between self-interest and that enthusiasm for virture? Why would I choose to be Cato tearing out his own entrails, rather than Ceasar at the height of his triumph? If you take away from our hearts that love of what is noble, you will take away all the charm of life. A man whose vile passions have stifled those exquisite feelings in his narrow soul, and who, by focusing all his attention on himself, has come to

love no one but himself, is no longer enraptured by anything; his cold heart no longer throbs with joy; no tender
emotion ever moistens his eyes; he enjoys nothing. Such a
wretched man no longer feels, or lives; he is already dead.

But however many wicked people there may be on
earth, there are few of those cadaverous souls who have
become insensitive, outside of their own interest, to everything that is just and good. Injustice is pleasing to them
only insofar as it works to their advantage; otherwise, like
everyone else, they always want the innocent to be protected. If, on a street or a road, we see an act of violence
and injustice, anger and indignation immediately well up
in our hearts and urge us to go to the defense of the victim; but a more powerful duty restrains us, and the law
deprives us of the right to protect the innocent. If, on the
other hand, we witness an act of clemency or magnanimity, what love and admiration it inspires in us! Is there
anyone who does not say to himself, "I wish I had done
the same"? It is surely of little concern to us whether a
man was good or bad two thousand years ago, and yet we
take the same interest in ancient history as if it had happened in our time. What do Catiline's crimes matter to
me? I am not afraid of being his victim. But why, then, do
I have the same horror of him as if he were my contem-
porary? We hate the wicked not only because they harm
us, but also because they are wicked. We want happiness
not only for ourselves, but also for others, and when their
happiness is not detrimental to ours, it increases it. And finally, we pity the unfortunate, independently of our will;
when we see their suffering, we ourselves suffer from it.
Even the most depraved of men cannot lose that inclination completely, and it often leads them into self-contradic-
tion. A bandit who robs travelers will still cover the na-
kedness of a pauper; a vicious murderer will support a
fainting man.

We speak of the voice of remorse that secretly punishes
hidden crimes and often brings them to light; we speak
from experience, for each of us, alas, has heard that un-
welcome voice himself. We would like to stifle that tyrannical feeling which causes us so much torment. Let us
obey nature, and then we shall learn how gently she reigns
and how pleasant it is, when we have listened to her, to
pass favorable judgment on ourselves. The wicked man
fears and avoids himself; he lifts his spirits by going out-

side himself; he looks around him with anxiety, seeking something that will divert him; if it were not for bitter satire and insulting mockery, he would always be sad; derisive laughter is his only pleasure. The virtuous man, however, finds serenity within himself; there is no malice in his laughter, but only joy, and the source of that joy is in himself; he is as cheerful alone as in company; he does not draw his contentment from those around him: he communicates it to them.

Look at all modern nations and read the histories of ancient ones. Among all those strange and harsh cults, amid that prodigious diversity of customs and behavior, you will find everywhere the same ideas of justice and integrity, the same principles of morality, the same notions of good and evil. Ancient paganism engendered abominable gods who, had they been mortals, would have been punished as scoundrels. But even though vice descended from the immortal realm armed with sacred authority, the moral instinct repulsed it from the hearts of men. While Jupiter's debauchery was celebrated, Xenocrates' continence was admired; chaste Lucretia worshiped shameless Venus; the dauntless Romans offered sacrifices to Fear; they invoked the god who mutilated his father, and died without a murmur at the hands of their own fathers. The most despicable divinities were served by the greatest men. The holy voice of nature, stronger than that of the gods, was respected on earth and seemed to relegate both crime and criminals to heaven.

There is thus within our souls an innate principle of justice and virtue by which, in spite of our maxims, we judge our acts and those of others as good or bad, and it is this principle that I call conscience.

But at this word I hear the clamor of supposedly wise men arising on all sides. "Childish errors! Prejudices of our upbringing!" they exclaim in concert. "There is nothing in the human mind that has not been brought into it by experience. We judge everything on the basis of acquired ideas." They go further: They dare to reject the obvious and universal agreement of all nations; and, to oppose the uniformity of human judgment, they go off into the shadows to seek out some obscure example known only to themselves. As though all the inclinations of nature were annihilated by the depravity of a single people! As though the existence of deformed individuals reduced the whole species to nothing! But what does the skeptical Montaigne accomplish by all his strained efforts to unearth in some corner of the world a custom opposed to the notion of justice? What good does it do him to attribute to the most untrustworthy travelers the authority that he denies to the most famous writers? Shall a few strange and doubtful customs, based on local causes that are unknown to us, destroy the general conclusion drawn from the agreement of all peoples, who differ in all other respects and concur only on this one point? O Montaigne, you who claim to be so frank and honest, be sincere and truthful, if that is possible for a philosopher, and tell me if there is any country in the world where it is a crime to keep one's promise and be merciful, kind, and generous; where the upright man is despised and the treacherous man is honored.

It is said that everyone furthers the public good in his own self-interest. But why, then, does a good man sometimes further it to his own detriment? Can anyone give up his life in his own self-interest? It is no doubt true that each man acts only for his own good; but if there is a moral good that must be taken into account, only the acts of the wicked can be explained by self-interest. It even seems likely that no one will ever attempt to do more than that. A philosophy in which the acts of the virtuous were a stumbling block would be too abominable; it could evade the difficulty only by inventing base intentions and dishonorable motives to account for them; it would be forced to malign Socrates and slander Regulus. If such a doctrine were to arise among us, the voices of nature and reason would immediately denounce it, and would allow none of its partisans the excuse of being in good faith.

It is not my intention to enter into metaphysical discussions which are beyond my understanding and yours, and which actually lead nowhere. I have already told you that I wanted not to philosophize with you, but to help you to consult your heart. If all the philosophers in the world prove me wrong, I shall still have achieved my purpose if you feel that I am right.

To achieve it, I have only to make you distinguish our acquired ideas from our natural feelings; for we feel before we know, and just as we do not learn to will our own good and avoid what is harmful to us, but receive that will from nature, love of good and hatred of evil are as natural to us as self-love. The acts of our conscience are not judgments, but feelings. Although all our ideas come from outside us, the feelings that evaluate them are within us, and it is solely by those feelings that we know the fitness or unfitness that exists between us and those things which we must respect or shun.

For us, to exist is to feel; our sensitivity unquestionably preceded our intelligence: we had feelings before ideas.[10] Whatever the cause of our existence may be, it has provided for our preservation by giving us feelings suited to our nature, and it cannot be denied that those feelings, at least, are innate. They are, so far as the individual is concerned, self-love, fear of pain, horror of death, and desire for well-being. But if, as cannot be doubted, man is sociable by nature, or at least capable of becoming so, he can be sociable only by other innate feelings, relative to his species, for if physical need were the only consideration, it would surely disperse men rather than bring them together. The impulsion of conscience arises from the moral system formed by the individual's double relation between himself and his fellow men. To know good is not to love it; man has no innate knowledge of it, but as soon as his reason leads him to know it, his conscience impels him to love it: it is this feeling that is innate.

I therefore do not believe, my friend, that it is impossible to explain the direct force of conscience as a consequence of our nature, independent of reason itself. But even if it could not be so explained, there would be no need to reject it, for since those who deny that force, accepted and recognized by the rest of the human race, do not prove that it does not exist, but merely say so, when we say that it does exist we have at least as much justification as they, and we also have in our favor the inner testimony of the voice of conscience, which speaks for itself. If the first gleam of judgment dazzles us and confuses our perception of the objects before us, let us wait until our weak eyes open again and become steadier; we shall then soon see those objects in the light of reason, as nature first showed them to us. Or rather, let us be simpler and less vain; let us limit ourselves to the first feelings we find within us, since inquiry always brings us back to them, when it has not led us astray.

Conscience! Conscience! Divine instinct, immortal and

celestial voice! You are the sure guide of a being who is ignorant and limited, but intelligent and free. You are the infallible judge of good and evil; it is through you that man resembles God; it is to you that he owes the excellence of his nature and the morality of his acts. Aside from you, I feel nothing in me that raises me above the level of the beasts, except the sad privilege of wandering from error to error by means of understanding without rules and reason without principles.

Thank heaven we are now delivered from the whole bewildering apparatus of philosophy! We can be men without being learned, we have no need to spend our lives studying morality; we have a more reliable guide, acquired at the cost of less effort, to help us find our way through the immense labyrinth of human opinions. But it is not enough to know that this guide exists: We must also be able to recognize and follow her. If she speaks to all hearts, why are there so few who understand her? It is because she speaks to us in the language of nature, which everything has made us forget. Conscience is timid, she loves retirement and peace; she is dismayed by the noisy tumult of worldly affairs. The prejudices to which her origin is attributed are actually her cruelest enemies. She either flees from them or falls silent before them; their loud voices cover hers and prevent it from being heard; fanaticism dares to imitate it, and to advocate crime in her name. After being rejected so often, she finally becomes disheartened; she no longer speakers to us or answers us, and when we have despised her so long, it becomes as difficult for us to call her back as it was to banish her.

How often I grew weary of the coldness I felt within me during my inquiries! How often sadness and boredom poured their poison into my first meditations and made them unbearable to me! My arid heart gave only languid, lukewarm zeal to my love of truth. I thought, "Why should I torment myself in seeking something that does not exist? Moral good is an illusion; there is nothing good but the pleasures of the senses." Once we have lost our taste for the pleasures of the soul, how hard it is to regain it! And it is still harder to acquire it if we have never had it. If there were a man so wretched as never in his life to have done anything whose memory made him satisfied with himself and glad that he had lived, he would be incapable of ever knowing himself; unaware of the good that was suited to his nature, he would have to remain wicked, and would be everlastingly unhappy. But do you believe that there is anywhere on earth a man so depraved that his heart has never yielded to the inclination to do good? It is so natural and attractive that it cannot be resisted always; and the memory of the pleasure it has once given us is enough to keep it in our thoughts. Unfortunately that inclination is at first difficult to satisfy; we have countless reasons for not giving in to it; false prudence restrains the heart within the limits of the human self, and venturing beyond them requires great efforts of courage. Taking pleasure in doing good is the reward of having done good, but we obtain that reward only after we have earned it. Nothing is more enjoyable than virtue, but we do not know that until we have experienced it. When we first try to embrace virtue, it assumes many alarming forms, like Proteus in the fable, and finally shows itself in its own form only to those who have not let go of it.

Constantly torn between my natural feelings, which spoke in favor of the common good, and my reason, which related everything to myself, I would have spent my whole life in that continual fluctuation, doing evil, loving good, and always in conflict with myself, if truth had not settled my opinions, determined my conduct, and put me at peace with myself. It is futile to try to establish virtue by reason alone; what solid foundation can we give it? It is said that virtue is love of order. But can that love prevail over love of my own well-being, and should it do so? Give me a clear and sufficient reason to prefer it. In reality, that so-called principle is only a play on words, for I can also say that vice is love of order, taken in a different sense. There is some sort of moral order wherever there is feeling and intelligence. The difference is that the good man orders his life in relation to all, while the bad man orders it in relation to himself. The latter makes himself the center of everything, the former measures his radius and remains at the circumference, so that his position is fixed in relation to the common center, which is God, and all the concentric circles, which are God's creatures. If there is no God, only the bad man reasons coherently, and the good man is a fool.

My son, may you some day feel what a great burden is lifted from you when, having exhausted the vanity of human opinions and tasted the bitterness of the passions, you at last find, so close to you, the path to wisdom, the reward of your labors in this life, and the source of the happiness that you had lost all hope of attaining. All the duties of natural law, once almost obliterated in my heart by the injustice of men, have now been engraved in it again in the name of eternal justice, which imposes them on me and sees me fulfill them. I feel that I am the creation and the instrument of the great Being who wills and produces what is good, and will bring about my own good if my will concurs with his and if I use my freedom rightly. I acquiesce in the order he establishes, certain that I shall some day enjoy it myself and find my happiness in it, for what sweeter happiness can there be than feeling oneself part of a system in which everything is good? When I am in the grip of pain, I bear it patiently, reminding myself that it is temporary and comes from a body that is not mine. If I do a good deed unknown to other men, I know that it has been seen, and I am aware of the bearing that my conduct in this life will have on the life to come. If I suffer an injustice, I say to myself, "The just Being who controls all things will compensate me for it. The needs of my body and the miseries of my life make the idea of death more bearable to me. There will be fewer bonds to be broken when I must leave everything."

Why is my soul subject to the domination of my senses, and chained to this body which enslaves and thwarts it? I do not know; God's decrees have not been explained to me. But I can, without rashness, make modest conjectures. I say to myself that if man's spirit had remained free and pure, he would have no merit in loving and following the order he finds established, since he would have no interest in disturbing it. He would be happy, it is true, but his happiness would lack its most sublime degree: the glory of virtue and a good opinion of himself. He would be like the angels, whereas the virtuous man will no doubt be more than they. But the soul is bound to a mortal body by ties as strong as they are incomprehensible. Its concern with the preservation of the body gives it an interest contrary to the general order. Yet it is capable of seeing and loving that order; the right use of its freedom then becomes both its merit and its reward, and it works toward everlasting happiness for itself by opposing its earthly passions and maintaining its original will.

If all our first inclinations are right, even in our debased state during this life, and if all our vices come from ourselves, why should we complain of being subjugated by them? Why should we blame the Author of all things for the enemies we make and the ills we bring upon ourselves? Ah, let us not corrupt man! He can always be good without difficulty, and happy without remorse. The guilty who say that they were forced to commit crimes are as untruthful as they are wicked. How can they fail to see that the weakness of which they complain is their own doing, that they voluntarily took the first step toward depravity, and that by yielding to temptation willingly they finally made it irresistible, so that they must yield to it whether they are willing or not? Although it is no longer within their power not to be wicked and weak, it was once within their power not to become so. We could so easily remain in control of ourselves and our passions, even during this life, if, before our habits were formed and while our minds were beginning to open, we kept our thoughts occupied with the things we needed to know in order to judge those that we did not know; if we sincerely wanted to enlighten ourselves, not so that we could win the admiration of others, but to be good and wise according to our nature, and to make ourselves happy by fulfilling our duties. This study seems boring and difficult to us because we think of it only now that we have already been corrupted by vice and enslaved by our passions. We fix our judgments and decide what is worthy of our esteem before we know good and evil, and then, measuring everything by that false standard, we give nothing its true value.

There is an age when the heart, still free, but ardent, anxious, and eager for a happiness that it does not know, seeks it with curious uncertainty, and deceived by the senses, finally fixes on a vain image of it and believes it has found it where it is not. In my case, those illusions lasted too long. Alas, I knew them too late, and I have not been able to destroy them completely; they will endure as long as the mortal body that causes them. But although they entice me, they at least do not deceive me; I know them for what they are, and I despise them even when I follow them. Far from seeing them as the object of my happiness, I see them as an obstacle to it. I long for the time when, freed from the shackles of the body, I shall be *myself*, without conflict or division; I shall then need only myself in order to be happy. Meanwhile I am happy even in this life, because I attach little importance to all its ills and regard it as almost foreign to my being, and I know that all the real good I can draw from it depends on me.

By means of lofty meditation I approach that future state of happiness, strength, and freedom as closely as it is now possible for me to do. I contemplate the order of the universe, not to explain it with vain systems, but to admire it unceasingly and worship the wise Maker whose presence I feel in it. I converse with him, I impregnate all my faculties with his divine essence, I am deeply moved by his kindness, and I give thanks to him for his gifts; but I do not pray to him. What could I ask of him? That he change the course of the world for me, that he perform miracles in my favor? Knowing that I must love above all else the order established by his wisdom and maintained by his providence, shall I ask him to disrupt that order for my sake? No, that audacious wish would deserve to be punished rather than granted. Neither do I ask him for the power to act rightly—why should I ask him for what he has already given me? Has he not given me conscience to love the good, reason to know it, and freedom to choose it? If I do evil, I have no excuse; I do it willingly, and asking him to change my will would be asking of him what he asks of me; it would be wanting him to do my work and let me reap the reward for it. To be dissatisfied with my state would be to wish to cease being a man, to want something other than what is, to desire disorder and evil. Good and merciful God, source of all justice and truth, I trust in you, and the supreme wish of my heart is that your will be done. When I join my own will to yours, I do as you do, I acquiesce in your goodness; I feel that I share in advance the supreme happiness that is its reward.

In my justified mistrust of myself, all that I ask of God, or rather what I expect of his justice, is to correct my error if I go astray and if that error is dangerous to me. I do not believe that my good faith makes me infallible; the opinions that seem truest to me may be so many falsehoods, for what man does not cling to his own opinions, and how many men are in agreement on everything? Although the illusion that misleads me comes from myself, only God can cure me of it. I have done all I can to reach truth, but its source is too high for me. If I lack the strength to go farther, am I at fault? I can now only wait for truth to come to me.

The good priest had been speaking fervently; he was deeply moved, and so was I.* I felt as if I had been hearing the divine Orpheus singing the first hymns and teaching men to worship the gods. Yet I saw many objections that I could have raised; I raised none of them, however, because they were less solid than perplexing, and I was basically persuaded in his favor. As he spoke according to his conscience, my own seemed to confirm what he said.

"The views you have just expressed to me," I said, "seem more unusual to me because of what you admit you do not know than because of what you say you believe. I see in them something very close to theism or natural religion, which Christians profess to equate with atheism or irreligion, though it is actually the exact opposite. But in the present state of my faith I would have to ascend, rather than descend, to adopt your opinions, and it would be difficult for me to remain precisely where you are, unless I were as wise as you. To be at least as sincere as you, I want to take counsel with myself. It is the inner voice that must lead me to follow your example, and you yourself have told me that after it has been silenced for a long time it cannot be quickly called back. What you have said will remain in my heart; I must meditate on it. If, after careful reflection, I am as convinced as you, you will be my last teacher, and I will be your disciple till death. But continue your teaching now; you have told me only half of what I need to know. Speak to me of revelation, of the Scriptures, of those obscure dogmas about which I have been undecided since my childhood, unable either to understand or believe them, to accept or reject them."

He embraced me and said:

Yes, my son, I will finish telling you what I think. I do not want to open my heart to you only halfway; but the desire you have expressed was necessary to make me feel justified in speaking to you without reserve. Till now I have told you nothing which I did not think would be of

---

*In this section the speaker is the young man who has been listening to the priest. (Translator's note.)

use to you, and of which I was not firmly convinced. The inquiry that remains to be made is quite different; I see in it only perplexity, mystery, and obscurity; I approach it with uncertainty and misgiving. I tremble at the thought of it, and I shall be telling you of my doubts, rather than of my opinions. If your views were more settled, I would hesitate to give you mine; but in your present condition it will be better for you if you think as I do.[11] Give my words only the authority of reason, however; I do not know if I am in error. In discussion it is sometimes difficult to avoid taking a decisive tone, but remember that all my assertions will be only reasons for doubt. Seek truth for yourself; as for me, I promise you only sincerity.

In the statement of my opinions you you see only natural religion; it is strange that another kind should be required. If so, how am I to know it? Of what am I guilty if I serve God in accordance with the understanding he has given to my mind and the feelings he has aroused in my heart? Is there any moral purity, any dogma that will help man and honor his Maker, which I can derive from a formal doctrine but cannot derive without such a doctrine by the right use of my faculties? Show me what can be added, for the glory of God, the good of society, and my own advantage, to the duties of natural law, and how a new form of worship could produce a virtue that would not be a consequence of mine. The greatest ideas of the Divinity come to us through reason alone. Look at the spectacle of nature, listen to the inner voice. Has not God presented everything to our eyes, our conscience, our judgment? What more can we learn from men? Their revelations only degrade God by attributing human passions to him. Far from elucidating our ideas of the great Being, specific dogmas seem to me to confuse them; far from ennobling them, they debase them; to the inconceivable mysteries that surround God, they add absurd contradictions; they make man haughty, intolerant, and cruel; instead of assuring peace on earth, they bring fire and the sword. I ask myself what is the good of all that, and I cannot answer. I see in it only the crimes of men and the misery of the human race.

I am told that a revelation was needed to teach men the way in which God wanted to be served; the diversity of strange cults that they have instituted is given as proof of this, but what is overlooked is that this very diversity comes from the vagaries of revelations. When nations began making God speak, each one made him speak in its own manner, and say what it wanted to hear. If men had listened only to what God says in their hearts, there would always have been only one religion on earth.

I am willing to grant that uniformity of worship was needed; but was it so important that the whole apparatus of divine power was required to establish it? Let us not confuse the rites of religion with religion itself. The worship that God asks of us is the worship that comes from the heart, and when it is sincere it is always uniform. It is foolish vanity to imagine that God takes such great interest in the form of a priest's garments, the order of the words he speaks, the gestures he makes before the altar, and all his genuflections. Remain standing at your full height, my friend, and you will still be close enough to the earth. God wants to be worshipped in spirit and in truth; that duty belongs to all religions, all countries, and all men. As for the external aspects of worship, if they must be uniform for the sake of order, that is entirely an administrative matter which requires no revelation.

I did not begin with all these reflections. Impelled by the prejudices of my upbringing and that dangerous vanity which makes man strive to go beyond his own sphere, and unable to lift my feeble thoughts to the great Being, I tried to bring him down to my level, to reduce the infinite distance that he has placed between his nature and mine. I wanted more immediate communication, more specific instructions; and not content with making God resemble his human creatures, I wanted supernatural knowledge so that I might be privileged among my fellow men; I wanted an exclusive kind of worship; I wanted God to tell me things which he had not told to others, or which others had not understood as I did.

Regarding the point I had reached as the common point from which all believers took their departure in order to arrive at a more enlightened worship, I found in the tenets of natural religion only the elements of all religion. I considered all the different sects that reign on earth and accuse each other of falsehood and error, and I asked, "Which one is right?"

"Mine!" answered everyone. "Only I and those who agree with me think rightly; everyone else is mistaken."

"How do you know that your sect is the right one?"

"God said so."[12]

"And who told you that God said so?"

"My minister. He knows. He told me to believe it, and I do. He assures me that those who say anything different are liars, so I do not listen to them."

And I thought, "What! Truth is not one? Can what is true in one place be false in another? If a man who goes astray follows the same method as a man who takes the right path, how can one deserve more praise or blame than the other? Their choice is the result of chance, and holding them personally responsible for it is unjust; it means rewarding or punishing them for having been born in a certain country. To dare to say that God judges us in that way is to insult his justice."

Either all religions are good and pleasing to God, or, if he prescribes only one to men and punishes those who do not observe it, he has given it obvious and unmistakable signs by which it can be distinguished and known as the only true religion. These signs must be the same in all times and places, equally recognizable to all men, great or humble, learned or ignorant, Europeans, Indians, Africans, or savages. If there were on earth one religion outside of which there were only eternal torments, and if anywhere in the world there were a single man of good faith who had not been struck by its obvious truth, the God of that religion would be the cruelest and most unjust of tyrants.

Do we seek truth sincerely? Let us grant nothing to the right of birth and the authority of fathers and ministers, but let us examine, in the light of conscience and reason, everything they have taught us from childhood. It is vain for them to tell me that I must subdue my reason; the same could be said to me by someone who wanted to deceive me. I must have reasons for subduing my reason.

All the theology that I can acquire for myself by observing the universe and rightly using my faculties is limited to what I have already explained to you. To know more, we must resort to extraordinary means. Those means cannot be the authority of men, for all men are of the same species as myself; I can therefore know anything that any man can know naturally, and another man can as easily be mistaken as I. If I believe what he says, it is not because he says it, but because he proves it. Thus the testimony of men is actually the same as that of my reason, and adds nothing to the natural means of knowing truth that God has given me.

"Apostle of truth, what have you to tell me that I cannot rightfully judge for myself?"

"God himself has spoken; listen to his revelation."

"That is another matter. God has spoken! What an impressive statement! To whom has he spoken?"

"To men."

"Then why have I heard none of his words?"

"He has told other men to report them to you."

"I understand: It is men who will tell me what God has said. I would rather have heard God himself; it would have been no more difficult for him, and it would have protected me from being misled."

"He protects you from it by proving that his spokesmen were really sent by him."

"How does he prove that?"

"By miracles."

"Where are those miracles?"

"In books."

"Who wrote those books?"

"Men."

"And who saw the miracles?"

"Men who attest to them."

"What! Always human testimony! Always men who report to me what other men have reported! How many men there are between God and me! Let us see, however, let us examine, compare, and verify. Ah, if God had deigned to spare me all that labor, would I have served him any less wholeheartedly?"

Consider, my friend, the terrible discussion in which I have now become engaged; consider the vast learning I must have in order to go back into remote antiquity, to examine, weigh, and compare prophecies, revelations, and all the religious documents offered by all countries of the world, to determine their dates, places, authors, and occasions! What accurate critical judgment I must have to distinguish true from false evidence; to compare objections and replies, translations and originals; to appraise the impartiality, common sense, and knowledge of witnesses; to know if anything has been omitted, added, transposed, altered, or falsified; to resolve the contradictions that remain; to decide what weight must be given to the silence of adversaries in the face of the charges brought against them, and if those charges were known to them, and if they took them seriously enough to deign to answer them, and if books were common enough at the time for ours to have reached them, and if we were sincere enough to let their books circulate among us, with the strongest objections in them left unaltered.

If all those documents are accepted as authentic, we must next consider the evidence for their authors' mission; we must know the laws of chance and probability to decide which predictions could not come to pass without a miracle; we must be well versed in the spirit of the original languages to know what is a prediction in those languages and what is only a figure of speech; we must know what is in the order of nature and what is not, so that we can judge the extent to which a clever man may delude the simple and even astonish the learned; we must determine what traits and authenticity a miracle must have, not only to be believed, but to make doubt of it a punishable offense; we must compare the evidence offered for both true and false miracles, and find reliable rules for distinguishing between them; and finally, we must explain why God has chosen to validate his words by means which themselves have such great need of validation, as though he were making sport of men's credulity and deliberately avoiding the true means of convincing them.

Assuming that the Almighty had condescended to make a man the medium for communicating his sacred will, would it be reasonable and just to demand that the whole human race obey that spokesman's voice without making him known as such? Would it be fair to give him no credentials but a few special signs that were witnessed only by a small number of obscure people and could never be known to the rest of mankind except by hearsay? If we were to believe all the miracles that simple and uneducated people all over the world claim to have seen, each sect would be the right one; there would be more miracles than natural events, and the greatest of all miracles would be that there were no miracles where fanatics were persecuted. It is the immutable order of nature that best shows the wise hand that guides it. If there were many exceptions to it, I would no longer know what to think of it. For my part, I believe in God too firmly to believe in all those miracles that are so little worthy of him.

Suppose a man were to say to us, "Mortals, I proclaim

to you the will of the Almighty. Recognize, by my voice, him who has sent me. I order the sun to change its course, the stars to form another arrangement, the mountains to become flat, the waves to rise, and the face of the earth to take on a new appearance." Seeing such miracles, who would not immediately recognize the master of nature? She does not obey impostors; they work their miracles on street corners, in deserts, or behind closed doors, and there they easily take in a small number of specators already disposed to believe anything. Who will venture to tell me how many eyewitnesses are required to make a miracle worthy of belief? If miracles performed to prove a doctrine must themselves be proved, they are useless, and performing them is a waste of time.

The most important question with regard to the proclaimed doctrine still remains to be examined. Since those who say that God works miracles on earth maintain that the devil sometimes imitates them, even the best-attested miracles leave us no better off than before; and since Pharaoh's magicians dared, in Moses' presence, to produce the same signs that he produced at God's command, why, in his absence, should they not have claimed the same authority, with the same justification? Thus, after the doctrine has been proved by miracles, the miracles must be proved by the doctrine,[13] lest we mistake the work of the devil for the work of God. What do you think of that way of begging the question?

If a doctrine comes from God, it must bear the sacred stamp of the Divinity; not only must it elucidate the confused ideas that reasoning sketches in our minds, but it must also offer us a form of worship, a morality, and guiding principles that are compatible with the attributes by which we conceive God's essence. If, then, it taught us only absurd and unreasonable things, if it aroused in us only feelings of aversion of our fellow men and fear for ourselves, and if it depicted only a wrathful, jealous, vengeful, and partial God who hates men, a God of war and combat, always ready to strike and destroy, always speaking of torments and penalties, and boasting of punishing even the innocent, my heart would not be drawn to that God, and I would certainly not give up natural religion to embrace that doctrine; for, as you can see, a choice would have to be made. "Your God is not ours," I would say to his followers. "A God who begins by choosing a single people for himself, and proscribing the rest of mankind, is not the common father of men; a God who dooms most of his creatures to eternal suffering is not the good and merciful God whom my reason has shown to me."

With regard to dogmas, my reason tells me that they must be clear, illuminating, and strikingly self-evident. If natural religion is inadequate, it is because of the obscurity it leaves in the great truths it teaches us; it is for revelation to teach us those truths in a way that the human mind can grasp, to bring them within our reach, to make us comprehend them so that we can believe them. Faith is made strong and firm by understanding; the best of all religions is necessarily the clearest. A religion that preaches a doctrine laden with mysteries and contradictions tells me by that very fact that I must mistrust it. The God I worship is not a God of darkness, he has not given me understanding so that he can forbid me to use it; to tell me to subdue my reason is to insult its Author. The minister of truth does not tyrannize my reason: he enlightens it.

We have set aside all human authority, and without it I did not see how one man can convince another by preaching an unreasonable doctrine to him. Let us pit those two men against each other for a moment, and see what they have to say in the harsh language usually employed by both sides.

THE MAN OF INSPIRATION. Reason tells you that the whole is greater than the part, but I tell you, on behalf of God, that the part is greater than the whole.

THE MAN OF REASON. Who are you to dare to say that God contradicts himself? And which shall I choose to believe: God who teaches me eternal truths through reason, or you who proclaim an absurdity on his behalf?

INSPIRATION. Believe me, because my teaching is less abstract; and I will prove to you conclusively that God has sent me.

REASON. What? You will prove to me that God has sent you to testify against him? What kind of proof will you use to convince me that it is more certain that God speaks to me through your mouth than through the understanding he has given me?

INSPIRATION. The understanding he has given you! Vain,

small man! As though you were the first unbeliever who had gone astray through his reason corrupted by sin!

REASON. Man of God, you will not be the first charlatan to give his arrogance as proof of his mission.

INSPIRATION. What! Do philosophers also use insults?

REASON. Sometimes, when saints set the example for them.

INSPIRATION. But I have a right to do it: I speak for God.

REASON. You ought to show your credentials before exercising your privileges.

INSPIRATION. My credentials are genuine; heaven and earth will bear witness for me. Please follow my reasoning carefully.

REASON. Your-reasoning? You cannot mean what you say! When you tell me that my reason deceives me, are you not refuting whatever it may say to me in your favor? Anyone who rejects reason must convince others without using it, for assuming that you were to convince me by reasoning, how could I know that it was not my reason corrupted by sin which made me accept what you said to me? Furthermore, what proof, what demonstration could you ever use that would be more self-evident than the axiom it was meant to destroy? It is no more difficult to believe that a good syllogism is false than that the part is greater than the whole.

INSPIRATION. What a difference! My proofs are unquestionable: they are of a supernatural order.

REASON. Supernatural! What does that word mean? I do not understand it.

INSPIRATION. Changes in the order of nature, prophecies, miracles, wonders of all kinds.

Reason. Wonders! Miracles! I have never seen any of those things.

INSPIRATION. Others have seen them for you. Multitudes of witnesses ... the testimony of whole nations. ...

REASON. Is the testimony of nations of a supernatural order?

INSPIRATION. No; but when it is unanimous, it is incontestable.

REASON. Nothing is more incontestable than the principles of reason, and an absurdity cannot be made acceptable by the testimony of men. Once again, let me see your supernatural proofs, because human declarations are not supernatural.

INSPIRATION. Hardened heart! Grace does not speak to you!

REASON. That is not my fault; according to you, no one is able to ask for grace unless he has already received it, so you must begin by speaking to me in its place.

INSPIRATION. That is what I am doing, and you will not listen. But tell me, what do you say about prophecies?

REASON. First, I say that I have no more heard prophecies than I have seen miracles. I also say that no prophecy could be conclusive for me.

INSPIRATION. Follower of the devil! Why could no prophecy be conclusive for you?

REASON. Because it would require three conditions that can never occur together: I would have to hear the prophecy, I would have to witness the event that fulfilled it, and it would have to be demonstrated to me that the event could not have coincided with the prophecy by chance. For if a prediction is made at random, even if it is as clear, precise, and unequivocal as an axiom of geometry, its clarity does not make its fulfillment impossible, and therefore if that fulfillment takes place it does not, strictly speaking, prove anything with regard to the man who predicted it.

Thus you can see that your miracles and prophecies, your supposed supernatural proofs, are all reduced to this: believing them on the word of others, and placing the authority of men above the authority of God speaking to my reason. If the eternal truths that my mind understands were to be vitiated in some way, there would no longer be any kind of certainty for me; and far from being convinced that you speak to me on behalf of God, I would not even be sure that he exists.

Here we have many difficulties, my son, and there are others. Of the different religions that proscribe and exclude each other, all are wrong but one, assuming that even one is right. To determine which is right, it is not enough to examine only one: we must examine them all. And here, as in all other matters, we must not condemn anyone without a hearing;[14] we must compare the evidence with the objections to it; we must know what charges each side makes against the others, and how each answers them. The more it seems to us that a certain view is clearly demonstrated, the more we must try to discover the grounds that so many people have for not accepting it. Only a simpleminded man would believe that listening to the theologians of his own religion was all he had to do in order to learn about the reasons given by adherents of an opposing religion. Where are we to find theologians who pride themselves on arguing in good faith? Where are those who, to refute the arguments of an adversary, do not begin by minimizing them? Each one shines in his own sect and is proud of his arguments, but he might cut a sorry figure with those same arguments among members of another sect. If you expect to find the answers to your questions in books, you will have to acquire great erudition, learn many languages, go through countless libraries, and do vast amounts of reading. Who will guide you in your choice? It is difficult in any country to find the best books of the opposing side, much less those of all sides; and if you did find them, they would soon be refuted. The absent are always wrong, and bad arguments stated with confidence easily override good ones stated with contempt. Furthermore, books are often extremely misleading and express their authors' views with great inaccuracy. When, after having lived among us, you tried to judge the Catholic faith from Bossuet's book, you found that you were very wide of the mark. You saw that the doctrine with which the Protestants are answered is not the same as the one which is taught to the people, and that Bossuet's book has little in common with what is said in sermons. To judge a religion correctly, you must not study it in the books of its adherents: You must learn it by living among them, which is a very different matter. Each religion has its own traditions, meanings, customs, and prejudices which form the spirit of its creed and must be taken into account in judging that creed.

How many great peoples print no books of their own and do not read ours! How are they to judge our opinions? How are we to judge theirs? We laugh at them and they despise us; our travelers hold them up to ridicule, but they would do the same to us if they traveled among us. In all countries there are sensible, sincere, honest people who love truth and seek only to know it in order to profess it. Yet everyone sees it in his own religion and regards those of other nations as absurd. Therefore either those foreign religions are not as preposterous as they seem to us, or the rightness we see in our own proves nothing.

We have three main religions in Europe. One accepts only one revelation, another accepts two, and another accepts three. Each one hates and curses the others, and accuses them of being blind, obdurate, stubborn, and untruthful. What impartial man will dare to decide among them without having first carefully weighed their evidence and attentively listened to their arguments? The one that accepts only one revelation is the oldest and seems the best established; the one that accepts three is the newest and seems the most consistent; the one that accepts two, and rejects the third, may well be the best, but it certainly has all prejudices against it, and its inconsistency is obvious.

In all three revelations, the sacred books are written in languages unknown to the peoples that follow them. The Jews no longer understand Hebrew, the Christians understand neither Hebrew nor Greek, the Turks and Persians do not understand Arabic, and even the modern Arabs no longer speak the language of Mohammed. Is it not foolish to teach people in a language they do not understand? Those books have been translated, it will be said. A fine answer! How can I be sure that they have been accurately translated, or even that it is possible for them to be accurately translated? And if God goes so far as to speak to men, why should he need an interpreter?

It will never be clear to me why everything that men are obliged to know should be enclosed in books, and why anyone who does not have access to those books, or to people who understand them, should be punished for his involuntary ignorance. Always books! What an obsession! Because Europe is full of books, Europeans regard them as indispensable, without considering that the inhabitants of three-quarters of the earth's surface have never even seen one. Were not all those books written by men? Why, then, should man need them in order to know his duties? And what means did he have of knowing them before those books were written? Either he can learn his duties by himself, or he is not obliged to know them.

Our Catholics loudly proclaim the authority of the Church; but what do they gain by it if, to establish that authority, they need as great an array of proofs as other sects need to establish their doctrines directly? The Church decides that the Church has a right to decide. Is that not a well-founded authority? If you go outside it, you return to all the difficulties we have discussed.

Do you know many Christians who have taken the trouble to examine carefully what Judaism has to say against them? If a few of them have read anything about it at all, it is in books written by Christians. An excellent way of learning their adversaries' arguments! But what other way is there? If anyone among us dared to publish a book openly favorable to Judaism, we would punish the author, the publisher, and the bookseller.[15] That is a sure and easy means of always being right. It is a pleasure to refute people who are afraid to speak.

Those of us who have the opportunity of conversing with Jews are little better off. Those unfortunate people feel that they are at our mercy; the tyranny exercised against them makes them apprehensive; they know how easily Christian charity can accommodate itself to injustice and cruelty. What can they venture to say without running the risk of being denounced for blasphemy? Our greed makes us zealous, and they are too rich not to be wrong. The most learned and enlightened among them are always the most cautious. You may convert some poor wretch who is paid to slander his religion; you may speak with some abject secondhand clothes dealer who agrees with you to gain your favor; you may triumph over their ignorance or cowardice while their theologians smile in silence at your stupidity. But do you think they could bo so easily overcome in a place where they felt safe? At the Sorbonne, it is perfectly clear that the Biblical prophecies concerning the Messiah refer to Jesus Christ. Among the rabbis of Amsterdam, it is equally clear that they have nothing to do with him. I will never believe that I have heard the arguments of the Jews until they have a free state of their own, with schools and universities where they can speak and debate without risk. Only then can we know what they have to say.

In Constantinople the Turks state their arguments but we do not dare to state ours; there, it is our turn to cringe. If the Turks require us to show as much respect for Mohammed, in whom we do not believe, as we require the Jews to show for Jesus Christ, in whom they do not believe, are the Turks wrong? Are we right? On what principle of justice can that question be answered?

Two-thirds of the human race are neither Jews, Mohammedans, nor Christians; and how many millions of people have never even heard of Moses, Jesus Christ, or

Mohammed! This is denied; our missionaries, it is said, go everywhere. That is easy to say. But do they go into the heart of Africa, still unknown to us, where no European has ever yet ventured? Do they go to the inner depths of Tartary to follow on horseback those wandering tribes which are never approached by any foreigner, and which, far from knowing anything about the Pope, have scarcely even heard of the Dalai Lama? Do they go into the immense continents of America, where whole nations do not yet know that people from another world have set foot in theirs? Do they go to Japan, from which their intrigues have caused them to be banished forever, and where their predecessors are known to the rising generation only as crafty schemers who came with hypocritical zeal to work toward gradually taking over the empire? Do they go into the harems of Asian potentates to proclaim the Gospel to thousands of poor slaves? What have the women in that part of the world done, that no missionary can preach the faith to them? Will they all go to hell for having been kept in seclusion?

Even if it were true that the Gospel had been preached all over the world, what would that change? When the first missionary arrives in a country, it is certain that someone has died the day before, without having been able to hear him. Tell me what we are to do about that someone. If there were in the whole world only one man to whom no one had ever preached Jesus Christ, the objection would be as strong for that one man as for a quarter of the human race.

When ministers of the Gospel speak to faraway nations, what do they tell them that can reasonably be accepted on their word and does not require rigorous verification?

"You tell me of a God who lived and died two thousand years ago, in some small town at the other end of the world, and you say that everyone who does not believe in that mystery will be damned. Those are strange things to be believed so quickly, entirely on the authority of a man I do not know! If your God wanted to make it my duty to learn about those events, why did he make them happen so far away from me? Is it a crime not to know what takes place on the other side of the earth? Could I even have guessed that in another hemisphere there was a Hebrew people and a town of Jerusalem? You might as well expect me to know what happens on the moon. You say that you have come to teach me all this, but why did you not come to teach it to my father, and why do you damn that good old man for never having known anything about it? Must he be eternally punished because of your laziness, when he was so good and kind, and sought only truth? Be honest and put yourself in my place, then tell me whether I ought to believe, on your word alone, all the unbelievable things you have told me, and how I can reconcile all that injustice with the just God you proclaim to me. First let me go and see that remote country where such wondrous things happen, things that are unknown here; let me go and find out why the inhabitants of that Jerusalem treated God as if he were a bandit. They did not recognize him as God, you say. Then what am I to do, when I have heard of him only from you? You add that they have been punished, dispersed, oppressed, subjugated, and that none of them now goes near that town. They surely deserved all that; but what do the present inhabitants of the town say about the deicide of their predecessors? They deny it; they, too, refuse to recognize God as God. The town could just as well have been left to the descendants of its first inhabitants.

"What! God has been recognized by neither the ancient nor the modern inhabitants of the town where he died; yet you want me to recognize him when I was born two thousand years later and two thousand leagues away! Do you not see that before I believe in that book which is sacred to you but incomprehensible to me, I must learn from people other than you when and by whom it was written, how it has been preserved, how it came to you, and the reasons given by those who reject it even though they know everything you have told me as well as you do? It should be obvious to you that I must go to Europe, Asia, and Palestine to examine everything for myself; I would have to be mad to listen to you before I had done that."

Not only does what I have just said seem reasonable to me, but I maintain that any sensible man should say something similar in similar circumstances, and send away any missionary who wants to teach and baptize him without delay, before his testimony has been verified. I also maintain that the same objections made against Christianity can be made against any other revelation with equal or greater force. From this it follows that if there is only one true religion, and if everyone is obliged to accept it under penalty of damnation, we must spend our lives thoroughly studying and comparing all religions, and traveling in the countries where they are established. No one is exempt from the first duty of man, no one has a right to rely on another's judgment. The artisan who lives only by his work, the plowman who does not know how to read, the shy and delicate young girl, the invalid who can scarcely leave his bed—everyone, without exception, must study, meditate, debate, and roam all over the world. There will be no more fixed and stable nations; the earth will be covered with pilgrims traveling at great cost of money and fatigue so that they can investigate, compare, and examine for themselves the religions that are followed in different countries. Then farewell to arts, crafts, human sciences, and all secular occupations; there will no longer be any study than that of religion. Only those who have enjoyed the best health, made best use of their time and reason, and lived longest, will be able to approach their goal by the time they reach old age, and they will be lucky if they do not die before learning in which religion they should have lived.

If they try to soften the rigor of that method by giving the slightest weight to human authority, you immediately surrender everything to it. If the son of a Christian is right to follow his father's religion without a thorough and impartial examination, why should the son of a Turk be wrong to do the same? I defy the intolerant to answer that question in a way that will satisfy a sensible man.

Hard pressed by these arguments, some prefer to make God unjust, rather than give up their barbarous dogma. Others solve the problem by obligingly sending an angel to instruct those who have led morally good lives in unavoidable ignorance. What a noble invention that angel is! Not content with making us slaves to their contrivances, they place God himself under the necessity of using them.

That, my son, is the kind of absurdity to which pride and intolerance lead when everyone is determined to achieve certainty and wants to feel that he is right while the rest of mankind is wrong. I call to witness the God of peace whom I worship, and whom I have proclaimed to you, that my inquiries were sincere; but seeing that they had been and always would be unsuccessful, and that I was adrift on a shoreless sea, I turned back and enclosed my faith within the limits of my first ideas. I was never able to believe that God had ordered me, under penalty of going to hell, to be learned. I therefore closed all books. There is only one that is open to all eyes: the book of nature. It is in that great and sublime book that I learn to serve and worship its divine Author. No one can be excused for not reading it, because it speaks to all men in a language intelligible to all minds. Suppose I had been born on a desert island, had never seen another human being, and had never learned what had happened in ancient times in another part of the world; if I exercised and cultivated my reason and made good use of the immediate faculties given to me by God, I would learn by myself to love him and his works, to will the good that he wills, and to fulfill all my duties on earth to please him. What more could all human learning teach me?

As for revelation, if I were a better reasoner or more erudite, I might perceive its truth and its usefulness for those who are fortunate enough to recognize it; but if I see evidence in its favor which I cannot oppose, I also see objections against it which I cannot resolve. There are so many solid arguments for and against it that, not knowing what to decide, I neither accept nor reject it. I reject only the obligation to recognize it, because that supposed obligation is incompatible with God's justice; far from removing obstacles to salvation, it would multiply them and make them insurmountable for most of mankind. With that exception, I remain in respectful doubt concerning the matter. I do not presume to think myself infallible. Other men have been able to reach a decision on what seems to me uncertain; I reason for myself, not for them; I neither blame nor imitate them; their judgment may be better than mine, but it is not my fault if mine is not the same as theirs.

I also admit that the holiness of the Gospel is an argument which speaks to my heart, and that I would regret finding a valid refutation of it. Consider the books of philosophers, with all their pomp: How small they are in comparison! Can it be that a book so sublime, yet so simple, is the work of men? Can it be that he whose story it tells is himself only a man? Is this the tone of a zealot or an ambitious sectarian? What gentleness and purity in his conduct! What touching grace in his teachings! What grandeur in his maxims! What profound wisdom in his sermons! What presence of mind, shrewdness, and soundness in his answers! What control over his passion! Where is the man, where is the sage who can suffer and die without weakness or ostentation? When Plato depicts his imaginary righteous man covered with all the opprobrium of crime and worthy of all the rewards of virtue, he gives an accurate description of Jesus Christ: The resemblance is so striking that all the Fathers of the Church were aware of it, and no one can fail to recognize it. What prejudices and blindness one must have, to dare to compare the son of Sophroniscus with the son of Mary! How far apart they are! Socrates, dying without pain, without ignominy, easily plays his part to the end; and if that easy death had not honored his life, one might doubt whether Socrates, with all his intelligence, was anything more than a Sophist. He is said to have invented morality, but others had practiced it before him; he only said what they had done, and used their examples in the form of lessons. Aristides was just before Socrates stated what justice was; Leonidas died for his country before Socrates made love of one's country a duty; Sparta was austere before Socrates praised austerity; Greece abounded in virtuous men before Socrates defined virtue. But where among his people did Jesus find that lofty, pure morality which he alone taught and exemplified?[16] The highest wisdom spoke in the midst of the most rabid fantacism, and the simplicity of the noblest virtues honored the vilest of nations. No one could wish for a gentler death than that of Socrates calmly philosophizing with his friends; no one could fear a more horrible death than that of Jesus expiring in torment, insulted, mocked, and cursed by a whole people. Socrates, taking the cup of poison, blesses the weeping man who presents it to him; Jesus, suffering atrocious torture, prays for his relentless executioner. Yes, if Socrates's life and death are those of a sage, Jesus's life and death are those of a God. Shall we say that the story in the Gospel is imaginary? My friend, one does not imagine such things; and the deeds of Socrates, which no one doubts, are less well attested than those of Jesus Christ. To regard the Gospel as imaginary is only to push back the difficulty without resolving it, for it is less plausible to assume that several men invented the same story than that one man was really the subject of it. The Jewish authors could never have imagined that tone and that morality; and the stamp of truth in the Gospel is so great and striking, so unmistakably genuine, that if the story had been invented, its inventor would have been more astonishing than its hero. Yet with all this, that same Gospel is full of incredible things, contrary to reason, which no sensible man can comprehend or accept. What are we to do in the face of all those contradictions? We must always be modest and cautious, my son; we must respect in silence what we can neither understand nor reject, and humble ourselves before the great Being who alone knows the truth.

Such is the involuntary skepticism in which I have remained; but it is by no means painful to me, because it does not extend to essential matters of practice, and I am firmly convinced with regard to the principles of all my duties. I serve God in the simplicity of my heart. I seek to know only what concerns my conduct. Unlike so many others, I do not trouble myself about dogmas that have no bearing on action or morality. I regard all particular religions as so many salutary institutions which in each country prescribe a uniform manner of honoring God in public worship, and which may all have been shaped by climate, government, the spirit of the people, or other local conditions that make one religion preferable to another in specific times and places. I believe that they are all good when God is properly served in them. The essential worship comes from the heart. God rejects no homage, in whatever form it may be offered to him, if it is sincere. Called to the service of the Church in the religion that I profess, I fulfill as scrupulously as possible all the duties that it prescribes for me, and my conscience would reproach me if I deliberately neglected them in any way. As you know, after a long suspension by the Church I obtained permission, through Monsieur de Mellarède's influence, to resume exercising my functions as a priest to earn my livelihood. In the past, I said Mass with the casual attitude that we eventually develop toward even the most serious things when we have done them too often; now that I have acquired my new principles, I say Mass with greater reverence; I am pervaded by the majesty of the Supreme Being, by his presence, and by the inadequacy of the human mind, which has so little understanding of everything related to its Maker. Aware that I am presenting to him the vows of the people in a prescribed form, I carefully observe all the rites; I recite attentively, I do my best never to omit a single word or act; as I approach the moment of the Consecration, I commune with myself in order to perform it in the frame of mind required by the Church and the greatness of the sacrament; I try to efface my reason before the Supreme Intelligence; I say to myself, "Who are you, to measure infinite power?" I speak the sacramental words with respect, and I give their meaning all the faith at my command. Whatever that incomprehensible mystery may be, I am not afraid of being punished on the Day of Judgment for having ever profaned it in my heart.

Honored by the sacred ministry, even though I am in its lowest rank, I will never do or say anything that will make me unworthy of fulfilling its sublime duties. I will always preach virtue to men, I will always exhort them to do what is right; and so far as I am able, I will always set an example for them. It is not within my power to make religion attractive to them or to strengthen their faith in the truly useful dogmas that every man is obliged to believe; but God grant that I may never preach the cruel dogma of intolerance to them, that I may never teach them to hate their neighbors or say to other men, "You will be damned. There is no salvation outside the Church."[17] If I were in a more conspicuous position, my unwillingness to do those things might bring me into difficulties, but I am too obscure to have much to fear, and I can hardly fall any lower than I am. Come what may, I will never blaspheme against divine justice, or tell lies against the Holy Ghost.

For a long time I aspired to the honor of becoming a parish priest; it is still my aspiration, but I no longer have any hope of attaining it. My dear friend, I feel that there is nothing nobler than being a parish priest. A good parish priest is a minister of kindness, as a good magistrate is a minister of justice. A parish priest is never required to do evil; if he cannot always do good himself, he is never out of place when he calls on others to do it, and he is often successful in persuading them, if he has been able to earn their respect. Ah, if only I could be assigned to minister to a congregation of good people in our mountains! I would be happy, for it seems to me that I would make my parishioners happy. I would not make them rich, but I would share their poverty; I would take away from it the stigma and contempt that are harder to bear than poverty itself. I would make them love harmony and equality, which often put an end to indigence and always make it tolerable. When they saw that I lived in contentment even though I was in no way better off than they, they would learn to accept their fate and be as content as I. In my teachings I would stress the spirit of the gospel more than the spirit of the Church. In the Gospel, dogma is simple and morality sublime; we see few religious practices in it, but many works of charity. Before teaching my parishioners what they ought to do, I would try always to practice it, so that they could see clearly that I believed everything I said to them. If there were Protestants living nearby or within my parish, I would make no distinction between them and my parishioners so far as Christian charity was concerned; I would urge them all to love one another, to look on one another as brothers, to respect all religions, and to live at peace with one another, each in his own religion. I believe that to ask anyone to leave the religion in which he was born is to ask him to do wrong, and consequently to do wrong oneslf. As long as our understanding remains limited, let us maintain public order; let us respect the laws in each country, and not disturb the worship that they prescribe; let us not incite the citizens of any country to disobedience, for we do not know with certainty that it would be good for them to abandon their present opinions in favor of others, and we do know with great certainty that it is bad to disobey the law.

My young friend, I have now stated my creed to you as God reads it in my heart; you are the first to hear it, and you will perhaps be the last. As long as any good belief remains among men, we must not trouble peaceful souls or alarm the faith of simple people with difficulties which they could not resolve and which would only distress them without enlightening them. But when everything is shaken, the trunk must be preserved at the cost of the branches. Consciences that are agitated, uncertain, and almost stifled, as I saw yours to be, need to be strengthened and aroused; and to reestablish them on the foundation of eternal truth, one must pull down the tottering pillars by which they think they are still supported.

You are at that critical age when the mind opens to certainty, when the heart receives its form and character, and when each of us becomes what he will be for the rest of his life, for better or worse. Later, the substance is hardened and new impressions no longer leave their mark.

Young man, receive the imprint of truth in your soul while it is still malleable. If I were surer of myself, I would have spoken to you dogmatically and decisively, but I am a man, ignorant and subject to error: What could I do? I have opened my heart to you without reserve; what I consider certain, I have given you as such; I have given you my doubts as doubts, my opinions as opinions; I have told you my reasons for doubting and believing. It is now for you to judge. You have said that you want to take time; that is a wise precaution which makes me think well of you. Begin by making your conscience willing to be enlightened. Be honest with yourself. Take from my views whatever has convinced you, and discard the rest. You have not yet been so perverted by vice as to be in danger of making a bad choice. I would offer to discuss the choice with you, but as soon as a dispute arises, tempers flare, vanity and stubbornness intervene, and sincerity vanishes. Never argue, my friend, because argument enlightens neither oneself nor others. As for myself, I came to my conclusions only after many years of meditation; I will continue to accept them; my conscience is at peace and my heart is content. If I were to decide to reexamine my views, I could not do so with a purer love of truth, and my mind, already less active, would be less capable of perceiving it. I will remain as I am, for fear that love of meditation might become an idle passion and gradually make me apathetic toward the fulfillment of my duties, and for fear that I might fall back into my former skepticism without having the strength to bring myself out of it. More than half my life is over; I now have time only to make good use of what is left, and to efface my errors by my virtues. If I am mistaken, it is in spite of myself. He who sees into the depths of my heart knows that I do not love my blindness. Since I am powerless to overcome it by my own understanding, my only means of freeing myself from it is to lead a good life; and if God is able to make children for Abraham out of stones,* every man has a right to hope for enlightenment when he makes himself worthy of it.

If my reflections lead you to think as I do, if my views are yours, and if we have the same creed, I give you this

---

*A reference to Matthew 3:9, in the New Testament. (Translator's note.)

advice: Cease exposing your life to the temptations of misery and despair; cease leading it ignominiously at the mercy of strangers; and cease abjectly eating the bread of charity. Go back to your country, return to the religion of your fathers, follow it in the sincerity of your heart, and never forsake it: It is very simple and very holy; I believe that of all religions on earth it is the one whose morality is purest and most acceptable to reason. As for the expenses of the journey, do not trouble yourself about them: they will be provided for. And do not fear the false shame of a humiliating return; we should be ashamed of making a mistake, not of repairing it. You are still at the age when everything is forgiven, but when one can no longer sin with impunity. If you are willing to listen to your conscience, countless empty objections will vanish at the sound of its voice. You will realize that in our state of uncertainty it is an inexcusable presumption to profess a religion other than the one into which we were born, and that it is duplicity not to practice sincerely the one we profess. If we stray from it, we deprive ourselves of a great excuse before the tribunal of the Sovereign Judge. Will he not be more inclined to forgive an error in which we were brought up than one which we dared to choose for ourselves?

My son, keep your soul in the state of always desiring God's existence, and you will never doubt it. Moreover, whatever your final decision may be, remember that the true duties of religion are independent of human institutions; that a righteous heart is the true temple of the Divinity; that in all countries and all sects, the epitome of the law is to love God above all else and one's neighbor as oneself; that there is no religion which absolves man from the duties of morality, and that they alone are truly essential; that inner worship is the first of those duties; and that without faith there can be no real virtue.

Shun those who, on the pretext of explaining nature, sow distressing doctrines in the hearts of men, and whose apparent skepticism is a hundred times more assertive and dogmatic than the confident tone of their adversaries. On the arrogant assumption that they alone are enlightened, truthful, and sincere, they imperiously try to impose their peremptory decisions on us and claim to be teaching us the true principles of things when they set forth the unintelligible systems that they have constructed in their imagination. Furthermore, by overturning, destroying, and trampling underfoot everything that men respect, they deprive the afflicted of their last consolation in their misery, and remove the only curb on the passions of the rich and the powerful; they tear out remorse from crime and the hope of virtue from men's hearts, and then they boast of being benefactors of the human race. Truth is never harmful, they say. I believe that too, and in my opinion it is strong proof that what they teach is not true.[18]

My good young man, be sincere and truthful without arrogance; know how to be ignorant: you will deceive neither yourself nor others. If cultivation of your talents should ever enable you to speak to men, always speak to them only in accordance with your conscience, without caring whether or not they applaud you. Misuse of knowledge causes incredulity. Learned men always scorn common opinions; each wants to have his own. Haughty philosophy leads to irreligion, as blind devotion leads to fanaticism. Avoid those extremes; always hold fast to the path of truth, or what appears to you as such in the simplicity of your heart, without ever letting yourself be turned away from it by vanity or weakness. Dare to confess God to philosophers; dare to preach humanity to the intolerant. You may have to stand alone, but you will have within you a testimony in your favor that will free you from dependence on the judgments of men. It will not matter whether they love or hate you, whether they read or disdain your writings. Say what is true, do what is right; what matters is to fulfill our duties on earth, and it is by forgetting ourselves that we work for ourselves. My son, self-interest deludes us; only the hope of the righteous man is never deceptive.

$\mathcal{N}OTES^*$

1. M. de La Condamine tells us, in his writings, of a people that could only count to three. Yet the men who composed that people had hands, and had therefore often seen their fingers without knowing how to count to five.

2. I grant that this rest is only relative; but since we observe greater and lesser degrees of motion, we clearly conceive one of the two extremes, namely, rest; we conceive it so well, in fact, that we are inclined to regard it as absolute when it is only relative. But if matter can be conceived at rest, it is not true that motion is an essential property of it.

3. Chemists regard phlogiston or the element of fire as scattered, motionless, and stagnant in the compounds of which it is a part, until external causes release it, concentrate it, set it in motion, and change it into fire.

4. I have made every effort to conceive of a living molecule, without success. The idea of matter feeling without having senses seems unintelligible and self-contradictory to me. To accept or reject this idea, one would have to begin by understanding it, and I admit I am not that fortunate.

5. Could one believe, if there were not proof of it, that human absurdity could be carried so far? Amatus Lusitanus claimed to have seen a one-inch man enclosed in a glass, whom Julius Camillus, like a new Prometheus, had made by alchemical science. Paracelsus, *De Natura Rerum*, teaches the method of making these little men, and maintains that pygmies, fauns, satyrs, and nymphs have been engendered by chemistry. To establish the possibility of such things, I see little more that needs to be done, except to assert that organic matter withstands the heat of fire, and that its molecules can remain alive in a furnace.

---

*In these notes, Rousseau is speaking in his own voice, rather than attributing his remarks to the priest. (Translator's note.)

6. It seems to me that, far from saying that rocks think, modern philosophy has discovered that men do not think. It no longer recognizes anything but sentient beings in nature; the only difference it finds between a man and a stone is that a man is a sentient being that has sensations, while a stone is a sentient being that has none. But if it is true that all matter feels, where am I to conceive the sentient unit, or the individual self? Is it in each molecule of matter, or in aggregate bodies? Shall I place it in fluids and solids alike, in compounds as well as elements? There are, it is said, only individuals in nature. But what are those individuals? Is a stone an individual or an aggregate of individuals? Is it a single sentient being, or are there as many in it as there are grains of sand? If each elemental atom is a sentient being, how shall I conceive that intimate communication by which one feels within another, so that their two selves are mingled in one? Attraction may be a law of nature whose mystery is unknown to us, but we at least understand that attraction, acting according to mass, is in no way incompatible with divisibility. Can you conceive the same thing with regard to feeling? The sentient parts have extension, but the sentient being is invisible and one; it cannot be divided, either it is a whole or it is nothing; therefore a sentient being is not a body. I do not know how our materialists view this, but it seems to me that the same difficulties which have made them reject thought should also make them reject feeling, and I do not know why, having taken the first step, they should not then take the next. What more would it cost them? And since they are sure that they do not think, how can they dare to assert that they feel?

7. When the ancients called the supreme God *optimus maximus*, they spoke truly, but if they had said *maximus optimus*, they would have been more accurate, since his goodness comes from his power; he is good because he is great.

8. "Not unto us, O Lord, not unto us, but unto thy name give glory, for thy mercy, and for thy truth's sake" (Psalm 115).

9. Modern philosophy, which acknowledges only what it explains, carefully refrains from acknowledging that obscure faculty called instinct which appears to guide animals toward some end without any acquired knowledge. According to one of our wisest philosophers, instinct is

only a habit that is void of thought, but is acquired by thinking. From the way in which he describes this development, we must conclude that children think more than adults, a paradox strange enough to be worth examining. Without entering into that discussion here, I ask what name I must give to my dog's ardent hunting of moles, which he does not eat; to the patience with which he watches for them, sometimes for hours on end; and to the skill with which he seizes them and pulls them out of the ground just as they emerge, then kills them and leaves them, without ever having been trained to hunt them or taught where to find them. I also ask, and this is more important, why, the first time I threatened that same dog, he lay on his back with his paws bent downward, in a posture well designed to touch me—a posture which he would certainly not have kept if, without letting myself be swayed, I had begun beating him as he lay there on the ground. What! Had my dog, almost a newborn puppy at the time, already acquired moral ideas? Did he know the meaning of clemency and magnanimity? On the basis of what acquired knowledge did he hope to appease me by thus abandoning himself to my mercy? All dogs in the world do more or less the same thing in similar circumstances, and anyone can verify what I am saying here. Let philosophers, who so disdainfully reject instinct, explain this fact solely by the operation of sensations and the knowledge we acquire from those sensations; let them explain it in a way that will satisfy any sensible man. If they can do that, there will be nothing left for me to say, and I will speak no more about instinct.

10. In some respects, feelings are ideas and ideas are feelings. Both words apply to a perception that directs our attention to its object and to ourselves, who are affected by it; the appropriate word is determined only by the order in which this directing of attention takes place. If we are first concerned with the object, and then with ourselves only by reflection, the perception is an idea; if our attention is first drawn to the impression received, and then only by reflection to the object that causes it, it is a feeling.

11. I believe that the good priest could now say this to the public.

12. "All men," says a good and wise priest, "say (and all use the same jargon) that their religion and their belief

in it have come to them not from man or any other
created being, but from God.

"But to speak truly, without disguising or misrepresent-
ing anything, that is not the case. No matter what may be
said, religions are received from human beings and trans-
mitted by human means; witness, first of all, the way in
which they were originally received into the world and are
still received every day by individuals: A man's nation,
country, and locality give him his religion. He belongs to
the religion of the place where he was born and raised.
We are circumcised or baptized, we are Jews, Mohammedans, or Christians before we know that we are men; we
do not hold our religion by choice and preference. Witness, next, how badly our lives and morals accord with
our religion. And finally, witness how we violate the
tenents of our religion for such slight and human reasons"
(Charron, *De la Sagesse*, Bordeaux, 1601; Bk. II, Ch. V,
p. 257).

It is quite likely that if the virtuous theologian of Con-
dom [Charron] had sincerely stated his creed, it would
not have been very different from that of the Savoyard
priest.

13. This is explicitly stated in many parts of the Bible,
in the thirteenth chapter of Deuteronomy, for example,
where it is said that if a prophet proclaims other gods and
supports his words with predictions of wonders which actually come to pass, far from being heeded, he must be
put to death. Therefore, when the pagans killed apostles
who proclaimed a strange god to them and proved their
mission by predictions and miracles, I do not see how we
could have made any objection to them which they could
not have turned against us. What is there to do in such a
case? Only this: return to reasoning and leave miracles
alone. It would have been better not to resort to them in
the first place. This is only common sense, which is obscured only by making distinctions that can at best be
called very subtle. Subtleties in Christianity? Was Jesus
Christ wrong, then, in promising the kingdom of heaven
to the simple? Was he wrong to begin his most beautiful
sermon by praising the poor in spirit, if it takes so much
intelligence to understand his doctrine and learn to believe
in him? When you have proved to me that I must submit
to what you say, all will be well; but to prove it, put yourself on my level, adapt your arguments to the understand-

ing of a simple mind, or I will not recognize you as a true disciple of your master, and it is not his doctrine that you are expounding to me.

14. Plutarch reports that, among other strange paradoxes, the Stoics maintained that in rendering a judgment it was unnecessary to hear both parties, for, they said, the first party has either proved his case or failed to do so; if he has proved it, there is nothing more to be said, and the other party must be condemned; if he has failed to prove it, he is in the wrong, and his case must be dismissed. I find that the method of all those who accept an exclusive revelation closely resembles that of the Stoics. Since each of those many parties claims to be the only one that is right, we cannot choose among them, without being unjust, unless we hear all of them.

15. Among many known cases, here is one that requires no comment. In the sixteenth century, when Catholic theologians had decided that all Jewish books without exception were to be burned, the illustrious and learned Reuchlin was consulted on the matter; he incurred terrible disfavor that was nearly fatal to him by merely stating the opinion that it would not be wrong to spare those Jewish books which said nothing against Christianity and dealt with matters irrelevant to religion.

16. See, in the Sermon on the Mount, the parallel that he himself draws between his morality and that of Moses (Matthew 5:21 et seq.).

17. The duty of following and loving the religion of one's country never extends to dogmas that are contrary to good morals, such as that of intolerance. This horrible dogma turns men against one another and makes them all enemies of the human race. The distinction between civil tolerance and theological tolerance is puerile and vain. Those two kinds of tolerance are inseparable; one cannot be accepted without the other. Even angels would not live in peace with men whom they regarded as enemies of God.

18. The two parties attack each other with so many sophisms that it would be a vast and rash undertaking to try to point out all of them; it is doing a great deal simply to note some of them as they arise. One of the commonest on the part of the philosophical party is to contrast a people supposedly composed of good philosophers with a people of bad Christians; as though it were easier to form a

people of true philosophers than a people of true Christians! I do not know if, among individuals, it is easier to find one than the other, but I do know that so far as peoples are concerned, we must assume that some will misuse philosophy without religion, just as ours misuse religion without philosophy; and this, it seems to me, puts the question in a very different light.

Bayle has clearly shown that fanaticism is more pernicious than atheism, and that is undeniable; but there is something equally true which he neglects to say: that fanaticism, although bloodthirsty and cruel, is nevertheless a great and powerful passion which lifts up man's heart, makes him despise death, gives him a prodigiously strong motivation, and needs only to be better directed in order to produce the noblest virtues, whereas irreligion, and the argumentative philosophical spirit in general, attaches man to life, softens him, degrades his soul, concentrates all his passions in the baseness of private interest and the abjectness of the human ego, and thus quietly undermines the real foundations of all society, for what private interests have in common is so slight that it can never balance what makes them opposed to one another.

If atheism causes no bloodshed, it is less from love of peace than from indifference to good: The so-called sage cares little what happens, as long as he remains undisturbed in his study. His principles do not cause people to be killed, but they prevent them from being born, by destroying the morals that multiply them, by detaching them from their species, by reducing all their passions to a secret selfishness that is as deterimental to population growth as it is to virtue. Philosophical indifference is like the tranquillity of a state with a despotic government; it is the tranquillity of death; it is even more destructive than war.

Thus fanaticism, though more harmful in its immediate effects than what is now called the philosophical spirit, is much less harmful in its consequences. Moreover, while it is easy to display fine maxims in books, the question is whether they are really related to the doctrine involved, whether they follow from it necessarily, and this has not yet been made clear. It remains to be seen whether philosophy, at ease on the throne, would control vainglory, self-interest, ambition, and the petty passions of men, and whether it would practice that humane benevolence which it extols, pen in hand.

In principle, philosophy can do no good that religion cannot do even better, and religion does much good that philosophy cannot do.

In practice, it is another matter; but we must still examine it. It is true that no one follows his religion, when he has one, on every point. It is also true that most people have hardly any religion and do not follow what little they have in any way at all. But some people do have a religion and follow it at least partially. There can be no doubt that religious reasons often prevent them from doing wrong, and cause them to have virtues and do praiseworthy deeds that they would not have had or done otherwise.

If a monk denies that money was entrusted to him, what conclusion can be drawn except that the man who entrusted it to him was a fool? If Pascal had done the same, it would have proved that he was a hypocrite, and nothing more. But a monk! ... Can it be said that those who turn religion to their own profit are religious? All the crimes committed within the clergy, as elsewhere, do not prove that religion is useless, but only that very few people are religious.

Our modern governments are unquestionably indebted to Christianity for the fact that their authority is more solid and their revolutions less frequent. Christianity has also made those governments less bloodthirsty. This can be shown by comparing them with governments of the past. Religion, better understood and abjuring fanaticism, has given more gentleness to Christian morality. This change has not been the work of literature, for humanity has not been more respected in those places where literature has flourished, as is evident from the cruelties of the Athenians, the Egyptians, the Roman emperors, and the Chinese. How many acts of mercy are the work of the Gospel! How many restitutions and reparations has confession led Catholics to make! The Hebrew jubilee made usurpers less grasping and did much to prevent poverty; the brotherhood of the Law united the whole nation, and there were no beggars within it. There are none among the Turks, either; they have countless charitable institutions and are hospitable as a matter of religious principle, even to enemies of their religion.

"The Mohammedans," writes Chardin, "say that after

the examination which will follow the universal resurrection, all bodies will cross a bridge called Poul-Serrho, which passes over the eternal fire. This bridge, they say, can be called the third and last examination and the true final judgment, because it is there that the good will be separated from the bad. (. . .) The Persians attach great importance to this bridge; when someone suffers a wrong that he cannot eradicate in any way at any time, his final consolation is to say, 'By the living God, you will pay me double for that on the last day! You will not cross the Poul-Serrho until you have given me satisfaction! I will cling to your coat and throw myself against your legs!' I have seen many eminent people, of all professions, who, for fear of being thus denounced on that awesome bridge, begged forgiveness of those who had complaints against them. It has happened many times to me personally. Men of high rank who, by their importunity, have made me do things that I did not want to do, have approached me when they felt that enough time had passed for my irritation to die down, and said to me, 'Please, *halal becon anchifra*,' that is, 'Make that matter right for me.' Some have even given me gifts and rendered me services to make me forgive them and say that I did it wholeheartedly. And the cause of all this is the belief that no one will cross the bridge over hell unless he has paid his debt in full to those whom he has wronged."

Am I to believe that the idea of this bridge, which makes amends for so many iniquities, never prevents any? If someone were to take that idea away from the Persians by convincing them that there was no Poul-Serrho, or anything like it, where the oppressed would have vengeance against their oppressors after death, is it not clear that oppressors would feel very much more at ease, having been freed of the need to concern themselves with appeasing their victims? It is therefore false that such a doctrine would not be harmful; and it would therefore not be the truth.

Philosophers, your moral laws are lofty and excellent, but please show me their sanction. Stop your mental wanderings for a moment and tell me plainly what you put in place of the Poul-Serrho.

The MENTOR Philosophers

A distinguished series of six volumes presenting in historical order the basic writings of the outstanding philosophers of the Western world—from the Middle Ages to the present time.

☐ **THE AGE OF BELIEF: THE MEDIEVAL PHILOSOPHERS edited by Anne Fremantle.** Basic writings of St. Augustine, Boethius, Abelard, St. Bernard, St. Thomas Aquinas, Duns Scotus, William of Ockham and others.
(#ME1536—$1.75)

☐ **THE AGE OF ADVENTURE: THE RENAISSANCE PHILOSOPHERS edited by Giorgio de Santillana.** Da Vinci, More, Machiavelli, Michelangelo, Erasmus, Copernicus, Montaigne, Kepler, Galileo, Bruno. (#ME1342—$1.75)

☐ **THE AGE OF REASON: THE 17TH CENTURY PHILOSOPHERS edited by Stuart Hampshire.** Bacon, Pascal, Hobbes, Galileo, Descartes, Spinoza, Leibniz.
(#MW1428—$1.50)

☐ **THE AGE OF ENLIGHTENMENT: THE 18TH CENTURY PHILOSOPHERS edited by Isaiah Berlin.** Locke, Berkeley, Voltaire, Hume, Reid, Condillac, Hamann.
(#MW1494—$1.50)

☐ **THE AGE OF IDEOLOGY: THE 19TH CENTURY PHILOSOPHERS edited by Henry D. Aiken,** Kant, Fichte, Hegel, Schopenhauer, Comte, Mill, Spencer, Marx, Nietzsche, Kierkegaard.
(#MW1452—$1.50)

☐ **THE AGE OF ANALYSIS: 20TH CENTURY PHILOSOPHERS edited by Morton White.** Peirce, Whitehead, James, Dewey, Bertrand Russell, Wittgenstein, Croce, Bergson, Sartre, Santayana and others.
(#MW1179—$1.50)

THE NEW AMERICAN LIBRARY, INC.,
P.O. Box 999, Bergenfield, New Jersey 07621

Please send me the MENTOR BOOKS I have checked above. I am enclosing $_____(check or money order—no currency or C.O.D.'s). Please include the list price plus 35¢ a copy to cover handling and mailing costs. (Prices and numbers are subject to change without notice.)

Name_____

Address_____

City_____State_____Zip Code_____
Allow at least 4 weeks for delivery

MENTOR Books of Special Interest

☐ **THE PHILOSOPHY OF NIETZSCHE edited with an Introduction by Geoffrey Clive.** A unique topical anthology of writings from the Oscar Levy English translation of 18 volumes and based on Karl Schlechta's new German edition of Nietzsche's works. (#MJ1474—$1.95)

☐ **LEISURE: THE BASIS OF CULTURE by Josef Pieper.** In a series of astonishing essays, the author indicts the 20th century cult of "work" and hectic amusements, which can ultimately destroy both our culture and ourselves. Introduction by T. S. Eliot.
(#MY1535—$1.25)

☐ **GREAT DIALOGUES OF PLATO translated by W. H. D. Rouse.** A new translation into direct, forceful modern English of "The Republic" and other dialogues.
(#MJ1520—$1.95)

☐ **THE CREATIVE PROCESS: A SYMPOSIUM edited by Brewster Ghiselin.** An explanation, in their own words, by thirty-eight brilliant men and women such as Albert Einstein, Friedrich Nietzsche, Katherine Anne Porter, and Vincent Van Gogh, of the creation of art, music, literature, and other arts. (#ME1500—$1.75)

☐ **BOOKS THAT CHANGED THE WORLD by Robert B. Downs.** Sixteen great books that changed the course of history are discussed here—books that caused people to revolt against oppression, start wars, and revolutionized man's ideas about himself and the world.
(#MY1352—$1.25)

THE NEW AMERICAN LIBRARY, INC.,
P.O. Box 999, Bergenfield, New Jersey 07621

Please send me the MENTOR BOOKS I have checked above. I am enclosing $_____(check or money order—no currency or C.O.D.'s). Please include the list price plus 35¢ a copy to cover handling and mailing costs. (Prices and numbers are subject to change without notice.)

Name_____

Address_____

City_____State_____Zip Code_____
Allow at least 4 weeks for delivery

Other MENTOR Books You'll Want to Read

☐ **THE PLEASURES OF PHILOSOPHY by Charles Frankel.**
A lively and provocative introduction to philosophy:
Plato on government; St. Augustine on the enigma of
time; Santayana on religion; Descartes on reason;
Dostoyevsky on irrationality; Nietzsche on primitive human drives; William James on temperament and
thought; and many others.   (#MJ1197—$1.95)

☐ **THE GREEK PHILOSOPHERS edited by Rex Warner.**
Basic writings of philosophers from Thales to Plotinus,
revealing the roots of Western philosophy in ancient
Greece.   (#MW1487—$1.50)

☐ **THE PHILOSOPHY OF ARISTOTLE newly translated by
A. E. Wardman and J. L. Creed,** with introduction and
commentary by Renford Bambrough.
          (#MW1217—$1.50)

☐ **TEN GREAT WORKS OF PHILOSOPHY edited with a
general introduction and commentaries by Robert Paul
Wolff.** Ten great works of philosophical speculation and
reflection by such great thinkers as Plato, Aristotle,
James, Aquinas, Hume, Descartes, Kant and others.
          (#MJ1401—$1.95)

☐ **TWO TREATISES OF GOVERNMENT by John Locke.** Introduction and Notes by Peter Laslett. A crucial book of
political philosophy which later strongly influenced the
American Federalists.   (#ME1492—$2.25)

Literary Classics in MENTOR Editions

☐ **THE INFERNO by Dante; translated by John Ciardi.** One of the world's great poetic masterpieces in a new verse translation into modern English. (#MW1271—$1.50)

☐ **DON QUIXOTE (abridged) by Miguel Cervantes; translated by Walter Starkie.** The entertaining mis-adventures of the dreamy knight-errant who tried to revive chivalry in Spain. (#ME1528—$1.75)

☐ **THE PRINCE by Niccolo Machiavelli.** The classic work on statesmanship and power, the techniques and strategy of gaining and keeping political control. (#MY1517—$1.25)

☐ **THE AENEID by Vergil; translated by Patric Dickinson.** The great Roman epic of adventure, war, and love, in a brilliant new verse translation by a noted English poet and classical scholar. (#MY1429—$1.25)